DEREK BEALES is Professor of History at the University of Cambridge and a Fellow of Sidney Sussex College. He was educated at Bishop's Stortford College and Sidney Sussex and received his Ph.D. in 1957. In 1965 he was a Visiting Lecturer at Harvard University, and in 1960 he was awarded the Prince Consort Prize and Seeley Medal at Cambridge. He is also the author of *England and Italy, 1859-60,* and *The Risorgimento and the Unification of Italy.*

THE NORTON LIBRARY HISTORY OF ENGLAND

General Editors

CHRISTOPHER BROOKE
*Professor of History, Westfield College,
University of London*

and

DENIS MACK SMITH
Fellow of All Souls College, Oxford

Already published:

ROMAN BRITAIN AND EARLY ENGLAND, 55 B.C.–A.D. 871
Peter Hunter Blair

FROM ALFRED TO HENRY III, 871–1272
Christopher Brooke

THE LATER MIDDLE AGES, 1272–1485
George Holmes

THE CENTURY OF REVOLUTION, 1603–1714
Christopher Hill

THE EIGHTEENTH CENTURY, 1714–1815
John B. Owen

FROM CASTLEREAGH TO GLADSTONE, 1815–1885
Derek Beales

MODERN BRITAIN, 1885–1955
Henry Pelling

Forthcoming:

THE TUDOR AGE, 1485–1603
M. E. James

From Castlereagh
to Gladstone
1815-1885

>>>>>>>>>>>><<<<<<<<<<<<

DEREK BEALES

W · W · NORTON & COMPANY

New York · London

First published in the Norton Library 1969
by arrangement with Thomas Nelson & Sons Ltd.

W. W. Norton & Company, Inc., 500 Fifth Avenue, New York, N.Y. 10110
W. W. Norton & Company Ltd., 37 Great Russell Street, London WC1B 3NU

Books That Live

The Norton imprint on a book means that in the publisher's
estimation it is a book not for a single season but for the years.

W. W. Norton & Company, Inc.

PRINTED IN THE UNITED STATES OF AMERICA

9 0

ISBN 0-393-00367-1

General Editors' Preface

The present series was planned in the conviction that a fresh survey of English history was needed, and that the time was ripe for it. It will cover the whole span from Caesar's first invasion in 55 BC to 1955, and be completed in eight volumes. The precise scope and scale of each book will inevitably vary according to the special circumstances of its period; but each will combine a clear narrative with an analysis of many aspects of history – social, economic, religious, cultural and so forth – such as is essential in any approach to English history today.

The special aim of this series is to provide serious and yet challenging books, not buried under a mountain of detail. Each volume is intended to provide a picture and appreciation of its age, as well as a lucid outline, written by an expert who is keen to make available and alive the findings of modern research. They are intended to be reasonably short – long enough that the reader may feel he has really been shown the ingredients of the period, not so long that he loses his appetite for anything further. The series is intended to be a stimulus to wider reading rather than a substitute for it; and yet to comprise a set of volumes, each, within its limits, complete in itself. Our hope is to provide an introduction to English history which is lively and illuminating, and which makes it at once exciting and more intelligible.

C. N. L. B.
D. M. S.

To my Wife

Preface

The list of Books for Further Reading on pp. 302–8 is necessarily incomplete, but it includes the works on which I have chiefly relied in writing this volume. Among the books listed, though, are some which have appeared too late for me to use them, such as the most recent writings of Professor H. J. Hanham, Dr E. J. Hobsbawm, Professor P. Mathias and Professor H. Perkin. In the footnotes I have been able only to indicate the sources of quotations and to give references in matters of controversy.

The President and Fellows of Harvard College made an important contribution to the writing of this book when they appointed me to be a Visiting Lecturer there in 1965.

It would be a lengthy undertaking to acknowledge all my debts to individuals, including my pupils at Cambridge and Harvard Universities. I should like to mention the following. Dr G. Kitson Clark, Dr R. C. Smail and the Master of Sidney Sussex College have given me continuous help and encouragement over many years. So has Mr D. Mack Smith, who also criticized my typescript. He and the others who read the book, or part of it, at earlier stages, Professor C. N. L. Brooke, Professor D. M. Joslin, Dr R. Robson and Dr J. P. W. Rogers, have much improved it. I have received valuable assistance in various ways from Mr R. P. Blows, Professor W. O. Chadwick, the late C. S. Colman, Mr E. H. Dancé, Mr E. E. Y. Hales, Dr R. J. Lambert, Professor S. E. Lehmberg, the late J. A. Reeves and Mr J. W. A. Thornely. The publishers have been exemplarily patient and co-operative. A special obligation is acknowledged in the dedication.

Sidney Sussex College,   D.B.
Cambridge
14 April 1969

Note to the Sixth Printing

For this reprint I have been able to make some corrections. I am grateful to readers and reviewers who have pointed out errors and confusions, and especially to Professor N.G. Garson for his criticisms of the passages on South Africa.

I have not been able to bring the bibliography up to date.

D.B.

1 September 1981

Contents

Abbreviation

The following abbreviation has been used in the footnotes and the bibliography:

    Econ.H.R.   *Economic History Review*

Note on Money Values

It is impossible to give a worthwhile overall index to show the change in money values between the period covered by this book and the present day. Some commodities, like food and travel, have relatively cheapened. Others, like houses, have become relatively dearer. In any case there was considerable variation between districts and between 1815 and 1885. However, it may be helpful to point out that in London, which was as now an expensive place, policemen of adequate quality could be recruited in 1829 for £1 1s (1.05) a week, and the Improved Industrial Dwellings Company reckoned it could make a profit at the end of the period by renting a room at an average of just over 2s (10p) a week. For wheat prices, see Appendix F.

List of Plates

Acknowledgements

Our thanks are extended to the bodies and individuals listed below for their help in providing illustrations and for permission to reproduce them. The sources of the plates are as follows: National Monuments Record (7 and 8); National Monuments Record and the Victoria County History (18); University Library, Cambridge (2, 3 and 5); H.M. Treasury and the National Trust (Egremont Collection, Petworth) (1); The Science Museum (6); The Gernsheim Collection, Humanities Research Center, University of Texas (Austin) (19, 20 and 21); *The Illustrated London News* (9 and 15); The National Army Museum, Camberley (16 and 17); the Vicar of St Paul's Church, Brighton and Mr F. Wackett (14); The Amalgamated Engineering Union and Weidenfeld and Nicolson Ltd. (11); the Reece Winstone Collection of *Bristol As It Was* (10 and 12); Mary Evans Picture Library (13); British Museum (4).

We are grateful to the Cambridge University Press for permission to reproduce statistical material in the appendices from P. M. Deane and W. A. Cole, *British Economic Growth 1688–1959*, and B. R. Mitchell and P. M. Deane, *Abstract of British Historical Statistics*.

Maps

I

Introduction

WITH the defeat of France under the Emperor Napoleon I at the battle of Waterloo in 1815, Britain was established again as the greatest of the Great Powers. She had first attained the primacy a century earlier, but France had won it back in the wars that followed her Revolution of 1789: around 1811, at the height of his success, Napoleon had controlled virtually the whole Continent. The battle of Waterloo completed the destruction of his Empire and made it possible to restore the political map of Europe to something like the position of 1789. Britain emerged even more powerful than before. Most obviously, her colonial Empire was far more splendid than that of any other country. She also had the largest navy and mercantile marine, the chief share of the world's trade, the most developed manufactures and even the most progressive agriculture. London was the biggest city and the financial capital of the world. Britain's superiority in these respects outweighed the comparative smallness of her army and her population.

In 1885 she was still ahead. But there were signs of relative decline. Her agriculture fell behind in the 'seventies. Already in the early 'eighties the United States manufactured more than Britain. Colonial rivalry was growing: France resumed her expansion outside Europe in 1881; the new Italy founded her first colony in 1882, the new Germany hers in 1884. 1885 is a less natural terminal date than 1815, but the seventy years between do have this degree of unity: they constitute the period when the British were least disputably 'top nation'.

From some other angles too, the period seems unified. Between 1815 and 1914 Britain fought many colonial wars, but, as far as her relations with European Powers were concerned, this was easily the most peaceful century in her history: she was involved in only one major European war, the Crimean (1854-6). The extensive reforming legislation of the period bore a distinctively Liberal stamp, whereas before 1815 there was hardly any reform at all and in the twentieth century all parties have promoted measures of a semi-socialist character. The internal combustion engine and the electric power station arrived only in the 'eighties. The early and middle nineteenth century were the age of steam and gas, and most prominently of railways. As it happens, 1815-85 is an identifiable period in the history of British dramatic and musical writing; in both cases the worst period of all since before the Renaissance. But the attempt to identify unities is not very profitable. For the most striking feature of the age is that during it things changed at an unprecedented rate.

British pre-eminence itself was maintained only because Britain changed exceedingly fast. Her Empire was immensely greater at the end of the period than it had been at the beginning, and was governed altogether differently. In order to preserve her naval supremacy she had to replace her wooden sailing ships with much bigger iron steamships. Similarly, her merchant fleet in 1815 was composed of rather more than 20,000 vessels, almost all of them sailing ships, with a total net tonnage of nearly 2½ million tons; in 1885, though she had only a few more ships, the tonnage amounted to over 7 million tons, of which steamships accounted for 4 million tons. Some idea of the growth of her trade can be gathered from the fact that her exports in the decade 1811-20 had an average value of about £40,000,000 a year, and in the decade 1881-90 of about £230,000,000 a year, or six times as much – prices having fallen in the meantime. Her output of manufactured cotton goods, her chief industrial product and export throughout the period, is not accurately known; but it must bear a close relation to her consumption of raw cotton, which rose from an average of 139,000,000 lbs. a year in 1816-20 to an average of over 1,700,000,000 lbs. a year, twelve times as much, in 1880-4.

This book will give quite a lot of statistical information. The historian of the nineteenth century is most fortunate, compared with the historian of earlier periods, in the range of such material available to him. However, these figures must not be regarded as absolutely reliable, only as conveying a just general impression. In the words of John Rickman, who was in effective charge of the first four British population censuses, of 1801, 1811, 1821 and 1831: 'Unavoidable inaccuracy will not influence the experienced mind to reject or even to discountenance approximations to useful knowledge, great part of which must always consist of imperfect information.'

The changes already mentioned were associated with countless others. The population of Britain rose from about 13,000,000 in 1815 to about 31,000,000 in 1885. In 1815 about a third of the British people were supported by agriculture, and only a fifth of them lived in towns with more than 20,000 inhabitants; in 1885 a mere eighth were supported by agriculture (that is, roughly the same absolute number as in 1815), while over half lived in such towns (that is, about six times as many as in 1815). At the time of Waterloo the fastest mode of land transport was by coach, the cheapest by canal; by 1885 the railways had long superseded both. At the beginning of the period fewer than 500,000 persons had the right to vote in Parliamentary elections; at the end 5,000,000 had that right. In 1815 the law excluded Protestant Dissenters to a great extent, and Roman Catholics almost entirely, from public office; by 1885 such 'religious tests' had almost disappeared. In 1815 trade unions were illegal 'combinations'; by 1885 strikes were lawful. These years saw the more or less drastic reform of Parliament, the Church of England, municipal corporations, the ancient English Universities, the English law and the English legal system. Over this period the scope of both central and local administration was much enlarged. In the recruitment of government employees 'patronage' was giving way to competitive examination, and, more slowly, the amateur to the professional. By a combination of public and private efforts some of the social machinery necessary to modern urbanized civilization was created. Education, a private matter in 1815, and then by no means available to all, had by 1885 been made compulsory for all children between the ages of five and ten, the State inspecting and giving grants to many schools. Other achievements of the period were the Public Health Code, and tolerable water supplies and sanitary facilities for the towns. To sum up the main trend: Britain was much wealthier, more densely-populated, more urbanized and industrialized in 1885 than in 1815, and she was rather more democratically, professionally and efficiently governed. Her old institutions had been sufficiently modified to function successfully in a changed and more complex society.

In the history of thought and religion, though there were great changes, it is not so easy to trace a clear process of development. The concept and theory of evolution, and in particular the ideas of Charles Darwin's *The Origin of Species* (published in 1859), became very influential. Literal acceptance of the Bible story, general at the beginning of the period, was unusual at the end. Catholicism, both Roman and Anglican, revived. Nearly all denominations prospered. The most conspicuous part of the period's legacy, apart from the railways, is the churches it built, at least 20,000 of them, commonly in some Gothic style.

The tale of change and achievement could be much extended. For the British themselves, as long as national feeling lasts, it will be natural to take a special interest in this period of their country's greatest power; and, national feeling apart, the age is important to the modern inhabitant of Britain because its institutional and legal changes, its methods and its ideas still exert much influence today. All those who speak and read the English language know this period as one of the most brilliant in the history of English literature. Further, the transformation of the life of Britain between 1815 and 1885 had an enormous impact on the rest of the world, both because it strengthened Britain's power and influence and also because it furnished a model of progress to other countries. The history of the world cannot be told without recounting much of the history of Britain during these years.

I have divided the period into four parts. This procedure necessarily creates difficulties, and in a few cases I have virtually confined treatment of a theme to one section of the book. For instance, the only survey of the 'Establishment' is in Part I, the only account of public schools and the cult of games in Part III. Within each phase I have borrowed the plan of Mr Christopher Hill's *The Century of Revolution* in this series: I give first a brief narrative of events, and then single out certain topics for further illustration, analysis and discussion. I hope the reader will bear with the use of certain terms in the narrative sections, which are not explained until later.

At least two of my usages may cause pain. I mean by 'Britain' the United Kingdom less Ireland, but I am conscious that Scotland receives inadequate attention. I use 'Establishment', in inverted commas, to signify 'the privileged', 'the governing class in Church and State'.

With regard to foreign and imperial affairs, I have confined myself almost entirely to considering British policy and activity from the British point of view. I have scarcely ventured to generalize about their impact on the rest of the world. In dealing with art, architecture, literature and thought I have limited myself chiefly to placing notable works in their period, though I have attempted some more constructive observations.

My prime emphases are on economic development; on its relation to social and political change; and on domestic reform and 'improvement'.

PART ONE

1815-1832

An old, mad, blind, despised, and dying king, –
Princes, the dregs of their dull race, who flow
Through public scorn, – mud from a muddy spring, –
Rulers who neither see, nor feel, nor know,
But leech-like to their fainting country cling,
Till they drop, blind in blood, without a blow, –
A people starved and stabbed in the untilled field, –
An army, which liberticide and prey
Makes as a two-edged sword to all who wield
Golden and sanguine laws which tempt and slay;
Religion Christless, Godless – a book sealed;
A Senate, – Time's worst statute unrepealed, –
Are graves, from which a glorious Phantom may
Burst, to illumine our tempestuous day.

P. B. SHELLEY, *England in 1819*

Turn where we may, within, around, the voice of great events is proclaiming to us, Reform, that you may preserve. . . . Renew the youth of the State. Save property, divided against itself. Save the multitude, endangered by its own ungovernable passions. Save the aristocracy, endangered by its own unpopular power. Save the greatest, the fairest, and most highly civilized community that ever existed, from calamities which may in a few days sweep away all the rich heritage of so many ages of wisdom and glory. The danger is terrible. The time is short. If this bill should be rejected, I pray to God that none of those who concur in rejecting it may ever remember their votes with unavailing remorse, amidst the wreck of laws, the confusion of ranks, the spoliation of property, and the dissolution of social order.

T. B. MACAULAY, *speech in the House of Commons on the First
Reform Bill, 2 March 1831.*

2

Narrative of Events
1815-1832

IN 1811, when King George III finally went mad, his eldest
son, a sophisticated bigamist, became Prince Regent. In the
following year the Earl of Liverpool, a very experienced and
thoroughly respectable administrator, was chosen Prime
Minister of the Tory Government. His principal colleague
was Viscount Castlereagh, who led the House of Commons
and conducted foreign policy, with much ability but without
panache. Viscount Sidmouth, formerly, as Henry Addington,
Prime Minister from 1801 to 1804, was Home Secretary. These
were the chief Ministers in office at the time of Waterloo, and
it was Castlereagh who represented Britain at the peace
Congress. He secured that by the Treaty of Vienna of 1815
Britain retained several of the territories which she had seized
from France or from France's satellites during the war, including Malta, the Ionian Islands and, ultimately much more
important, the Cape of Good Hope. On the Continent, the
defeat of Napoleon's attempt at European domination had
re-established Russia, Prussia and Austria as effective rivals to
France. Britain was now a thoroughly satisfied Power, with
everything to gain from peace. At first Castlereagh promoted
the novel idea of holding regular international Congresses of
the Great Powers, which he hoped would help to prevent war
in Europe. Britain took part in the Congress of 1818. But in
1820, when revolutions occurred in Spain, Portugal and Naples,
the other Powers tried to use a Congress to co-ordinate action
against the rebels, with whom on the whole Britain sympathized. She therefore ceased to participate fully.

In internal affairs two major issues of principle divided
politicians: Parliamentary reform and Roman Catholic
emancipation. People had been advocating Parliamentary

reform for over 150 years – and with good reason, as will appear. In the late eighteenth century the two Pitts took up the cause; and Pitt the younger, when he was Prime Minister, in 1785 actually introduced a Bill to transfer 72 seats from small boroughs to large towns and populous counties, though without success. The question was not much discussed during the war, but, of the two national parties, most of the Whigs of 1815 had at some time publicly supported some measure of Parliamentary reform, while most of the Tories were known to be opposed to any. There were, of course, many different schemes of reform, ranging from proposals more moderate than Pitt's to the extremist programme of manhood suffrage, the secret ballot, annual Parliaments and the redistribution of seats in strict accordance with population. After the war the first Whig motion in favour of Reform was brought forward in 1819 by Lord John Russell, one of the most promising younger representatives of the great aristocratic families; but not until 1822 did he go beyond Pitt, by asking for the transfer of 100 seats.

When the Act of Union with Ireland in 1800 joined Ireland to the existing United Kingdom and made Parliament at Westminster supreme over four million Irish Roman Catholics, Emancipation, that is, the concession of political rights to them and to their co-religionists in Britain, became a serious issue. Pitt the younger resigned the Premiership because George III would not allow him to propose it. By 1815 most of the statesmen of the day were sympathetic; and so, generally, by a small majority, was the House of Commons. But the Regent, the House of Lords and, probably, a large proportion of British Protestants were opposed to it.

Fiscal questions were also important after the war. In 1815 Parliament passed a Corn Law prohibiting the importation of foreign corn into Britain until the price on the home market reached 80 shillings a quarter. In 1816 the House of Commons revolted against the Government and refused to continue the income tax, first levied in 1798. As a result, tariff rates had to be increased in the Budget of 1819. In that year also it was decided to return to a gold currency, abandoned in 1797.

In 1816 there appeared all over the country a network of societies, the Hampden Clubs, appealing to working-men by a low subscription of 1d. a week, and advocating radical Parliamentary reform. Supporting the same cause, William Cobbett's

Political Register, by an evasion of stamp duty, sold from the middle of November 40,000 a week at 2d. Mass meetings were held at Nottingham, Liverpool, Manchester, Paisley, Glasgow and in London, where a petition to the Regent was approved and signed. In varying degrees the movement was patronized by the City of London and by radical aristocrats like Sir Francis Burdett. But in January 1817, alarmed by an attempt on the life of the Regent, the Government carried through Parliament, with very little opposition, a Habeas Corpus Suspension Act and an Act banning most public meetings. Cobbett left for the United States. However, the Habeas Corpus Suspension Act soon lapsed, and a new agitation arose in 1819. A series of mass meetings culminated at St Peter's Fields, Manchester, on August 16. The magistrates ordered the yeomanry to arrest the speaker, Henry Hunt. The yeomanry failed, and had to be rescued by regular cavalry. Eleven people were killed and 400 wounded. This was 'the Peterloo massacre'. The Government's reaction was to congratulate the magistrates, to increase the size of the army and to obtain from Parliament 'the Six Acts', the chief provisions of which were a still severer limitation of the right of public meeting and a further restriction of the freedom of the Press. On this occasion many of the Whigs opposed the Government.

George III died in January 1820, and the Prince Regent succeeded as George IV. The new King forced the Government to proceed against his Queen, Caroline, from whom he had long been separated, for a divorce. The hearing lasted for some months in the House of Lords. His case against her was strong, but not so strong as hers against him. She became a popular heroine, and the Whigs took her side. In the end, though there was a majority against her in the Lords, it was too small for the Government to be able to pursue the matter in the Commons. But she was not acknowledged as Queen, was turned away from the doors of Westminster Abbey on Coronation day, and died later in 1821.

Castlereagh (Marquis of Londonderry in the last year of his life) died in 1822, and his place was taken by George Canning, an abler and much livelier man, with great oratorical gifts and a flair for publicity. 'A poet,' wrote Halévy, 'had succeeded the man of prose.'[1] His foreign policy seemed very different

---

[1] E. Halévy, *The Liberal Awakening, 1815–1830* (London, 1949), p. 165.

from Castlereagh's. He not only refused to assist the suppression of a Liberal movement in Spain. In 1825 he recognized the new republics of Buenos Aires, Mexico and Colombia – all former Spanish colonies; he helped to establish Brazil, a former Portuguese colony, as an independent state; in 1826 he sent troops to aid the constitutionalist party in Portugal; and in 1827 he concluded a treaty with Russia and France under which Turkey was to be forced to grant a measure of independence to the Greeks, who had rebelled in 1821. The result of this treaty was the battle of Navarino Bay (fought in October 1827, two months after Canning's death) in which the allied fleet altogether destroyed the Turkish fleet. Greece became fully independent in 1830.

From about the time when Canning succeeded Castlereagh, the Tories became domestic reformers. Early in 1822 Lord Sidmouth had been replaced as Home Secretary by Robert Peel, the very able heir to a fortune made in the Lancashire cotton industry; in the following year F. J. Robinson became Chancellor of the Exchequer, and William Huskisson President of the Board of Trade. All these men, like Lord Liverpool himself, were moderate Free Traders; and in the next few years, particularly in the Budget of 1825, the Government somewhat reduced tariff rates and greatly simplified the exceedingly complicated tariff system. It was a time for removing restrictions and anomalies of all sorts. The customs barrier between Britain and Ireland was abolished in 1825. The Navigation Acts, designed in the seventeenth century to protect English shipping against Dutch competition, were modified, and the colonies were allowed to trade more freely with foreign countries. In 1820 Sir James Mackintosh, an Opposition leader, had carried Bills abolishing the death penalty for a number of preposterous offences, such as being disguised within the Mint, injuring Westminster Bridge, and personating out-pensioners of Greenwich Hospital. In 1823 Peel took up the cause, and abolished the death penalty for a further 100 offences. He also reformed the system of paying judges, and began the work of consolidating the criminal law into relatively few statutes. These were the years of 'Liberal Toryism'.

Early in 1827 Lord Liverpool had a stroke, and resigned. For the next three years politics were confused. Canning became Prime Minister. Peel and many other Tories refused to serve under him, but he obtained the assistance of some Whigs. When he died in August, Robinson, now Viscount Goderich, succeeded him. But by January 1828 he found it impossible to go on, and the King resorted to the Duke of Wellington, who had commanded the British troops at the battle of Waterloo and served in Liverpool's Cabinets from 1818 onwards, a man of conservative prejudices controlled by massive realism. Wellington gave office to Peel and his sympathizers, but lacked the support of the Whigs and, after a brief period of cooperation, of the 'Canningites'. In the confusion Parliament passed in March the repeal of the seventeenth-century Test and Corporation Acts which, in theory at least, had debarred Dissenters from public office. The Government modified the Corn Law, so that corn would be imported when the home price reached 52 shillings, but only at a high rate of duty, which fell as the home price rose. The Metropolitan Police Act of 1829, Peel's work, founded the modern police force.

In April 1829 Wellington carried Catholic emancipation. This was an astonishing reversal of form, since Peel had been the most prominent opponent of the measure and the Government was the nearest approach possible to a 'Protestant' Ministry. Emancipation had been forced on the Government by the campaign of the Catholic Association in Ireland, under the leadership of Daniel O'Connell. This organization, closely associated with the Catholic priesthood, obtained a large revenue from the Irish peasantry by a subscription of 1d. a month. It had been founded in 1823, suppressed by statute in 1825, but re-formed. At the General Election of 1826 it showed its strength by winning two constituencies normally in the control of Protestant landlords. In 1828, when Vesey Fitzgerald, one of that class, newly appointed by Wellington President of the Board of Trade, stood for re-election in County Clare, O'Connell, though disqualified as a Catholic from sitting in the House, put up against him and won. It was plain that only O'Connell's present moderation was preserving order in Ireland, and that the Association would win other seats at the next General Election; 25,000 of the 30,000 troops in the United Kingdom were engaged in watching the situation in Ireland. Wellington decided that Emancipation must be granted; and he prevailed on Peel not to resign, on the King not to obstruct the measure, and on the House of Lords not to reject it. There were certain safeguards in the Act: a Catholic had to swear an elaborate oath before taking office; he could not aspire to be Regent, Lord Chancellor, Lord Lieutenant of Ireland, or – save the mark! – High Commissioner to the General Assembly of the Church of Scotland; he could not make church appointments; and there were provisions 'for the gradual suppression and final prohibition of' male religious orders. At the same time, to preserve 'the Protestant ascendancy' in Ireland, the Parliamentary franchise there was greatly restricted.

George IV died in June 1830, and was succeeded by his eldest surviving brother, an undignified, jovial sailor, as William IV. In December 1829 Thomas Attwood, a fanatical currency reformer, had founded the Birmingham Political Union to agitate for Parliamentary reform, which he thought was the essential preliminary to other desirable changes. The Union soon had imitators all over the country. Not only Whigs and popular societies, but Tory gentry, disgusted at the concessions of Wellington's Government, were advocating Parliamentary reform. 'For two years,' wrote G. M. Young, 'beginning with the Paris Revolution of July 1830, England lived in a sustained intensity of excitement unknown since 1641.'[1] A serious labourers' revolt broke out in the southern agricultural counties in August. In November Wellington declared himself totally opposed to any reform of Parliament, and found that he had aroused general indignation. He resigned, and Earl Grey, an elderly, respected Whig who had entered Parliament before the Revolution of 1789 and had last held office in 1807, became Prime Minister. He formed a Cabinet pledged to propose a Reform Bill. It included several Canningites, among them Goderich as Colonial Secretary, Viscount Palmerston, hitherto best known as a 'man about town', as Foreign Secretary, and the cynical and indolent Viscount Melbourne as Home Secretary. A Tory reformer, the Duke of Richmond, also entered the Cabinet. Of the Whigs Viscount Althorp, a man of solid integrity whose main interest was in the family estates, became leader of the House of Commons; the Earl of Durham, virtually a Radical, was made

---

[1] G. M. Young, *Portrait of an Age* (London, 1936), p. 27.

Lord Privy Seal; and Henry Brougham, a fine orator and a great legal reformer, Lord Chancellor.

The Government introduced its Reform Bill for England and Wales on 1 March 1831. In charge of it in the Commons was Lord John Russell, who became a member of the Cabinet in June. It transferred 168 seats from small boroughs to large towns and counties; and standardized the franchise in the boroughs and extended it in the counties, so that it was calculated that the total electorate would be doubled. On 23 March the Bill was read a second time by 302 to 301 in the largest vote or 'division' ever recorded in the unreformed House of Commons. In April, however, the Government was defeated on a clause reducing the number of English Members, and after some hesitation the King agreed to dissolve Parliament, coming to the Lords in person just in time to prevent the House from passing a resolution deploring his action. A very rapid General Election took place, purely and simply on the question of the Reform Bill, and the Government won a majority of over 100. In September a second Bill, much like the first, passed the Commons. On October 8 the Lords rejected the second reading by a majority of 41. An extraordinary manifestation of popular feeling followed, with monster petitions, mass meetings, the foundation of a National Political Union in London and serious riots in several cities. Nottingham Castle and the Bishop's palace in Bristol were burned down. The Lords passed the second reading of a third Reform Bill in April 1832. But they were still determined to alter it in committee. Grey asked the King to create enough peers (about fifty) to force the Bill through as it stood. The King refused, Grey resigned, and another storm broke in the country. Petitions urged the Commons not to grant supplies, and there was a threat of a run on the Bank of England. Wellington considered it his duty to agree to take office, with the idea of bringing in a more moderate Bill. But Peel refused to help him, being unwilling again to bring forward a measure which was opposed to principles long maintained by himself and his party. The King was forced to recall the Whigs and to promise to create as many peers as might be needed to coerce the Lords. The Lords then yielded, Wellington giving the lead by announcing his intention of abstaining, and the Bill passed into law on June 7.

3

Economic Background
1815-1832

The Industrial Revolution

IN the 1780s the British economy began to change very rapidly – at a rate, in fact, unprecedented in the history of the world. This increase of tempo marks the decisive point in the development towards modern industrialized, urbanized society, the point which Rostow has strikingly christened 'the take-off into self-sustained growth',[1] after which the progressive exploitation of new sources of power and new techniques has made possible a long-term economic growth-rate once unimaginable but now considered normal. In order to understand what happened after Waterloo, it is essential to know something about the beginnings of this revolution and to appreciate its significance.

Many industries were affected, but three most prominently: coal, iron and cotton. It is thought that coal production rose from about 6,000,000 tons in 1780 to about 25,000,000 tons in 1830. The output of pig-iron in 1788 was estimated at 61,000 tons, in 1806 at 227,000 tons, in 1830 at 700,000 tons. Most remarkable, in 1781 the cotton industry consumed 5,000,000 lbs. of raw material, in 1800 56,000,000, from 1816 to 1820 an average of 107,000,000 a year, and from 1826 to 1830 an average of over 220,000,000 a year.

It is the story of the cotton industry which is the most significant. An industry which had been of little importance before 1780 was already, around 1815, exporting more, both by value and by volume, than the woollen industry, which had been Britain's staple since the Middle Ages. In 1830 half the whole value of British exports was made up of cotton manu-

---

[1] W. W. Rostow, *The Stages of Economic Growth* (Cambridge, 1960).

factures, cotton twist and yarn, despite a great fall in cotton prices and a great rise in total exports.

Not only was it a new industry in the sense that it had virtually grown from nothing in fifty years. It was new in its character. Before 1815 a series of machines had been invented which made it possible to transform both the process of cotton-picking in the United States and the processes of spinning and weaving in Britain so that production could be vastly increased and costs dramatically reduced. The essential change in spinning and weaving was the displacement of human motive power. First water-power was applied, then steam-power. A new opportunity now existed for a man who could afford capital outlay on the new machines, and consequently a new social structure emerged in the industry: the capitalist owner set over against a mass of wage-earners who had no share in the property of the enterprise. Further, it was now desirable to concentrate both the spinning and the weaving, hitherto often conducted at home in the country, into large factories which, when steam-power was applied to the process, were best located in towns. There was naturally a time-lag between the inventions and their widespread application, and different processes were affected at different times. In 1815 weaving was still mainly 'domestic'. But spinning was already mono-polized by mills, some driven by water but many by steam; and

the size of the average steam spinning mill in the chief manufacturing centres, even in 1815–16, was something unprecedented in British industry. Forty-one Glasgow mills averaged 244 workpeople each . . . and, at New Lanark, Dale and Owen employed over 1600. In England, the Strutts, at Belper and Millford, had 1494 workpeople. A list of forty-three important mills, in and about Manchester, gave an average employment figure of exactly 300. . . . In the year of the Reform Bill, a similar list of about the same number of Manchester mills gives a figure of nearly 401.[1]

Power-loom weaving had spread further by 1832, but was still not typical; so at first the other inventions brought into existence, as well as factories, armies of handloom or domestic weavers, a quarter of a million of them in 1830.

Unprecedented also was the widespread application of the motive power of steam in the cotton industry. Steam provided

---

[1] J. H. Clapham, *Economic History of Modern Britain*, vol. I (London, 1930), pp. 184–5.

probably three-quarters of its inanimate power by the 'thirties. This had become possible only after successive inventions, again in the late eighteenth century, had improved the old steam pumping-engines, long used in coalmines. Man thereby acquired a new 'prime mover', the first to have been discovered in historic times. He was no longer dependent on rivers, wind, and the labour of men and animals, and the new source of power was evidently far more generally effective than its competitors. The cotton industry in 1815, still more in 1832, appeared revolutionary in its wholesale use of machines, in the size, number and location of its factories and in its reliance on steam-power. It was also, as will be seen, revolutionary in its relation to world trade.

Innovation in the iron industry was less spectacular. The most important changes were those which made possible the use of coal rather than wood for smelting. As a result of this development Britain had become by about 1800 a net exporter instead of a net importer of iron, which was of course an essential raw material for the construction of machines, railways and so on. As for coal, the industry was a breeding-ground for inventions, like the steam-engine and the railway, which were influential chiefly outside it. However, coal as a raw material was of vast and growing importance: gas from coal was just beginning to be used for lighting around 1815, more and more heating processes were being converted from scarce timber to plentiful coal, and steam-engines always used coal. 'Coal and steam,' Landes has written, 'did not make the Industrial Revolution; but they permitted its extraordinary development and diffusion.'[1]

It must not be supposed that all British industries were revolutionized during this period. Before 1780 many had been well-established and highly-developed, especially coalmining, copper and tin mining and wool manufacture. Large numbers of workmen had long been gathered together in arsenals, mines, breweries and silk-mills, where capital and labour were separated. Though nearly all industries expanded greatly between 1780 and 1850, and though most benefited from some invention or other, the cotton industry was still at the latter date unique in its degree of mechanization, concentration

---

[1] D. S. Landes, in *Cambridge Economic History of Europe*, vol. VI (i) (Cambridge, 1965), p. 329.

and reliance on steam power. However, most historians have accepted that it is appropriate to use the term 'Industrial Revolution' with reference to this period, given the great expansion and transformation of the cotton industry and the lesser expansion and developments of other industries. The concept is not generally taken to refer to industrial developments in isolation. It connotes the complex of changes which were associated with industrialization and urbanization. Of these the most fundamental was the growth of population. By comparison with the Britain of 1885, or still more with the Britain of the 1960s, the Britain of 1815 was an empty country. But its population was twice as great as that of the Britain of the early eighteenth century. At the first census in 1801 it was 11,000,000; by 1831 it was 16,000,000. The rate of population growth in the years after Waterloo was the highest in British history.

This increase was by no means evenly spread over the country. In England the population of the South grew, but not nearly so fast as that of the North. In Scotland Highlanders increased in number, but not nearly so fast as Lowlanders. The most densely populated English counties in 1700 were Middlesex and Surrey (owing to the spread of London's suburbs), followed by some of the southern and South Midland counties. By 1801 Lancashire came second after Middlesex, Surrey was third, and then came Warwickshire, the West Riding of Yorkshire and Staffordshire. Only these six had a density of population higher than 200 per square mile. In 1831 the order was the same, but the six now had a density higher than 340 per square mile, and eight other counties had a density above 200.[1] Another way of looking at the matter is to compare the rates of growth of counties between 1801 and 1831. Two British counties more than doubled in population, Monmouthshire and Lanarkshire; Lancashire almost did so. Eight other counties gained 70 per cent or more: Surrey, Midlothian, Glamorgan, Cheshire, the West Riding, Ayrshire, Staffordshire and Sussex. At the other end of the scale several Welsh and Scottish counties grew hardly at all; while in England Rutland, the North Riding, Herefordshire and Wiltshire grew by less than 30 per cent.

---

[1] The average density in the modern U.K. is nearly 600 per square mile.

Urban population increased much more rapidly than rural. Manchester and Glasgow furnish the most spectacular examples of town growth on a large scale. In 1757 Manchester and Salford had roughly 20,000 inhabitants; in 1801 90,000; in 1831 228,000. Between 1801 and 1831 Glasgow grew from 77,000 to 202,000. For many centuries the greatest towns of England after London had been the ancient cathedral cities of Bristol and Norwich. As late as the third quarter of the eighteenth century Bristol, with in 1750 about 60,000 inhabitants, was still England's second city. But by the first census in 1801 Bristol had dropped to fifth place, behind Manchester, Liverpool and Birmingham, the three great cities of the future. Manchester was the centre of the Lancashire cotton industry, Liverpool its chief outlet to the sea and the busiest Atlantic port, Birmingham the capital of the metal-working trades. By 1831, even though Bristol had continued to grow and had reached 100,000 inhabitants, it had been overtaken by another upstart, Leeds, the centre of the growing woollen industry of the West Riding. London, indeed, remained supreme, its population increasing from 865,000 in 1801 to 1,474,000 in 1831. But it had closer rivals now than for many centuries, and these rivals were parvenus: as yet Manchester and Birmingham were not even boroughs. In Scotland the Capital was actually displaced as the most populous city: Glasgow, port and cotton town, overtook Edinburgh around 1815.

Why population increased so rapidly is a matter of acute controversy, or perhaps it would be truer to say of intense speculation. For the eighteenth century the figures of total British population are all estimates made by later students on the basis of incomplete returns worked out from defective parish registers. Even for the early nineteenth century census totals are not wholly reliable. When it comes to the statistics of births, marriages and deaths, on which any attempt at explaining the growth of population must be founded, there is the same difficulty for the early nineteenth as for the eighteenth century: it is known that many of these events went unrecorded even after more efficient registration was established in 1836, and the figures must be still less complete for earlier dates. Further, there seems to be no satisfactory theory of population growth, and in particular there appears to be little justification for the assumption commonly made that 'prosperity' or 'economic advance' naturally produces a high birth-rate. Again, attempts to explain the rise of population in Britain often fail to allow for the fact that, while Britain alone in the eighteenth and early nineteenth centuries underwent an Industrial Revolution, in most of the countries of the world population was growing fast.

The most hopeful approach promises to be that of Deane and Cole, who distinguish between areas within England and between stages in the whole story.[1] Broadly, they suggest this picture for the first thirty years of the nineteenth century. In London and the surrounding area it is hard to deny that there was a fall in the death-rate between the middle of the eighteenth century and 1830. This was presumably the result of somewhat improved sanitary arrangements and living conditions, somewhat better medical services (including the spread of vaccination) and an absence of great epidemics, with the necessary precondition that food supplies kept pace with the rise in numbers. It is difficult to find evidence for London of a rising birth-rate. About half the increase in its population seems to have been due to migration, and London and the Home Counties apparently gathered people from all over the South.[2]

In the North-west, the principal industrial area, on the other hand, the effects of a sustained rise in the birth-rate in the late eighteenth century would appear to have been enhanced by a fall in the death-rate in the early nineteenth century. Migration was comparatively small and local, apart from a growing influx from Ireland. The rise in the birth-rate is explained partly by economic opportunity, especially because it encouraged earlier marriage. It has been suggested by Habakkuk, with great plausibility, that Britain's overall pattern of population growth diverged from Continental Europe's in the early years of the nineteenth century, industrialization explaining the faster increase in Britain.[3] But it is so difficult to be sure of the pattern and of the statistics of

---

[1] P. M. Deane and W. A. Cole, *British Economic Growth, 1688–1959* (Cambridge, 1967), ch. III.

[2] Cf. E. A. Wrigley, 'London's Importance 1650–1750', *Past and Present* 1967.

[3] See H. J. Habakkuk's article 'The Economic History of Modern Britain' (*Journal of Economic History*, 1958), reprinted in D. V. Glass and D. E. C. Eversley (eds.), *Population in History* (London, 1965). For the whole question, Glass & Eversley, and the review article of G. S. L. Tucker in *Econ.H.R.* 1967.

birth and death-rates that it is impossible to substantiate this suggestion, and it is hard to reconcile it with the case of Ireland, an almost purely agricultural country which until the 1840s had a population rising as fast as any.

To account for the location of the growing industrial districts is somewhat easier. Deposits of coal were near all of them, making domestic as well as industrial heating cheaper. However, before coal was much used in manufacture, Yorkshire was competing successfully with the woollen industry of the South, cotton was established in Lancashire, and Liverpool was outdistancing Bristol in the slave and sugar trades of the North Atlantic. The previously underdeveloped North seems to have afforded better opportunities than the South for new enterprise.

As well as new industries, the oldest, agriculture, developed greatly in the eighteenth and early nineteenth centuries. In fact it has been common to speak of an Agricultural Revolution of the same period as the Industrial Revolution. However, if the agricultural changes are to be regarded as revolutionary, they must be seen against thousands of years of development. For the advances were slow, and much less radical than those in industry. They were of two kinds. First, methods of farming on existing farmland were improved. Secondly, the area of farming was extended. Both were age-old processes. The former had speeded up in the late seventeenth and early eighteenth centuries, when the cultivation of turnips and similar crops became more general in Britain, making it unnecessary to leave fields fallow for one year in two, three or four, and when serious efforts began to improve the breeds of sheep and cattle. The extension of farming, especially arable farming, became more rapid in the late eighteenth century, with the pressure of growing population and the sharp rise in food prices during the wars with France. An index of these developments was the increase in the frequency of 'enclosures', or redrawings of the rural map of ownership. Sometimes they took the form of replacing long-standing arrangements of a partially feudal or communal character by strict division into individually-owned and compact farms; sometimes it was a matter of taking into cultivation and ownership waste or common (communally-owned) land; often it was a bit of both. Generally it required an Act of Parliament; and 3554 enclosure acts were passed in the reign of George III, mostly for the Midlands and during the wars. They made possible greater efficiency in farming. But the scale of the changes must not be exaggerated. It has long been normal for historians to cite the effect of better techniques on the rental of Thomas Coke of Holkham in Norfolk, later Earl of Leicester. His rents are usually said to have gone up ten times in forty years before 1816. This is an error: on a constant area they only doubled, and that in a time of rising prices.[1] This is a fair indication of the rate of change – far from spectacular, but considerable. Progress continued after 1815, but the emphasis was different. Livestock farmers continued to prosper, but, though grain yields rose, the area of arable cultivation probably fell slightly.[2]

More dramatic were the improvements made in communications. In the 1750s the canal age began. By the 1820s there were 3000 miles of canals in Britain, almost all in the North and Midlands. They made little difference to the traveller, but they made it possible to carry large non-perishable loads to parts of the country previously difficult or impossible of access by water, at a time when heavy bulk transport by road was hardly feasible. They also reduced transport costs by perhaps three or four times. The roads were not neglected. This was the age of the 'turnpike trusts', which took upon themselves the duty, supposed to be that of the ordinary local authorities, of bringing main roads into a tolerable condition. There were about 20,000 miles of turnpikes in the 1820s. The most spectacular achievement they made possible was the introduction of rapid mail and passenger coach services between the principal towns of Britain. In the middle of the eighteenth century it had taken nearly a week to travel from London to Edinburgh by road, and well into the nineteenth century people preferred to make the journey by sea; but the coach time had been cut to less than 48 hours by 1830. The government took some part in improving roads where military considerations operated, as in the Highlands of Scotland and with the route to Holyhead, the port for Ireland. Some of the most beautiful British road bridges date from this period, perhaps the most striking being the Menai bridge between

---

[1] R. A. C. Parker, 'Coke of Norfolk and the Agrarian Revolution', *Econ.H.R.* 1955.
[2] For this and subsequent sections on agriculture see E. L. Jones, *The Development of English Agriculture, 1815–1873* (London, 1968) and works cited in his bibliography.

Anglesey and the mainland of Wales, opened in 1826, designed,
like hundreds of lesser structures, by Thomas Telford.

These developments were necessarily accompanied by the
growth of 'special commercial organizations'. Over the period
of the Industrial Revolution the number of London and country
private banks increased enormously. A century after the first
foundation of a country bank in 1716, there were about 900.
The Stock Exchange, which had started very informally, was
by 1815 well-organized and publishing a list of securities, mostly
government stocks, in which the public might invest. Insurance
against fire and other risks also developed considerably.

Better communications and financial organization were
associated with a great expansion of the internal market.
But the high rate of growth attained during the Industrial
Revolution would have been impossible to achieve but for the
existence of huge overseas markets, some under Britain's
political control, some not, which her industry was able to
exploit. The cotton industry tapped a mass market of unprecedented size. It also had a novel relationship with world
trade. Before the rise of the cotton industry Britain had imported few commodities in bulk: only timber, sugar, and in bad
years grain. She had exported relatively little too, chiefly woollen goods. But the cotton industry required enormous imports
of raw cotton, most of which, by the 'thirties, came from the
United States; and it exported more of its manufactured products than it sold at home. Not only did it capture large markets
in both North and South America, but between 1820 and 1840
its competition destroyed the cotton industry of India.

> This was not merely a gratifying extension of Lancashire's markets. It
> was a major landmark in world history. For since the dawn of time
> Europe had always imported more from the East than she had sold
> there. . . . The cotton shirtings of the Industrial Revolution for the
> first time reversed this relationship.[1]

The Industrial Revolution had made Britain even by 1815
certainly the richest and most industrialized, and probably
the most urbanized, country in the world; and she had established such a lead, possessed such good natural resources and
had access to such excellent markets that for much of the
period covered by this book the gap between Britain and other

---

[1] E. J. Hobsbawm, *The Age of Revolution* (London, 1962), p. 35.

countries widened. As far as Britain herself is concerned, many of the trends of the Industrial Revolution persisted throughout the period and beyond. The high rate of population growth was sustained until the 1880s. Up to the First World War cotton, iron (with steel) and coal, together with wool, remained the staple industries of the country. The same nine British cities which were the largest at the census of 1801 are the largest still, in a slightly different order. Much of this book must be devoted to tracing these trends and their impact on British society down to 1885.

Economic Vicissitudes

I have been writing of the Industrial Revolution as though economic development was proceeding smoothly and beneficently in the late eighteenth and early nineteenth centuries. In fact the process was far from smooth, and, though the general trend was doubtless towards greater prosperity all round, many people suffered economic hardship.

In the first place, account must be taken of the impact of the war with France and its aftermath. It cut links between the mainland of Europe and the rest of the world, especially after 1807, when Napoleon inaugurated his 'Continental System', designed to make the territories under his control as nearly self-sufficient as possible and to eliminate all trade with Britain, and when Britain began to retaliate with Orders in Council intended to establish a complete blockade of his Empire. These measures were not entirely successful, but they did virtually close overseas markets to the products of the Continent, and they did give Britain almost a monopoly of the carrying trade, so that such non-European goods as reached the countries of Napoleon's Empire came in British ships. On the other hand, between 1812 and 1814 Britain was at war with the United States, and both the imports and exports of the cotton industry were drastically reduced. The war created exceptional demand for such things as iron, ships and woollen goods. By cutting Britain off from Continental grain supplies, it encouraged the development of her agriculture. After the war foreign competition returned to overseas markets and the carrying trade. But for the Corn Law, it would have seriously affected British agriculture. The demand for iron, ships and woollen goods fell. However, some European markets and the trade with the United States were reopened. It may be that the war was decisive in permitting Britain to keep control of certain markets, especially the South American. But otherwise it would seem that the short-term gains of wartime were offset in peacetime, and that the war should be thought of as distorting rather than furthering British economic development as a whole.

This is particularly evident when the effects of the wartime activities of the government are considered. Britain by 1815 had been at war, with one short break, for twenty-two years. Taxation rates and government expenditure, over £100,000,000 a year in 1814 and 1815, were higher than at any later date in the period covered by this book. The impact of the war on the economy was comparable with that of the First World War. After 1815 government expenditure dropped sharply, taxation somewhat less sharply, and 300,000 men were thrown on to the labour market by the demobilization. The combined effects of these changes, of depreciation of the currency and of the disruption of trade was to raise prices during the war and lower them when peace came. There were other factors affecting prices, of course. Cotton prices fell more than general prices after the war, because the technological changes in the industry made possible reductions in costs. The overall picture is that, as compared with the beginning of the war in 1793, prices had nearly doubled by 1813, and were back to their old levels by 1821.

Many factors other than the war worked against smooth economic development. One was the weather. The quality of the harvest was still of crucial importance to the whole economy. A bad harvest meant high bread prices, higher still given the Corn Law. Dear bread meant a drastic reduction in the power of ordinary people to purchase commodities other than food. This limited the market at home for the products of British industries. Even if overseas demand remained good, high domestic consumption was necessary to maintain full employment in industry. So there was likely to be heavy industrial unemployment just at the time when food prices were high. In other words, the industrial worker lost twice over.

Further, there were superimposed on to the effects of the war and the effects of the weather the fluctuations of the business cycle. When goods are selling well, it is likely that too many workers will be taken on, too much capital invested and too many goods produced. There then comes a point when the goods no longer sell, workers lose their jobs and capacity is idle. The cycle still occurs in the second half of the twentieth century, but it is now much less evident because controlled by governments. In the early nineteenth century it was allowed to operate with a minimum of interference. These were some of the difficulties. Manufacturers, traders and investors were working largely in the dark, especially in their dealings outside Europe, now more important than ever before. It took several weeks to cross the Atlantic, several months to get to India; there was no telegraph; people in Britain could have very little idea of conditions in such areas as South America. The success of British exports depended not only on willingness to buy, but also on ability to pay. Many countries could take British exports only if they could provide Britain with useful imports, and development of their resources might depend on attracting British investment. Britain throughout this period imported more goods from the rest of the world than she exported; her balance of payments was generally favourable, but only because of earnings from shipping, services and foreign investment. Of these, foreign investment was growing in importance. Some of it, however, was in the nature of the case in dubious projects in areas with unsettled governments and unreliable banks. The most remarkable instance was a loan of £200,000 subscribed in 1822 to the 'Kingdom of Poyais' which did not exist. So there were periodical crises of confidence following upon defaults, repudiations and bank failures. Each crisis resulted in a drain of gold from Britain and therefore in credit restriction and recession at home. In this period the early 1820s were years of high foreign investment, and by 1825 the total was almost £100,000,000, four times that of 1815. Then in 1825 came the crash. This crisis also revealed the weakness of English country banks, about 70 of which failed.

For all these reasons there were marked fluctuations in production, exports, imports, wages and prices from year to year. To take prices, although their trend was downwards after 1813, the annual variations were very large. In 1812 the average wheat price was 126 shillings a quarter, the highest ever; in 1815 it was down to 66 shillings, hardly more than half what it had been three years earlier; in 1817 it was 97 shillings; in 1822 45 shillings; in 1825 68 shillings again. It helps to understand political history to know that there were particularly high wheat prices in 1812–13, 1816–19, 1824–5 and 1828–31, those of 1824–5 being offset by boom conditions.

There were also longer-term trends operating against the British economy. Until the 1840s the prices of imports, mainly raw materials, tended to rise and the prices of exports, mainly manufactured goods, to fall. Hence the great increase in the volume of exports brought relatively little benefit.

State action often made matters worse. The tariff system was ill-adapted to the British economy, in general as well as in particular. The end of the income tax, and the imposition of the Corn Law and of other tariffs to replace the revenue previously derived from the income tax, increased the burden of taxes on the poor, thus reducing the demand for cheap manufactured goods. There was a duty on the import of raw cotton, small it is true, but manifestly harmful. There was a heavy duty on imported timber, which Britain needed in large quantities. There was a duty on the export of coal, of which Britain produced a considerable surplus and other countries were short. High excise duties were levied on 'printed calicoes and muslins', that is, on the main products of the cotton industry, and on glass and paper, when made and sold in Britain. Further, the export of machinery was prohibited; skilled labourers might not emigrate; and trade was in many cases restricted to English ships.

During the period 1815–32, as has been seen, Ministers tried to make improvements. Most statesmen accepted, with growing conviction as the years went by, that, while tariffs were clearly necessary to raise revenue, they were unlikely to promote economic development. The views of the 'political economists', and especially of Adam Smith and David Ricardo, had partially won over educated opinion. What prevented Governments from reducing duties further was partly their belief that the House of Commons, probably reflecting public opinion, would not tolerate the income tax in peacetime. But, further, the Corn Law was admitted to be a special problem; there was much support for colonial preference, entrenched in the tariff system; and manufacturers and shippers clung to protective measures. An Act of 1826, which took away the Bank of England's monopoly of joint-stock banking, was an attempt to assist economic development in another way, by encouraging the formation of stronger country banks than those which had proved inadequate in 1825. Parliament was also slowly repealing, in the name of *laissez-faire*, the old laws which restricted apprenticeship and terms of employment and had attempted to regulate industrial production.

So the economy as a whole, despite the great advances of the Industrial Revolution, could hardly be said to be in a happy state. Although there were some very good moments, especially in 1824–5, when output, investment, exports, profits and employment were all high, there were too many bad moments. The uncertainties of commerce and the sharp fluctuations of the economy caused much hardship. Manufacturers, traders and investors were liable to find themselves suddenly bankrupt. The special case of the farmers was important. Although protected by the Corn Law, they saw the general level of agricultural prices fall. Many of them had borrowed money during the war to carry out some improvement and found themselves after 1815 paying the interest out of lower receipts. All farmers were discontented, a few were ruined. This is when the small farmer suffered, rather than in the war years. The new conditions favoured larger-scale farming and pasture farming.

Much more serious than the farmers' difficulties was the hardship of wage-earners. Wages in the northern industrial districts were in general high, and workers in the new factories were well paid in good times. But in periods of unemployment their position would be appalling. Workers in some trades were not merely thrown out of work from time to time, but saw the craft in which they had been trained and by which they had lived eliminated by technical advance. Fear of this led to opposition to mechanization. The years 1811–12 had been particularly notable for 'frame-breaking', in some areas rather as a means of drawing the attention of employers to workers' grievances, but in others as a protest against the introduction of labour-saving machinery. As yet large numbers of handloom weavers were necessary to the textile industries. But their wages were falling in relation both to the cost of living and to the wages of workers in factories. In the South especially, the agricultural labourer too was the victim of grave hardship.

Migration from the South to the North was difficult and un-
common, the surplus population of predominantly rural areas
found few opportunities open, and real wages in many southern
counties were lower after the war than before it. Something of
the same technological threat existed for the agricultural as
for the industrial worker. The labourers' revolt of 1830 in the
southern counties was directed partly against the introduction
of threshing machines.

The situation was complicated by the law, especially the
Poor Law. The basis of the Poor Law was the Act of 1601.
It provided, humanely, and as few countries' laws provided
even by the early nineteenth century, that the individual had
a right to the bare necessities of life. The old, the sick and the
insane were to be kept alive, if need be, by their parish, through
a rate levied on owners and occupiers of landed property;
children and others who, though capable of work, were unem-
ployed were to be 'set on work' in special 'workhouses'. By later
legislation it was laid down that a man should be 'chargeable'
only to a parish in which he acquired a 'settlement', either by
birth or residence. These were the laws which of all laws meant
most to the ordinary Englishman, offering him his only security
against starvation. From the late eighteenth century the problem of poverty began to grow, and new methods were adopted
to deal with it. It became more common for parishes to group
together to build a workhouse, which was made generally possible by Gilbert's Act of 1782. In 1795, at a time of high prices,
the magistrates of Berkshire, gathered in Quarter Sessions at the
Pelican Inn, Speenhamland, took a decision which was quickly
imitated elsewhere. They decided that the money raised by the
poor rate should be used to supplement wages according to a
scale based on the price of bread.

> When the Gallon Loaf of Second flour, weighing 8 lb. 11 ozs. shall
> cost 1s.
> Then every poor and industrious man shall have for his own support
> 3s. weekly, either produced by his own or his family's labour, or an
> allowance from the poor rates, and for the support of his wife and every
> other of his family, 1s. 6d. . . .
> And so in proportion, as the price of bread rise or falls . . . 3d. to the
> man, and 1d. to every other of the family, on every 1d. which the loaf
> rises above 1s.

This and other forms of 'outdoor relief' had been known

before, but now they became more general in the South of England. By 1830 there was scarcely any work done in the so-called workhouses, which had become refuges, but the amount spent on poor relief was much greater than in the eighteenth century.

Year(s)	Annual expenditure on poor relief in England and Wales	
1748–50	under	£700,000 (annual average)
1783–5	just over	£2,000,000 (annual average)
1818	almost	£8,000,000
1821–30	over	£6,000,000 (annual average)

It seems that the sum spent in the 1820s would have kept the whole population at the bare level of subsistence for rather less than five weeks, or between 8 and 9 per cent of the population for the whole year. The total rate represented a sum comparable with the yield of the land tax, the principal national direct tax levied after the income tax lapsed. In fact the receipts and expenditure were spread unevenly over the country, being highest in southern agricultural districts not under the influence of London and highest of all in Sussex. The Poor Law kept the poor alive, with relatively few exceptions. But the way in which it was administered after 1795 came to be regarded as unfortunate. In the worst areas, it was thought, wages were deliberately kept low by employers in order that rates, paid by owners and occupiers, should supplement them; labourers' earnings were thus maintained at or below subsistence level, and the law of settlement discouraged them from migrating to areas where wages were higher. In Scotland, where the law was different, and in some industrial districts, poor relief was given sparingly, and a better hope of high wages was balanced by a sharper fear of starvation.

Much discussion has ranged around the question of whether the standard of living of the worker rose or fell during and because of the Industrial Revolution. Many of the factors which enter the discussion are social rather than economic, and will be considered elsewhere. It must first be said that it makes a considerable difference whether one takes 1780 or 1800 as the starting date, and 1830, 1850 or the end of the depression of 1837–42 as the final date. But the conclusion cannot in any case be straightforward and confident. According to such calculations as have been made, average real wages were rather higher in Britain in the 1820s than in the 1780s. But the early 1820s were especially good years in this respect. During the war standards seem to have declined. 1800, incidentally, was a particularly bad year. Further, the statistics ignore unemployment and are unable to take proper account of the redistribution of the labour force; and the average real wage will be higher than the real wage of the average man. As has been seen, conditions varied enormously from area to area, trade to trade, and year to year. It would seem that the Industrial Revolution increased the uncertainties and fluctuations of the economy and the number of people exposed to their full effects. Given these vicissitudes, the high levels of poor relief expenditure and indirect taxation in the 1820s, and the size of two groups of workers whose real wages were then lower than before the war, the handloom weavers and the southern agricultural labourers, it is hard to accept a picture of general improvement in the standard of living of the working classes since the 1780s, at least down to 1832.[1]

It is important, however, not to romanticize the pre-industrial age, when poor people often suffered appallingly; and it must always be remembered that the rise of population was to a large extent independent of the Industrial Revolution, and that hardship would have been vastly greater in Britain if numbers had grown without an Industrial Revolution.

---

[1] J. E. Williams, 'The British Standard of Living, 1750–1850', *Econ.H.R.* 1966, gives the references to earlier articles and carries the discussion a stage further.

4
Society and Politics
1815-1832

FOR convenience of analysis the 'Establishment' will be first treated on its own, then 'other forces of society', and only later the interrelationships. This division is of course unreal, and will exaggerate the power, conservatism and solidarity of the 'Establishment' and the degree of its isolation from the working and middle classes, Nonconformity and the new industrial towns. But the exaggeration is salutary, for in many accounts of the nineteenth century the old governing class has been bowed off the stage much too soon.

The 'Establishment'
Although Britain's economy was developing so fast, the social structure of the country was changing only slowly. The great hereditary landlords, whose chief economic concern was agriculture, still dominated British society.[1] In some respects their position was even growing stronger. The progress of farming increased their revenues. Further, during the eighteenth century the trend had been for large estates to get larger, and this trend seems to have continued, though more slowly, into the second half of the nineteenth century. Both law and opinion favoured the transmission of entire estates to one male heir, rather than their division among several heirs. The first survey of land-ownership was not made until 1873, and was inadequate in many ways; but it is believed that a reliable general picture can be formed from it, the broad outlines of which apply to the previous sixty years as well. In 1873 363 persons each owned more than 10,000 acres in England. To look at the position in

---

[1] For much of this Section see F. M. L. Thompson, *English Landed Society in the Nineteenth Century* (London, 1963).

another way, half the land of England and Wales was owned by about 4,000 persons. Something of the same pattern was to be found in Scotland. Only in Eastern Europe were great land-owners so great as in Britain. Very roughly, 10,000 agricultural acres might be expected to yield £10,000 a year in rents.

Until the early twentieth century no mere businessman could compete with the greatest landlords in wealth, let alone in power and status. It was they, rather than British merchants and industrialists, who rivalled the ostentatious spending of the great American millionaires. Here are two instances of archi-tectural extravagance. The sixth Duke of Bedford, Duke from 1802 to 1839, already the owner of several large houses, built another at Endsleigh in Devon, starting in 1810. The grounds were landscaped by the famous Repton, whose scheme included a little cottage to be constructed across the river Tamar, not for habitation, but so that a fire could be lighted in it to produce a whiff of smoke at an appropriate point in the view. This was quite a common feature of 'picturesque' gardening. Less typically, the fifth Duke of Portland, Duke from 1854 to 1879, in order to be able to escape without being observed from his mansion, Welbeck Abbey in Nottinghamshire, had a tunnel made leading out of the grounds, a mile-and-a-half long. One of the strangest of eccentric peers was the fourth Marquess of Hertford, Marquess from 1842 to 1870, with perhaps £240,000 a year, who lived in Paris, devoted himself to collect-ing pictures, used the largest of his London houses as a store-room, only occasionally visited one of the others, never resided at either of his principal country houses, and finally left the bulk of his property to his illegitimate son, Sir Richard Wallace. His widow gave it, as the Wallace Collection, to the British nation.

As well as wealth, the great landowners possessed political power. Most obviously, they dominated the House of Lords, which before 1832, in practice as well as theory, was nearly as powerful as the House of Commons. Just over half of the 363 owners of 10,000 acres in England in 1873 were hereditary peers, and no doubt the position in this regard was much the same in 1815. There were a fair number of peers who owed their titles to their own or their ancestors' services in the armed forces, politics or the legal profession; but the idea that there were as yet, or indeed at any time in the period covered by this book, many peers drawn from the business world is quite mistaken. The sum total of businessmen created peers during the early decades of the Industrial Revolution is two, both bankers, both of whom had acquired vast landed estates before their elevation. The ownership of a substantial estate was considered a necessary attribute of a peer. Wealth derived from business had to be converted into land before it qualified.

In the House of Commons the great landowners were hardly less powerful. The fact that Members of Parliament were unpaid meant that only men of some wealth could serve, and this was more effective in restricting membership than the technical property qualification. But these were not the reasons for the special power of the great landlords. In order to understand this, it is necessary to know something of the crazy system of Parliamentary representation.

The House of Commons from 1801 to 1885 had 658 Members.[1] Before the First Reform Act Irish constituencies elected 100, Scottish 45, Welsh 24 and English the remaining 489. The great bulk of the constituencies were classified either as 'counties', usually covering the whole area of a county, or as 'boroughs', usually covering only a small area and identified with a town or village. Before 1832 English and Irish counties elected two Members each,[2] Welsh counties one, and Scottish counties either one each or one between two. The total of county Members was 188. In England, Wales and (until 1829) Ireland the electorate in the counties consisted of those males who were held to possess a freehold of the value of 40 shillings a year; in Scotland it was much more restricted. Every county in the United Kingdom sent Members to Westminster, but only those towns did so which had been accorded the privilege by the Crown in past centuries. The boroughs of England in general elected two Members each; the boroughs of Wales, Scotland and Ireland one each or one to a group. In the boroughs there was every variety of franchise. The extreme cases were Preston, where all the adult male inhabitants had the vote, and Old Sarum, the classic 'rotten' borough, which no longer had any inhabitants and whose seven 'burgage holdings' were the property of the Earl of Caledon. All voting

---

[1] Except that individual constituencies were disfranchised from time to time for corruption at elections, so that the total number of Members fell slightly.

[2] Except that after 1821 Yorkshire elected four Members.

was by public declaration. There was no limit to the number of different constituencies in which a man might qualify to vote, but in an individual constituency no one had more votes than there were M.P.s to be elected. Peers could not vote.[1]

Although there were so many more borough than county constituencies, this did not on the whole give power to urban rather than rural interests. The Parliamentary boroughs did not include some of the largest towns like Manchester, Birmingham, Sheffield and Leeds, whose inhabitants, if qualified, voted in their counties. Many of the boroughs were mere villages, most of them were no more than little market towns. In relation to population, the agricultural South of England was grossly over-represented by comparison with the industrial North, and England was over-represented by comparison with the other parts of the United Kingdom. Most of all, the great landlords, even as compared with other rural interests, had exceptional influence over the composition of the Commons.

Great landowners sometimes, as in the case of Old Sarum, owned a borough outright. More often a landlord had enough property in a constituency or could exert enough pressure on the voters to be virtually sure of the election of his nominee. Such pressure might include 'illegitimate influence', threats of eviction or withdrawal of custom, bribery, even violent intimidation. In many of the more open constituencies a landlord might still exercise enough of what contemporaries called 'legitimate influence' (a concept of which more will be said later) to have a good chance of returning his man. It was thought in the 1820s that over two-thirds of the constituencies were at least under the strong influence of some landlord, usually a peer. 261 M.P.s were supposed to be effectively nominated by a patron. A mere seven peers either nominated or strongly influenced the election of 51 M.P.s: the Dukes of Devonshire, Norfolk and Rutland, the Marquess of Hertford, and the Earls of Darlington, Fitzwilliam and Lonsdale. This kind of aristocratic influence had actually grown during the early Industrial Revolution. Further, more than a quarter of the House of Commons consisted of peers and sons of peers.[1]

By custom all the great officers of state came from one or other

---

[1] Irish peers (like Viscount Palmerston) could vote, and sit in the Commons.

House of Parliament. Before 1834 Cabinets always contained a majority of members of the House of Lords, and the more aristocratic M.P.s were better represented in Ministries than the common run. As well as power, tenure of the principal posts brought very large salaries, of the order of £5000 per annum. To a relatively impecunious peer, like Palmerston before his marriage in 1839, office made the difference between debts and affluence.

Parliament's acts, as much as its composition, reflected the dominance of landlords. The Corn Law is one instance. Another is the Game Laws. In the early years of the nineteenth century organized shooting of game on a large scale became a popular gentleman's sport, and game preservation became a fetish. This development was accompanied by a progressive stiffening of the law against poaching, which was at its most severe between 1816 and 1827. Until 1827 landowners were permitted to use spring-guns to trap and injure poachers, and from 1816 to 1828 any person found at night, armed and with a net for poaching, in any forest, chase or park was to be tried at Quarter Sessions and, if convicted, sentenced to transportation for seven years. Unarmed poachers were liable to imprisonment, with hard labour if caught with another person, and with whipping for second offences. Here landlords were at their most tyrannous, using their dominance of Parliament to carry utterly selfish legislation which they or their sporting companions, in their capacities as magistrates, were able to enforce locally. Between 1827 and 1830 one in seven of all criminal convictions were under the Game Laws.

More generally, the whole character of Parliament's activities reflected the landlords' dominance. As a result of the constitutional struggles of the seventeenth century, Parliament had become indisputably the sovereign legislature; it had also won control over the central executive; that executive had lost most of its power over the localities; and property rights had been sanctified, so that only statute, that is, Act of Parliament, could disturb them. Parliament's victory was the landlords', who used it, not to make large changes, but to preserve 'the ancient constitution' as they conceived it and to ensure that they were the masters in their counties. Parliamentary supremacy was employed to make local adjustments at the

behest of the local landlords. The main occupation of the
Parliaments of George III's reign was passing local acts:
enclosure acts; acts establishing turnpike trusts, bodies of
'improvement commissioners' and the like; acts for the construction of canals; acts for the restoration of church towers.
Many acts of wider application, like Gilbert's, were permissive
only. Where there was any question of disturbing property
rights, mandatory general legislation was suspect.

Hence, partly, the persistence of inefficiency, abuses and
anomalies. It seemed much more important to the landowners to keep control of the localities and stave off central
interference than to rationalize the system of government.
Already anomalous when they won their victory over the
King in the seventeenth century, this system had been deliberately preserved. No new Parliamentary constituency was
created between 1677 and 1832. It was maintained that the
system was nonetheless perfect, that places and interests not
visibly represented in Parliament were 'virtually' represented
there. Rationalization was unnecessary, and would in any
case be dangerous. This attitude had recently been reformu-
lated in a newly elevated manner by Edmund Burke, especially
in his *Reflections on the Revolution in France* (1790). He denounced
'economists and calculators' who made rationalist plans from
first principles. What already existed, however irrational it
seemed, had something to be said for it or it would not exist.
'The wisdom of the species' could be relied upon. Admittedly,
change was sometimes necessary, but the onus of proof lay
with the reformer. Burke's writings apart, it was widely
believed that the story of the French Revolution proved the
danger of violent and fundamental change. The brutality
and licence of the Terror, the tyranny and militarism of
Napoleon, were just the horrors that should be expected to
follow on the disturbance of the old French constitution, the
confiscation of aristocratic and ecclesiastical property, the
execution of the monarch, the denial of Christianity. So every
anomaly was defended: Old Sarum, the historic parish
boundaries, obsolete forms of law and unenforceable statutes.
Here are some extreme instances. A lucky few continued to
receive huge sums for offices which were now without duties,
like the second Lord Ellenborough, with nearly £10,000 a
year as chief clerk of the Court of King's Bench. The Duke of

Norfolk, excluded twice over, as peer and Roman Catholic, from the franchise, continued to return eleven M.P.s, Anglicans, to the House of Commons.

To understand fully the attitudes of the early nineteenth century it is necessary to go back in history much further than the French Revolution. Britain had preserved, to a degree almost unique in Europe, her medieval constitution. In the Middle Ages law had been regarded not as the command of the sovereign but as the custom of the community. The 'Common Law', enshrining this outlook, was still the dominant element in English law at the beginning of the nineteenth century. It consisted of statutes, many of them originally designed as clarifications rather than changes of the law, and 'precedents', that is, decisions of the courts interpreting these statutes and the law as a whole, decisions which were binding unless superseded by Act of Parliament. The reluctance to use Parliamentary sovereignty to put through general legislation reflected, as well as the interest of landlords in local autonomy and the security of property, the traditional views of Common Lawyers, who formed the largest and most influential part of the legal profession. They hallowed precedent rather than statute, and shared the landlord's reverence for property. It was their attitudes which Burke was reformulating.[1]

A few words must be said about other elements in English law. The monarch possessed a 'prerogative' covering executive action, foreign policy and so on; but its wider applications, of a legislative character, had been curbed in the seventeenth century, and even the royal 'veto' on Bills passed by both Houses of Parliament had fallen into disuse during the eighteenth century. There survived ecclesiastical courts with jurisdiction not only in matters of heresy and blasphemy but also over wills and marriages. More important, there was a rival system of law to the Common Law, namely 'equity', administered by a Court of Chancery separate from the Common Law courts. This system derived from the efforts of Chancellors of the late Middle Ages and the early modern period to supplement and circumvent the Common Law in the interests of the King or of a notion of justice. Chancery had a mode of procedure quite different from that of the Common

---

[1] J. G. A. Pocock, 'Burke and the Ancient Constitution', *Historical Journal* 1960.

Law courts. An obvious and important variation was that a defendant in Chancery had to give evidence, but could not do so at Common Law. Although the two systems were maintained technically and theoretically distinct from each other, and few lawyers practised under both, they were often concerned in the same questions. When that happened, cases passed to and fro between courts, as decisions were required which fell within the competence of first one and then the other system. At a time when legal procedure was especially dilatory and complex the Court of Chancery was even slower and more intricate than the Common Law courts.

With anomaly went disorder. The yeomanry was inefficient at controlling crowds of rioters, and the parish constables were no deterrent to serious crime. Highwaymen were notoriously numerous and successful. After dark, there was little security in the unlit towns. Most criminals escaped detection, while a few were punished very severely. But the creation of a proper police force was associated with Continental despotisms, and the story of the 1688 Revolution made people wary of allowing a sizable standing army to be maintained at home. Violent crime and violent punishments were regarded as part of the price of liberty, and violent sport too: 'A late eighteenth-century bill advertises "that Most antient, Loyal, National, Constitutional and Lawful Diversion: BEAR-BAITING".'[1] Violence and corruption at elections were equally condoned.

The great landlords, then, took the trouble to dominate Parliament and do much of the work of central administration in order to be sure of dominating the localities. The county was the most important unit of local government; only certain 'incorporated' boroughs (not necessarily the same as Parliamentary boroughs) were partly independent of county officials. The chief of these officials was the Lord Lieutenant, usually the greatest landowner of the district. He commanded the militia, the armed force which was supposed to combat invasion and rebellion, of which the yeomanry were the cavalry section. The militia consisted of officers drawn from the landed gentry, each higher rank requiring a higher property qualification, and of men to be supplied by the gentry. It was

---

[1] E. P. Thompson, *The Making of the English Working Class* (London, 1968), p. 96n.

on the recommendation of the Lord Lieutenant that the Justices of the Peace were appointed. The statutory qualification for a County Justice of the Peace was the possession of landed property to the value of £100 a year, but in practice most J.P.s were better off than this, that is, they came from among the substantial landowners. These Justices, about 2,000 of them in England and Wales, individually or in small groups, and especially in Quarter Sessions, the gathering of all the Justices of a county, had much judicial power, much power which looks like executive power, and even some power which is difficult to distinguish from legislative power. The extent of their judicial power is illustrated by the case of the Game Laws, already mentioned. They were the only significant local executive officials except in the boroughs, which had their own, less powerful J.P.s. Anything which Parliament or the central executive wanted done locally it told Justices to do. They found themselves with an astonishing range of duties, including even, after 1802, the regulation of factory conditions. They could levy 'rates', the local equivalent of taxes. Their quasi-legislative activity was nowhere better displayed than in the Speenhamland decision, which had far wider effects than most Acts of Parliament and which the Parliament of the day would never have dared to initiate. The Justices had originally been the principal agents of the King in the localities. Now they themselves were the kings. British local government was controlled by people who as leisured amateurs tended to distrust professional men and as landowners tended to despise traders and manufacturers. Anything in the nature of democracy survived in local government only anomalously, in parish institutions and in some boroughs.

Closely associated with the dominance of the landlords was the Church of England, technically, after 1801, 'the United Church of England and Ireland'.[1] Negatively, until 1829 Roman Catholics could not become M.P.s or J.P.s or take a seat in the House of Lords or vote in a British (as opposed to an Irish) Parliamentary election. Protestant Nonconformists or Dissenters, though not debarred from the House of Commons, were excluded until 1828 from public office, except in so far as

---

[1] The separate Established Church of Scotland had rather different associations. It will receive some treatment in Part II.

the less strict among them 'conformed', that is, took the sacrament of the Church of England, or took advantage of the Indemnity Acts remitting the penalties incurred by officials who had neglected to do so, Acts which by this time were passed regularly. In fact, almost all important office-holders were, nominally at least, Anglicans. Conversely, for certain parish offices, which were sometimes onerous, Nonconformists were not only eligible but might be compelled to serve: it was quite common for a Nonconformist to be a churchwarden, generally under protest. Dissenters were liable to have to pay rates for the upkeep of their parish church, and sometimes it was the duty of a Nonconformist churchwarden to levy the rate. Jews were virtually without rights. Religious toleration was far from complete: only Anglican priests and, strangely enough, Quakers and Jews, could perform marriages valid in law. There was no secular or civil marriage.

Positively, the Church of England was bound to the land, to its owners and to agriculture. The clergy were supported partly by proceeds from property belonging to the Church, partly by tithe, a tax on owners and occupiers. The upper clergy, appointed by the Crown, included 26 English and 4 Irish Archbishops and Bishops who sat in the House of Lords. Some of the sees provided an income which only a few laymen could surpass: the Archbishop of Canterbury and the Bishop of Durham each had £19,000 a year. Most of the lesser clergy were appointed by some lay landlord, who often chose a member of his family. The ecclesiastical geography of Britain was so tied to property rights that it could not be altered except by Parliament, and it had become hardly less anomalous than the system of Parliamentary representation. In the country there was still generally one parish to one village. In old towns there were often far too many parishes in the centre, while in new towns and in the suburbs of old towns there might be tens of thousands of people served by one small church and one ill-paid clergyman. There was a parish whose rector was paid more than £7000 a year, but about three hundred were worth less than £50. Some fortunate clergymen, usually those with noble connexions, held several rich 'benefices' together. Bishop Bagot of Oxford, son of Lord Bagot, was also Dean of Canterbury Cathedral and Rector of two Stafford-shire parishes to which his father had appointed him. The

8th Earl of Bridgewater was from 1780 to 1829 a 'prebendary' of Durham Cathedral, had two family benefices in Shropshire, and lived in Paris, surrounded by cats and dogs dressed as humans.[1] The value of benefices had been rising with other land values, and the social status of the clergy with it. They were now being taken into partnership in local government by the secular landlords, and many were J.P.s, perhaps half the total strength of the Bench. In some urbanized areas of counties the only residents considered qualified to be J.P.s were clergy. At the time of the Peterloo Massacre the Chairman of Salford Quarter Sessions, whose area included Manchester, was the Rev. W. R. Hay, Prebendary of York Minster, Rector of Ackworth and Vicar of Rochdale. In Wales and Ireland the association of the landlords with the Established Church was even more oppressive, since there the Church was not the Church of the majority of the population, which in Wales was Nonconformist and in Ireland Roman Catholic. The State still treated the Church of England as deserving of grants of public money. In 1818 £1,000,000, and in 1824 a further £500,000, was voted by Parliament for church-building. The law not only endorsed many of the doctrines of the Church, but also identified Christianity with the Church of England. 'A Trust', said the Tory Lord Chancellor, Eldon, 'for the worship of God pure and simple is a Trust for maintaining and propagating the Established Religion of the country.'[2]

Education, it must be understood, was largely an Anglican monopoly. There were only two English Universities until 1828, Oxford and Cambridge, and they were staffed almost entirely by clergymen of the Church of England. No one could take a degree at either unless he would subscribe to the Thirty-nine Articles. In the small group of undergraduates, fewer than 3,000 altogether at any given time in the 1820s, a majority of young men destined for holy orders mixed with a minority of prospective secular landlords. Oxford University could be described as 'the most illustrious body of the English Constitution'.[3] The great public schools and most grammar

---

[1] W. O. Chadwick, *The Victorian Church*, vol. 1 (London, 1966), p. 560.

[2] Quoted in B. L. Manning, *The Protestant Dissenting Deputies* (Cambridge, 1952), p. 58.

[3] Lord E. Somerset, M.P., at a Gloucestershire Pitt Club dinner (*Felix Farley's Bristol Journal*, 5 August 1826).

schools were all strongly clerical, and so were the village schools, often conducted in the parish church.

Finally, though a woman might become the Queen Regnant, and other women might succeed to some of the more ancient peerages and, so long as they were unmarried, own property, they could not sit in Parliament or vote for an M.P., and once they married were legally subordinate to their husbands. If anything, the rights of women were dwindling. It was considered anomalous that a few had the local government franchise in some places, and the new professions excluded them from membership. They could not go to University, and little attention was given to their education at any level.

This, then, was the core of the social, political, religious and educational 'Establishment', of the early nineteenth century, comprising a tightly-knit group, headed by the great peer landowners and tied to landed property. By the exercise of 'patronage' this small group made its influence felt throughout society. They thought it natural, and they were in a position to ensure, that those of 'good family' should hold the majority of offices in the government service, including commissions in the armed forces, as well as the bulk of ecclesiastical benefices. In 1858, the great Radical, John Bright, could still illustrate the point as follows:

> We have what is called diplomacy. We have a great many lords engaged in what they call diplomacy. We have a lord in Paris, we have another in Madrid, another in Berlin, another . . . in Vienna, and another lord in Constantinople; and we have another at Washington; in fact, almost all over the world; particularly where the society is most pleasant and the climate most agreeable, there is almost certain to be an English nobleman to represent the English Foreign Office. . . .[1]

It was true of most areas of administration until the second half of the century that they constituted 'a gigantic system of out-door relief for the aristocracy of Great Britain'.[2] Many offices could be purchased, and some became virtually hereditary. There were no pension schemes, and so people did not retire. An office held for life was treated, even in law, as a piece of freehold property. The men who obtained these posts by the operation of the patronage system were often diligent

---

[1] G. M. Trevelyan, *The Life of John Bright* (London, 1913), p. 274.
[2] ibid. p. 277.

and efficient. Property was admitted to have its duties as well as its rights. Similarly, landowners were expected to feel an obligation to pass on their estates to their children in an improved condition. It was also proper for them to behave well to their tenants and employees, and thus win 'legitimately' greater respect and influence than they could obtain by the ruthless deployment of their wealth and legal powers. But if the property-owner, whether landlord or office-holder, refused to acknowledge that he had duties, it was seldom possible to compel him to perform them.

Despite all the abuses, anomalies and injustices associated with the 'Establishment', it might have seemed unchallengeable. But between 1828 and 1846 it was severely mauled. The symbol of its decline was the passage of the Reform Act of 1832. The rest of this section will describe other forces of English society, the relationship between them and the 'Establishment', how reform occurred, and in particular how the unreformed Parliament came to reform itself.

Other Forces of Society

It is possible to distinguish several forces of society as being wholly or largely outside the 'Establishment'.

First, some attempt must be made to treat the activities of the working class, or, in the more realistic terminology of contemporaries, 'the working classes'. The 1790s were a decade of developments in this field hardly less remarkable than the economic changes of the 1780s. Before this time there was virtually no sign of continuous organized political action by workers. Popular discontent showed itself frequently in outbreaks of rioting, usually in times of high food prices and generally directed against them. Sometimes the rioters attacked particular government measures or particular groups such as foreigners, Scots, Jews and Roman Catholics. But there was little if any continuity between the outbreaks. In the last years of the century, however, while this kind of protest continued, more constructive means of expression appeared. The most striking development was the foundation in 1791–2, during the early years of the French Revolution, of working-class societies in many towns, of which the London Corresponding Society became the chief, for the 'acquisition and dissemination of POLITICAL KNOWLEDGE'. Though so novel, this was a movement which affected many thousands of working-men. The

kind of political feeling it embodied can be most easily discovered from Tom Paine's *Rights of Man*. This was a reply to
Burke's *Reflections*. Part One, published in 1791, at 3 shillings,
the same price as *Reflections*, is supposed to have sold 50,000
copies in its first year, against Burke's 30,000 in two years.
Part Two, more radical and published in 1792 at 6d., is
supposed to have sold 200,000 in its first year. These figures
far exceed anything previously known. Apart from the Bible
and one or two classics, *Rights of Man* must have been the most
widely-read book of the 1790s and the next decades. At this
time about half the adult population was capable of reading,
after a fashion.

Like the 'Establishment', its extreme opponents appealed
to an old constitution, the mythical Anglo-Saxon constitution.
'Conquest and tyranny', wrote Paine, 'transplanted themselves
with William the Conqueror from Normandy into England,
and the country is yet disfigured with the marks.'[1] The Conquest had brought the hereditary monarchy and aristocracy,
primogeniture and grossly uneven land distribution, and had
led to the imposition of high taxes to pay for foreign wars.
Paine, though he did not actually summon the people to
revolution, thought and hoped it was very near: 'I do not
believe that monarchy and aristocracy will continue seven
years longer in any of the enlightened countries in Europe.'[2]
He advocated also the liberalization of the Poor Law and the
redistribution of property, together with a pacific foreign
policy founded on friendship between nations. Paine had been
involved in the American Revolution, to which he paid as
much attention as to the French Revolution. In general, as
the latter became discredited even among radicals, the example
of the United States was emphasized more strongly. Here was
a country in which most adult males had the vote and most were
freeholders, where there was no monarchy, no official aristocracy, and something like equality of opportunity. It became
too a refuge for English radicals during periods of persecution.

Repressive measures drove this kind of working-class
activity underground during the wars. Some of the leaders
were tried for treason, and societies like the London Corre-

---

[1] Tom Paine, *Rights of Man* (Thinker's Library, London, 1937), p. 41.
[2] ibid. p. 127.

sponding Society were declared illegal by an Act of 1799. Paine had fled from England as early as 1792, and did not return during the remaining seventeen years of his life. There was very great discontent, however, which expressed itself in outbreaks of violence at times of economic crisis, worst in 1811–12, when, with wheat more expensive than ever before or since, disturbances in the Midlands occupied a large military and civil force, including an army of 12,000. The riots of these months were not associated with a movement for political reforms. But with the Hampden Clubs working-class political activity influenced by the ideas of Paine came to the surface again. 'The peculiar interest of reformist politics under the Regency,' it has been said, 'is to be found in the race . . . in which the popular leaders were engaged for the harnessing of economic discontent to the cause of political reform.'[1] The 'Establishment' has never been more bitterly hated than in the years of renewed economic crisis just after Waterloo, and there were protests of all kinds directed against it. But political change was coming to be more generally regarded as a necessary preliminary to economic and social betterment. This did not necessarily exclude the use of force: there were serious attempts at revolution, most notably the 'Pentridge rising' of 1817, in which a small group of labourers set out from Derbyshire to march on London, expecting the rest of the country to rise in their support and overthrow the 'Establishment', and the 'Cato Street conspiracy' of 1820, a plot to kill the Cabinet at dinner, with the same expectation. But societies like the Hampden Clubs generally disclaimed violence and the desire to redistribute property, and asserted that they were pursuing their political aims by constitutional means alone. More and more, this approach commended itself. No doubt the teachings of the churches and the rigours of the law helped in this direction. But so did the leaders of the working classes, in particular Cobbett, chiefly through the Press. His *Political Register*, especially in its first flush of 1816, caught popular imagination to the extent that he came to rival Paine as the prophet of the underprivileged. His straightforward graphic style, anticipating modern journalistic writing, and his use of illustrations from everyday rural life, ensured him an audience

---

[1] R. J. White, *From Waterloo to Peterloo* (London, 1963), p. 102.

wider than any British newspaper had ever commanded
before. His motley prejudices, anti-intellectual, anti-clerical,
monarchist, Anglican, rural, provincial, and insular to a
degree, and the fact that he deliberately set himself up against
theorists, revolutionaries and even political societies, helped
to moderate the extremism of protest. Although his personal
influence was reduced by his flight to America, it revived in
the 'twenties, to be powerful again in 1830–2.

The law continued to discourage all working-class as well
as much middle-class political activity. Under one of the Six
Acts of 1819, notice of any public meeting of a political
character involving more than fifty persons, except for a
'county meeting', had to be given to a J.P.; and, if the meeting
was to be held in a town, no one might attend it unless he was
a freeman, a householder or a considerable landowner. Apart
from the special legislation enacted, some of it for limited
periods only, in 1817 and 1819, frequent prosecutions of those
who wrote and sold newspapers and pamphlets, under the
Common Law of blasphemous, seditious and obscene libel,
put severe constraints on publications intended to reach a wide
public. It was avowed by the Government and the Courts
that what would be considered unobjectionable in an expensive
book might be regarded as criminal in a cheap newspaper.
Stamp duty remained at 4d. on every copy of a newspaper,
and evasion was made more difficult by one of the Six Acts.

These measures, however, still left the Government and
the 'Establishment' with inadequate powers for a policy of
total repression. They were most successful in dealing with
revolutionary attempts: Ministers knew all about the Pentridge
rising and the Cato Street conspiracy long before the event,
and those involved were heavily punished. But large meetings
were difficult both to prevent and to control, especially before
the Act of 1819 was passed and after it lapsed, in 1825. County
meetings were never prohibited; nor was large-scale petitioning
of Parliament, though it was of recent growth. In particular,
the popular Press could not be eradicated. The law did not in
general permit the intervention of the Government until after
objectionable matter had been published. Once the publication had occurred, while there were many ways of harassing
those concerned, there were also many difficulties in the way
of securing their conviction. Those who broke the law were

often left alone either because the forces of order and the Courts could not cope with all offenders or because there was reason to fear that a jury would not convict. Fox's Libel Act of 1792 had made juries the judge of law as well as of fact, and in several cases, especially in London, they refused to enforce the law. Many defendants were acquitted on technicalities, which were easily exploited under the unreformed legal system. Though many persons were imprisoned, some of them were so determined to protest that they ran their newspapers from prison, or persuaded their families and friends to continue their work. After Peterloo, and more emphatically during the Queen's trial, upper and middle-class opinion swung against the King and his Government and their repressive measures. From the mid-'twenties, though the lesser penalties for infringing the stamping regulations were still exacted, the Press was left almost untouched by prosecutions for libel. The cause of radicalism profited from the constitutionalism, legalism, inefficiency and anomalies associated with the rule of the 'Establishment'.[1]

During the 'twenties economic conditions were so much better that there was slight danger of working-class violence, and the scale of popular activity was reduced. However, during the crisis of 1829–32 all types of protest were made: there were riots and machine-breaking and rick-burning; but also there appeared over thirty newspapers for the poor, successfully defying the law by sheer weight of numbers. The public catered for was wider again than in 1816–19. Some of the leaders worked to harness discontent to a moderate political programme, like Francis Place in London; others would accept nothing short of the programme of Paine or of the extreme Parliamentary reformers like William Lovett; and a new group was preaching the gospel of 'co-operation', something like communism, associated with the name of Robert Owen, who was both cotton manufacturer and socialist visionary. But the moderates were successful to the extent that mass support was given to the Birmingham Political Union, with its middle-class leaders, which was calling for peaceful and not very radical Parliamentary reform. Many politically-conscious

---

[1] See W. H. Wickwar, *The Struggle for the Freedom of the Press, 1819–1832* (London 1928); White, *From Waterloo to Peterloo*.

workers were willing at this stage to settle for the Act of 1832 as a first step towards democracy, and to put constitutional change before social reform.

The working classes developed also over this period two related economic institutions, the 'friendly society' and the trade union. Friendly societies took the subscriptions of their members in order to insure them against death, illness, burial expenses and so on. In the late eighteenth century there was a great increase in the number of these societies, and in 1815 they probably had a million members. In other words, at least a million working-men had some savings. This movement, in so far as it was separable from the trade union movement, commanded the approval of the 'Establishment' even at the worst period of repression, and was assisted by Acts of Parliament from 1793 onwards. On the other hand, combinations of working-men to obtain increases of wages and better conditions of work were illegal under an Act of 1800, if not before. In fact they flourished, though half-secretly. In the 1820s the Government was persuaded, largely through a campaign run by Place, that legal suppression of combinations of this kind only drove them underground and made them more dangerous, and by an Act of 1824, somewhat restricted in 1825, they ceased to be illegal as such, though they had no positive status in law and were greatly limited in the means they might use to enforce their agreements. Working-class activity with economic rather than political aims was also becoming more continuous and pacific.

All these activities were essentially the sphere of the more skilled workmen, men of some education, standing and financial security. The line between these men and the rest of the working classes was in many ways more important than the lines usually discerned between the upper, middle and lower classes.[1] Below this line, sporadic riots and violent strikes remained the means of expressing feelings of grievance. Above it, the artisans were, from one point of view, betraying their fellow-workers, adopting the organizations and methods, and even the attitudes, of their social superiors, in accepting that change must come slowly, by legal and peaceful means, without expro-

---

[1] E. J. Hobsbawm, 'The Labour Aristocracy in Nineteenth-Century Britain', in his *Labouring Men* (London, 1964).

priation, and that political rights must be earned by good conduct; from another point of view, they were making the exclusiveness of the 'Establishment' seem preposterous and preparing the way for the political and social emancipation of all working-men.

Secondly, of course, the new industrial towns were for the most part outside the 'Establishment'. Unlike London and the old county towns they were not centres where the landed interest gathered for social and administrative purposes; nor were they, like lesser ancient towns, bound to agriculture. Many were governed, quite inappropriately, as villages, and many were short of parishes, churches, clergy and social amenities. It was not until the next period that the impact of the Industrial Revolution became a general concern of politicians and writers, but already the great new towns aroused alarm and wonder. Contemporaries were struck by the rift which was appearing between the class of manufacturers and capitalists on the one hand and the class of workers on the other in towns where factory industry was well-developed. Manchester was the type of the town which was not in any real sense a 'community', and its class divisions as well as its lack of government and of Parliamentary representation reduced its direct influence. Birmingham, on the other hand, where small-scale industry predominated, was a town of better relations between the classes, and therefore well-qualified to become the centre of the Reform agitation in its later stages. Liverpool, by chance, was an incorporated borough, and fittingly became a centre of Liberal Toryism, with Canning and Huskisson as its M.P.s. It was also a model municipality, using its large revenue from port dues, in addition to rates, for a wide range of purposes: to construct docks; under Acts dating from 1748, to light, cleanse, widen and police the streets; to build Anglican churches and schools associated with the Church of England; even to lay out public walks and gardens, and to provide public baths.

Towns in general were related to the 'Establishment' in a most complex way. Those which had special status as 'cities' or incorporated boroughs, about 200 altogether, many of them tiny, often had governments as undemocratic, Anglican, corrupt, inefficient and anomalous as could be imagined. However, they all had some measure of independence of the

county, appointing some J.P.s of their own; and the greater
towns might rank as counties themselves. The City of London
had far the most important corporation. In the eighteenth
century, as in Charles I's reign, it had set itself up as defender
of the liberties of the subject, whether against King or Parliament, and its legal privileges and its economic power were so
great that Governments had often had to bow before them.
In the early nineteenth century, though the Capital was
relatively less important both politically and economically, it
still presented a unique problem to the 'Establishment'. The
literacy rate was much higher there than in the rest of the
country, and the circulation of news and political information
far better. Before the railways made nationwide political
action easier, London was the natural leader of the forces of
protest. Like the City Corporation of neighbouring Westminster,
that of London was unusually democratic, and often expressed
the opinions of the urban lower classes. The M.P.s for the two
Cities were commonly popular leaders. So this was almost a
rival 'Establishment', commercial, bourgeois and radical.
It was nonetheless propertied, inefficient and anomalous.
There were by now large urbanized areas beyond the Cities'
boundaries, many of them governed by parish vestries with
radical views. The whole county of Middlesex was dominated
by urban influences, and returned popular M.P.s to Parliament.
But the power of the two Corporations was too great to permit
municipal reform in the Capital until long after the general
reforms of the 1830s.

To confuse the picture further, in nearly all towns which
lacked the privileges of incorporation and in many which
possessed them, there had been established during the second
half of the eighteenth century, under local Acts, bodies usually
called 'improvement commissioners' to pave, light, cleanse and
police the streets. There were about 300 of them, nearly 100
being in the metropolitan area outside the Cities. The Manchester Police Commissioners were uniquely adventurous,
and actually themselves supplied gas to the public before
the death of George III. However, the good work done by
most of these bodies was narrowly restricted in scope: they
covered small areas, and made no attempt to provide such
amenities as parks, libraries, houses, schools and baths. They
usually consisted of a group of more or less self-appointed and

self-perpetuating local notabilities, though during the 1820s some became elective, as pressure for representative government grew.

The third force in this category is Nonconformity. The Dissenters fall into two main groups, the 'old denominations' of Presbyterians, Congregationalists and Baptists, and the newer Methodists. To these should be added the Quakers and the Unitarians, smaller and theologically more extreme groups of great importance. The Presbyterians as such were in decline, and tending to merge with the Unitarians. The Congregationalists and the Baptists were advancing, but not so rapidly as the Methodists, the body evoked by John Wesley in the eighteenth century, with a theology scarcely distinguishable from the Anglicanism of the day, but socially not acceptable to the 'Establishment'. The total number of Nonconformists was already great, 2,000,000 at the very least, and growing fast. The Methodists especially tended to be most numerous in places where there was inadequate Anglican provision, that is, often in new industrial areas; but there were Dissenting strongholds in many other places, around London, in East Anglia and the Fens, and in the South-west. One of the contributions of Nonconformity at this period was the secondary education offered by the 'dissenting academies', not confined, as most Anglican education was, to divinity and classical literature, and more progressive in its methods. However, since they were an underprivileged minority, much of Dissenters' energy was spent on trying to improve their legal position. Here the denominations were able to exert pressure through a long-standing body, the Protestant Dissenting Deputies. Though it had something of a national status, this group was elected from the London area only, a commentary on the state of eighteenth-century communications. The Government treated it with respect, and it supplemented the efforts of the small number of Nonconformist M.P.s. When there was a move in 1811 to restrict itinerant preaching by statute, the Deputies were joined in protest by a short-lived national Protestant organization, a portent of what would prove possible later in the century. Not only was the Bill defeated, but in the result some gains were recorded, such as the legal toleration of Unitarians granted in 1813. The Deputies were again prominent in securing the repeal of the Test

and Corporation Acts. By 1832 Nonconformity was ready to move over to the offensive against the Church of England and the whole 'Establishment'.

Next must be considered the growth of 'the middle classes' and of middle-class consciousness, as partially separable from the forces previously discussed. The factory system contributed to distinguishing owners from labourers, as has been seen. But the middle classes are wider than the class of manufacturers, and their numbers increased as in the eighteenth and nineteenth centuries professions other than the Church and the Bar were consolidated and grew in 'respectability'. Attorneys, for instance, were universally disparaged in the early eighteenth century. By the time of Waterloo they were cultivating the name 'solicitor' and were much more highly regarded and better organized.[1] The Law Society was incorporated in 1831. Some branches of the medical profession showed the same development, and the story can be extended to engineers, architects and others. There were more well-to-do manufacturers, merchants and professional men than ever before; and there were more people living wholly or partly on interest derived from stocks and shares, mostly government stock.

> In 1823 the number of people with money invested in government securities exceeded 288,000. . . . There were . . . about 53,000 people drawing dividends exceeding £50 a year – and, incidentally, just about the same number of people employing one or more male servants (a rather larger number – 72,000 – owned a carriage). More than 148,000 people kept a horse for pleasure, and more than 40,000 had more than one.[2]

These were the people for whom Jane Austen wrote, not careless of property, but with more goods and money than land, conscious of their professional skill and sobriety, valuing it more highly than mere birth and extravagant sports, the people who were taking over Bath from the aristocracy and helping to make Brighton the fastest-growing of all towns in this period.

All the forces I have mentioned continued to grow in importance throughout the period of this book. Together,

---

[1] R. Robson, *The Attorney in Eighteenth-Century England* (Cambridge, 1959).
[2] Ed. A. Aspinall and E. A. Smith, *English Historical Documents*, vol. XI (London, 1959), p. 55.

they contributed to the growth of the 'public'. The idea of the public arises when relationships within society become manifestly incomprehensible in terms of personal relationships, and when the state of communications and education makes the number of persons able to form a reasonable opinion on national affairs too great to be included within an 'Establishment'. This situation had existed for some time in Britain before 1815. But the fact and the notion of the 'public' developed considerably between Waterloo and the First Reform Act. Working-class development has already been discussed. By the 'Establishment' the public, as well as the 'people', was still conceived narrowly, as 'the well-informed and weighty parts of the community', but this category was widening all the time. The circulation figures of the stamped, respectable newspapers, assisted by the use of steam to drive the printing machines, rose more rapidly than the population. The size of their readership now made it possible for them to emancipate themselves from the control hitherto exercised by the Government through subsidies. By the 1830s Sunday newspapers sold in aggregate 110,000 copies, which, given the punitive stamp duties, probably meant over a million readers. *The Times* sold 10,000 a day in the 1820s. Another symptom of this development was the appearance of societies in enormous numbers dedicated to all sorts of subjects and causes, such as the improvement of the condition of chimney-sweeps, missionary activity abroad, most notably the abolition of slavery. Circulating libraries multiplied. Some progress was made in the provision of amenities like museums, almost entirely by private benefactions. The Dulwich Art Gallery dates from just before Waterloo, the Fitzwilliam Museum at Cambridge from just after. In the late 1820s the rebuilding of the British Museum began. The many London club foundations on either side of 1830 are part of a similar process.

Among the respectable public, as well as among the working classes, there was a strong body of opinion in favour of radical reform. In *Reflections on the Revolution in France*, Burke also attacked British sympathizers with the revolutionaries. Over the whole of Europe during the eighteenth century the dominant trend of educated opinion had been that of the 'Enlightenment', progressive, inclining to believe in the perfectibility of Man, sceptical about mystery and miracles, expecting society to work as an elaborate mechanism rather than a complex organism. It was widely held that there were laws of politics not much more subtle than those of physical science as then conceived. If men would only take cognizance of the conclusions of rationalist writers, they would have a blueprint for the improvement, if not the perfection, of society. The test of a law, like the test of an action, was not tradition nor religious doctrine, but 'utility'. Despite the powerful impact of Burke's criticism and of the 'excesses' of the French Revolution, this attitude survived, and spread again during the 1820s. The thinker who is most often taken as its main respectable representative or advocate in early nineteenth-century Britain is Jeremy Bentham. In his twenties, in 1776, he had published *A Fragment on Government*, ridiculing the traditional attitudes of the Common Lawyers as expressed in Blackstone's *Commentaries*. For Bentham, the law should not grow by accretion of precedents. Anomaly was indefensible. Parliament or some other single source of law must remodel the whole system by the test of 'utility'. His main concern was always the reform of the law, but in later life he became more interested in deeper constitutional questions. In 1818 he brought out a pamphlet announcing his conversion to the view that Parliament, before it could carry through effective reforms, must itself be drastically reformed and universal adult male suffrage introduced. In the 1820s he gathered a number of able followers round him, most notably James Mill, and through the *Westminster Review* (founded in 1824) they influenced a wide public, while at meetings of their Political Economy Club Whig statesmen were indoctrinated. In 1828 they established a non-sectarian College in rivalry to Oxford and Cambridge, which became University College, London, in 1836. It must not be supposed that Bentham had many personal followers or readers. But he was the most productive, long-lived and down-to-earth of a group which was of great importance in that it had some influence on public opinion at large, more on political leaders, and more still, as will be seen later, on practical administration. They were known as the Philosophic Radicals. Certain points should be noted about their thinking. They were individualists in the sense that, unlike Burke, they wished to abolish groups like old corporations and parties which intervened between the individual and the government, considering them all 'sinister interests'. They were less radical than their fundamental doctrines might have led them to be about the social order: they did not question the institution of property or demand its redistribution. They were anti-clerical and sometimes anti-religious. And, though they were associated with economists who thought State intervention in the economy undesirable, they were quite prepared to give rein to the power of the State in social legislation on such matters as the provision of schools and the control of factories.

It must be pointed out that the relationship between the Industrial Revolution and these rising forces was not a simple cause-and-effect relationship, except, more or less, in the case of the great towns. Though industrialists were often Dissenters, and so were the majority of the churchgoing inhabitants of the new cities, the affiliation was incomplete. The strength of the growing professional middle class was in the South, in the established towns and the suburbs of London. Friendly societies were strongest in Lancashire, but trade union activity was, if anything, more evident outside the factory towns than in them. Middle-class radicalism, though tied to Dissent, was not tied to the industrial North. Methodism at this period was not on the whole reformist. Cobbett, the most influential of the popular political writers of the period, cut across every line. Further, it was not the classic split between Capital and Labour which signified in politics. There was a more important division, between the 'Establishment' – what Cobbett called 'the THING' – and the rest. Workmen at this time were fighting the entrenched landed interest in Church and State rather than their employers.

The 'Establishment' and Reform

Entrenched though the 'Establishment' was, and, bound to agriculture, Anglicanism and anomaly, it was not uninfluenced by these other forces. Nor was it monolithic. If businessmen seldom became peers, peers often became businessmen. Many members of the House of Lords had financial, commercial and mining interests, and profited by selling or developing land for urban housing. There were even extreme radicals, though not Nonconformists, among the aristocracy: the sixth Lord Byron pilloried the monarchy and the forces of order in his poetry, and spoke on behalf of machine-breakers in the Lords; Shelley, whose denunciation of the system is quoted at the head of this Part, was heir to a baronetcy. The Scottish Universities provided a non-Anglican education for liberal-minded Englishmen. About a third of both peers and M.P.s in the 1820s were Whigs, in almost permanent opposition to the Government. More will be said of Whiggism later, and more also of the relationship between the 'Establishment' and the other forces of society. First, attention will be given to a movement of reform which was generated largely within the 'Establishment'.

THE 'EVANGELICAL' MOVEMENT

Its leaders are usually identified as the 'Evangelicals', chief of whom was William Wilberforce, friend of the younger Pitt, whose special cause was the abolition of slavery. But it is better to think of the movement in a broader context than is evoked by the term Evangelical, which specifically denotes a man of quasi-Calvinist religious views. At its widest, it can be regarded as the sum of efforts to make the existing 'Establishment' more worthy of its position. It did not wish, like the reforming movements so far mentioned, to overthrow or at least greatly enlarge the 'Establishment'. Its central aim, so far as institutions were concerned, was not political reform, but the reform of the Church of England, to make it better capable of fulfilling its function as the Established Church of ministering to the whole people, thereby bringing nearer the moral 'reformation' of the country at large. It had before it the ideal of the parish system, that in every village and every district of a town there should be resident clergymen, who should be:

> ... the Friends and Benefactors of the Community – the Promoters and Guardians of Piety, Decorum, and Good Order – the liberal, intelligent, and instructive associates of the Rich – the humble, candid, compassionate and charitable teachers of the Poor – the public and accredited Voice of the Church; to instruct the ignorant, reclaim the guilty, exhort the erring, confirm the wavering, and console the afflicted;—to diffuse and extend that knowledge of the Lord, which is the only true wisdom; and proclaim those Good Tidings, which are 'Glory to God in the Highest, and on Earth, Peace, Good-will towards Men'.

To attain this ideal, it would be necessary to increase the number of clergy and educate them better, to create new parishes and build new churches, to redistribute and perhaps augment the wealth of the Church, to enforce residence and abolish pluralism, and virtually to create a national system of education for the poor. The movement, like Methodism, was partly a response to the social changes of the late eighteenth century and partly a protest against complacency and abuses within the Church. It was as much a lay as a clerical movement. The parish, it was hoped, would be blessed with a benevolent and godly squire, who would support the clergyman morally and financially, also dispense charity, and provide wholesome amenities such as better cottages for his employees and perhaps some sort of club facilities. Further, Sunday should be better observed, the clergy should desist from hunting and other pursuits considered unbecoming to their cloth, and laymen should institute the practice of family prayers in their households. A main motive of the stricter Evangelicals was fear for the established political and social system. 'Nothing is more certain', wrote Robert Southey, the Poet Laureate, in 1829, 'than that religion is the basis upon which civil government rests, . . . And it is necessary that this religion be established for the security of the state, and for the welfare of the people.' 'The best Christian', said a preacher in 1820, 'was the most loyal subject.' A famous sermon of 1793 had been entitled 'The Wisdom and Goodness of God in having made both Rich and Poor'. But there was more to the movement than this. Whereas many churchmen and laymen of the upper classes doubted the wisdom of educating the poor at all, the zeal of the Evangelicals for establishing schools was great and genuine; since 1780 Sunday schools had been set up all over the country, and two societies to promote popular education, less directly under Evangelical influence, had been founded in the years before Waterloo, the British and Foreign Schools Society, a joint Anglican and Nonconformist organization founded in 1807, and the National Society of 1811, a purely Anglican body.

In 1831 it was calculated that nearly half a million children were being educated – or, as the writers pleasantly phrased it, 'were educating' – in Sunday schools. In 1819 it was reported that in other schools there were over 600,000 children. By 1831 the figure was supposed to be 1,000,000 just for schools 'acting on the same principle' as the National Society, that is, using the 'monitorial system', under which, in the absence of enough adult teachers, the first set of pupils taught had to pass on to other children what they had learned. It is presumed that, against all odds, illiteracy was declining as a result of this educational effort.

So important and pervasive was the influence of 'Evangelical' feeling throughout the period covered by this book, and in all denominations, that it is worth quoting a long extract to show what it involved. The writer is describing the 'Various Means of Doing Good Bodily and Spiritually' recommended by a late eighteenth-century Evangelical, Dr Stonehouse.

> The means of doing good spiritually . . . included promoting schools and religious societies, helping the really talented to get on, the encouragement of private and family prayer and Bible-reading, and visiting the sick 'and comforting or admonishing them'; 'talking seriously and affably with children and servants, at any time or place, when a proper opportunity offers'; and 'dispersing printed or written slips of paper, against particular sins, as sabbath-breaking, swearing etc. in order to be given away occasionally, or enclosed in a letter, or put into a book, or dropt in any part of the house, where the reproved would be likely to meet with it . . .'

> The means of doing good bodily were even more comprehensive and practical, and . . . illustrate very well the kind of activities which their sense of social responsibility was more and more to press upon the well-to-do. '1. By giving to the poor bread, coals, shoes, stockings, linen, coats, or gowns, which may be bought much cheaper than they can buy them. 2. By paying their house-rent or part of it. 3. By sending them wine, herb teas, or spoon meats, when sick, and sometimes proper dinners on their recovery, suitable to their weak state. 4. By paying their apothecary's bill, or part of it. 5. By giving rakes, prongs, or spades, to day labourers, or some implements of their trade to poor industrious workmen. 6. By seldom giving *money*, unless to those who live at a distance, and then we should be well assured that their case is truly stated, and that we cannot relieve them by any other method. 7. By subscribing to an Infirmary, where we may procure that relief for some real objects of compassion, which they cannot obtain elsewhere; and without which, perhaps, they must perish, or remain hopeless of any cure, and burdens to society. 8. By discouraging idleness in man, woman, or child; and by contriving work for those who are unemployed. 9. By defending the poor against oppression; especially such of them as are too often most grievously oppressed by hard-hearted parish officers, who have the power over them.'[1]

---

[1] All the quotations in this section come from G. F. A. Best, *Temporal Pillars* (Cambridge, 1964), ch. IV.

The condescension is nauseating now; yet not only the attitude, but also the word itself, was adopted then without irony. That is not to say that all recipients of crumbs from great men's tables were willing to take up the corresponding attitude of grateful and uncritical 'deference' to their superiors, at least in their hearts. But most people paid lip-service to the twin concepts. And, however objectionable the spirit of this 'doing good' may seem, it undoubtedly produced some unobjectionable results. Even education in Sunday schools and National Schools was bound to enlighten minds more than no education at all. Among the well-to-do, the achievement was remarkable. The eighteenth-century aristocracy had been notoriously libertine and free-thinking; by the middle of the nineteenth century many of the great lords were sincerely religious, perhaps teaching in Sunday schools themselves, certainly conducting family prayers, while those who were less sincere were still regular church-goers and generous benefactors to good causes, and made some attempt to conceal the fact when they took a mistress. With increased stuffiness there certainly came increased responsibility. The process was the upper-class counterpart of the development of moderate working-class organizations, to which the same spirit contributed, but commonly under Methodist rather than Anglican auspices.

Although for many the movement was especially concerned with reforming, and so strengthening, the Church of England, it should not be supposed that much emphasis was laid on theological differences between denominations. In fact, until the 1830s, there was little interest in these matters. Evangelicals acknowledged a debt to Methodism. There was often ready co-operation between reformers inside and outside the Established Church. Further, Evangelicals worked with Radicals, even free-thinking Radicals. They had many aims in common: the enforcement of order, economy in public expenditure, encouragement of individual self-reliance in economic affairs, elimination of abuses in the Church and elsewhere. And there was more similarity between the beliefs of pious reformers and secularist Radicals than might be expected. This was a reforming Bishop's definition of Christianity: 'no other than THE UNION OF PURE DEVOTION WITH UNIVERSAL BENEVOLENCE'. 'Happily', wrote Bentham, 'the dictates of religion seem to approach nearer and nearer to a coincidence with those of utility every day.'[1] Though strict Evangelicals held strict doctrines, and though fundamentalist interpretations of the Bible were usual, little was heard of the authority of the catholic Church, and theological writing was often simple-mindedly rationalist and mechanistic. Paley's *Evidences of Christianity*, a stock University textbook, began with the naivest of comparisons between the human individual and a pocket-watch. The Church was often spoken of as though it were merely the most important of public utilities. Again, interest in the Church as a spiritual body, with a life of its own, was not evident until the 1830s.

Reformers of these various persuasions also collaborated in humanitarian causes. One of the characteristic developments of the eighteenth century was a greater concern for helpless living things: animals, children, prisoners, emigrants and slaves. This impulse tended to cut across progressive economic attitudes when it was a question of employing children in factories. But, though the working conditions of children in factories were shocking, this was less of a novelty than that many disinterested people should care about it and try to improve matters. By 1832 the first statutes had been passed to regulate the treatment of animals (1822), protect children working in cotton factories (1802, 1819), safeguard emigrants (1803 and others), and abolish the slave trade so far as Britain was involved in it (1807). More effective than Acts of Parliament, opinion was making the traditional violent sports ever less respectable.

Many of these measures were promoted by private Members. But the Tory Ministers of these years showed some degree of sympathy with this reforming movement, especially in relation to the Church. Lord Liverpool's ecclesiastical appointments, though seldom specifically Evangelical, were much less influenced than those of previous Prime Ministers by political and party considerations, the whims of the Sovereign, and the aristocratic connexions of the candidates. As well as granting money for church-building, his Government had passed an Act in 1813 to raise curates' stipends.

---

[1] Best, *Temporal Pillars*, p. 141n. J. Bentham, *Introduction to the Principles of Morals and Legislation* (ed. W. Harrison) (Oxford, 1948), p. 241.

POLITICS AND REFORM

Some minor reforms, then, are largely attributable to the spontaneous sympathy of Ministers and other politicians, especially Tories, with the movement for a moral reformation and the reawakening of the Church of England. But full 'Liberal Toryism' is incomprehensible in these terms, the passage of the Reform Act even more so. It is striking that the moral reformation movement itself, as well as exercising influence from within the governing class, found it worthwhile to perfect means for bringing pressure to bear from outside. It had replied to the London Corresponding Society and to *Rights of Man* with hundreds of Constitutional Clubs and anti-sedition tracts by the million. It now used popular organization and wide publicity in campaigning for reform. The Anti-Slavery Society, founded in 1823, set a new pattern and standard of organization for pressure-groups. A large Central Committee kept in touch with affiliated societies, over a thousand of them eventually, in every part of the country; meetings were held; tracts and placards distributed; petitions to Parliament prepared, with tens of thousands, sometimes hundreds of thousands, of signatures. The Parliamentary reform agitation used the same techniques on the same scale in 1831–2, as did the Catholic Association in Ireland before 1829. This was the most impressive kind of manifestation of opinion, with respectable leadership and mass support. But the upper-class Press was also increasingly effective: articles in the quarterly reviews, the Tory *Quarterly*, the Whig *Edinburgh* and the Radical *Westminster*, or in the daily *Times*, were now based on full published reports of Parliamentary debates, fair knowledge of the way M.P.s voted, and moderately reliable facts and figures revealing abuses in Church, State and society. It was fifty years since the proceedings of Parliament had ceased to be virtually private, but the repression of the war years had intervened. Politicians only now felt the force of the change. They reacted in different ways. To take Tory Ministers, Castlereagh found unpopularity 'more convenient and gentlemanlike'[1] than popularity, while Canning took delight in courting 'that mighty power of public opinion, embodied in a Free Press, which pervades, and checks, and

---

[1] Quoted in J. A. R. Marriott, *Castlereagh* (London, 1936), p. 297.

perhaps, in the last resort, nearly governs the whole constitution'.[1] But, whether they liked it or not, M.P.s had to pay
some attention to the new force.

In the first place, there were some weaknesses in the armour
of the 'Establishment'. As the Press discovered, the anomalies
of the system could be exploited against it. Seats in the House
of Commons could be literally bought, and some were purchased by men who had made their money in trade or manufactures. One man who became an M.P. in this way was
Sir Robert Peel, senior, father of the Prime Minister, a wealthy
calico-printer of Bury, Lancashire. Only ability could ensure
success at the Bar, and the first two Lord Chancellors of the
period were the sons of a Newcastle coal-factor and an
American painter. Even under the unreformed constitution,
there were some direct ways of bringing pressure to bear on
the 'Establishment' from outside. The British electorate was a
larger proportion of the population than had the vote anywhere in the Old World between 1815 and 1848, and there
were many 'open' constituencies in which a broad electorate
could return M.P.s pledged to support reform. There was more
prestige in winning a county seat or a seat for a large town
than in entering Parliament by way of aristocratic nomination.
In the General Election of 1830, and still more in 1831, representatives of great families found themselves threatened with
defeat in constituencies normally considered to be under
their control: if they would not support Reform, they were told,
they must retire. It was an essential part of the background
of the Reform Act that the county electorates pronounced for
it, the lesser landowners and the tenantry expressing their
resentment at the power which the great landlords derived
from rotten boroughs, and demanding better representation
for the landed interest as a whole (the agricultural labourers,
of course, excluded). The loss by the Government of one by-
election could change policy, as the County Clare election of
1828 demonstrated. Finally, the threat of civil war and revolution could overbear the 'Establishment', as the passage of the
Catholic Relief Act showed in 1829. Politicians habitually
claimed that they would never bow to the mob, to violent

[1] 30 August 1822 (*Speeches of the Right Honourable George Canning delivered on Public Occasions in Liverpool* (Liverpool, 1825), p. 365). I owe this reference to Dr R. Robson.

expressions of opinion by the lower orders, that it was only to the peaceful pressure of respectable opinion that they would listen. But this claim is belied by the history of the period. Catholic emancipation apart, members of the 'Establishment' were certainly more ready to pay attention to the demands of the respectable for Parliamentary reform when they were reminded by the riots and working-class agitation of 1831–2 how dangerous it might be to alienate moderates altogether. No other attitude was consistent with the refusal of the great majority of the ruling class to entertain the idea of keeping the country down by enrolling a large standing army. All but the most extreme conservatives justified suspensions of Habeas Corpus and restrictions on the right of public meeting only as temporary emergency measures. The worst of the Six Acts lapsed in 1825. In the last resort, the position of the 'Establishment' rested on consent, and it knew it.

Already a significant if modest role in the relationship between the public and the 'Establishment' was played by the political parties. In 1815, and until after the passage of the Reform Act, there were no more than traces of party organization outside Parliament; but there was party feeling. There were not many contested elections in this period: 100 seems to have been the average number at General Elections before 1832. But, when a contest took place, for whatever reason it took place, the names 'Whig' and 'Tory' were likely to be applied to the candidates; and there was a clear general distinction between the political attitudes associated with the two names. While there were many issues which were not party issues, Whigs were on the whole friendly to Roman Catholics and Dissenters, less inclined to repressive measures, more inclined to fundamental reforms, and had tended to oppose the wars with France. Tories were friends of the Church of England and its privileges, more inclined to repressive measures and less inclined to fundamental reforms, and had been in power during the wars.

In the two Houses of Parliament, at the beginning of the period, the situation was less simple. One powerful group of political leaders with considerable backbench support opposed another, Whigs versus Tories, though Tories themselves were reluctant to acknowledge the name. These parties were quite well-organized with recognized leaders, regular Whips and occasional full meetings. But in the Commons there were also perhaps as many as 100 uncommitted M.P.s, often, in effect, apolitical or absentee; and there were some small groups composed of the followers of leaders who were not incorporated into the two main parties: principally, the supporters of Grenville[1] and Canning. From about 1821 to 1827 the position was clearer. The 'independents' excepted, the House of Commons was divided into only two groups. These parties did not vote solidly on all issues. But on matters like Parliamentary reform, and if the question was raised 'which group of politicians shall form the government', they could normally be relied on. A further period of fragmentation from 1827 to 1830 was followed by the formation of Grey's Ministry, which, though more than a party Ministry, restored the simple dual pattern, again excepting the 'independents'. Then, during the Reform Bill debates, 'independence', virtually disappeared, nearly all Members ranging themselves on one side or the other: this is the significance of the size of the divisions.

At the high political level the parties had further differences of attitude: they were divided on a great constitutional question, the role of the King. To a large extent it was old battles which the parties were fighting rather than battles which mattered to the public opinion of the 1820s. The Whigs could claim a measure of continuity, both of personnel and attitudes, since the 1670s, and traditionally stood for the rule of the great aristocracy, put forward as the natural guardians of the people's rights against the monarchy, and for the interpretation of the maxim 'The King can do no wrong' to mean that, whether he did right or wrong, some Minister must be responsible for the act, not the King himself. The Tories, though longer pedigrees were and might be constructed for them, stemmed for practical purposes from those who in the 1760s had stood for the 'independence' of the King, his right to Ministers of his choice and to a say in policy. It must be emphasized that the Parliamentary parties, though they cannot be imagined without sympathizers outside, were generated within the aristocratic 'Establishment' and within a more or less closed Parliament. On the one hand, political loyalties and attitudes were often handed down from father to son, and

---

[1] Lord Grenville had been Prime Minister in 1806–7.

political memories were long and detailed. On the other hand, as had happened with the Whigs under Walpole, the long tenure of office by the Tories, at a time of crisis, when the King was becoming progressively less able to act on his own account, strengthened the solidarity of the leaders as against the initiative of the King and also as against the Opposition, so that the Tories themselves whittled away royal power and that 'crossing the floor of the House' was not to be undertaken lightly.

In the early years of George III's reign public opinion and party feelings were never strong and sometimes scarcely perceptible, and the King personally played an important part in the choice of Ministers, in holding Ministries together and in framing policy. His Court and the offices of his Household were of great political importance, and he had considerable influence over the disposal of patronage which would later have been regarded as the Administration's rather than his. 'Time's worst statute', the Septennial Act of 1716, which made it unnecessary to hold General Elections more often than once in seven years, had operated in fact so that every Parliament between that of 1715 and that of 1774, inclusive, lasted for at least six years. In any case, even when there was a General Election, it was rare for the electorate, let alone the people, to make much impact on the composition of the House of Commons. In the 1760s George III had succeeded in establishing, without special reference to the electorate, that Governments could be formed and could survive without the support of the great Whig lords who had controlled affairs under his two predecessors. In 1784, by which time party feeling had grown and public opinion was more active, the King, although his policy towards the American colonies had just failed disastrously, was able to maintain his choice of Ministers against the wishes of a majority of the House of Commons. He had the House of Lords on his side, and, using his power of dissolution creatively, to remove a Parliament only four years old, he also won the support of the electorate. In 1807 he executed a somewhat similar manoeuvre, dissolving a Parliament less than a year old and thereby increasing the majority for a Ministry opposed to Catholic emancipation. In 1811, when his son became Regent, it was generally supposed that, if he had so wished, he could have changed to Whig Ministers and made good his choice at a General Election.

However, the King had never been absolutely unfettered in his choice of Ministers. There were limits to what the most servile Parliaments would tolerate. And by the 1820s his choice was much more circumscribed than in the 1760s. At the beginning of George III's reign there had been perhaps 250 M.P.s who were 'placemen', that is, who held government offices of some sort. In George IV's reign Opposition spokesmen often claimed that this 'influence of the Crown' was increasing, and thus accounted for the acquiescence of the House of Commons in Tory rule. But in fact the number of 'placemen' M.P.s had been falling ever since George III's accession, and in 1822, looking high and low, the most reformers could find was 89, fewer than in a modern House of Commons. To bring about this change, the pressure of opinion and of the Opposition had acted on the government, but so had a desire for 'purity', economy and efficiency on the part of George III and his Ministers themselves. Further, the King's personal influence over appointments, even Household appointments, had been much reduced, largely as a result of the greater solidarity of Cabinets; and whereas George III had at least been generally popular and respected, George IV's prestige was minimal, especially after the Queen's trial. Again, the King and his Ministers now had many fewer seats at their disposal at elections. So in Parliament Ministers depended for a secure majority on party feeling, and at elections they depended on the combination of some popular support and some favourable aristocratic patronage.[1]

Now the House of Lords had a large Tory majority. While the size of the House had remained almost constant between 1719 and 1784, thereafter George III had used his prerogative of making peers as purposefully as his prerogative of dissolution. The membership of the Lords had been almost doubled by 1815, and those ennobled were often 'boroughmongers' and generally reactionaries. So, if the King decided to change to Whig Ministers, he had to be prepared to coerce the House

[1] W. R. Brock, *Lord Liverpool and Liberal Toryism, 1820–7* (Cambridge, 1941); A. Mitchell, *The Whigs in Opposition, 1815–1830* (Oxford, 1967); A. S. Foord, 'The Waning of the Influence of the Crown', *English Historical Review* 1947; D. Large, 'The Decline of "the Party of the Crown" and the Rise of Parties in the House of Lords, 1783–1837', ibid. 1963; D. Beales, 'Parliamentary Parties and the 'Independent' Member, 1810–1860' in *Ideas and Institutions of Victorian Britain* (ed. R. Robson) (London, 1967).

1 A Fête in Petworth Park, 1835, from a painting by W. F. Witherington. Greville has a fine description of this or an almost identical scene (*Memoirs*, Vol. III, pp. 84–5). The Earl of Egremont, owner of Petworth, annually feasted 'the poor of the adjoining parishes (woman and children, not men). . . . Fifty-four tables, each fifty feet long, were placed in a vast semi-circle on the lawn. . . . Tickets were given to . . . about 4,000; but, as many more came, the old Peer . . . ordered the barriers to be taken down and admittance given to all. They think 6,000 were fed. Gentlemen of the neighbourhood carved for them. . . .' This was an occasion when the romantic-conservative picture of rural relationships was realized in fact. Note that the New Poor Law had just been passed, and that Petworth is in Sussex, the county notorious for spending the largest sum per capita on 'outdoor relief'.

Column 1.			Column 2.			Column 3.			Column 4.		
Ages	Males.	Females.	Ages	Males.	Females.	Ages	Males.	Females.	Ages	Males.	Females.
Under One Year			3	20	20	30	7	5	60	7	5
			4	17	20	31	4	3	61	4	5
			5	10	11	32	4	1	62	5	4
			6	4	2	33	3	6	63	3	3
			7	2	3	34	4	1	64	3	5
			8	5	2	35	7	—	65	2	2
			9	4	3	36	7	2	66	6	5
			10	—	2	37	6	6	67	3	5
			11	—	4	38	2	5	68	2	6
			12	1	4	39	3	2	69	1	4
			13	—	—	40	7	3	70	1	5
	159	131	14	3	2	41	3	5	71	2	2
			15	2	1	42	4	2	72	1	2
1			16	—	2	43	7	2	73	2	2
			17	5	3	44	1	6	74	1	5
			18	2	—	45	7	4	75	4	5
			19	2	4	46	1	4	76	3	3
			20	1	3	47	3	3	77	2	4
			21	3	3	48	2	3	78	—	2
			22	3	3	49	3	1	79	1	1
	83	59	23	5	2	50	4	6	80	3	5
			24	2	4	51	3	2	81	1	1
2			25	6	1	52	7	1	82	—	2
			26	7	6	53	4	4	83	—	1
			27	7	4	54	4	2	84	2	3
			28	5	6	55	6	5	91	—	1
			29	6	4	56	6	3	86	1	—
	56	39				57	—	3	89	2	—
						58	2	4	88	—	1
	297	229				59	5	3	87	—	2
				139	130		127	97		62	91

Defective Registry of Ages - - [tally] — 2
[tally] — 10

In Burial Grounds of Dissenters, Jews, and others - - -

2	} 7	1	} 9
4		6	
1		2	
139		130	

SUMMARY.

	Males.	Females.	Total.
1st Column - - -	297	- 229	- 526
2d Column - - -	139	- 130	- 269
3d Column - - -	127	- 97	- 224
4th Column - - -	62	- 91	- 153
Total - -	625	- 517	- 1.172

2 A specimen page of a parish return of deaths, from the census of 1831. The cross-stroke marks each tenth death in each category.

of Lords by appealing to the people against them, and perhaps
by a massive creation of peers – not a course to be embarked
upon unless he positively desired to bring about a revolutionary situation.

In any case, George IV inherited from his father one political
principle, opposition to Catholic emancipation; and he also
wished to maintain as much as possible of his 'independence'
as King. In 1811 and for most of the period the Whigs were
determined not to take office unless they were allowed to bring
forward Catholic emancipation; they were pledged to restrict
the independence of the monarch; and they would not join a
Ministry except as a party. So it would have been unnatural
for George to choose a Whig Ministry. But, even among the
Tories, he was left with no choice of importance so long as
Liverpool led the broad-based Government which in 1819-21
had taken in the followers of Grenville and Canning. Only after
Liverpool's stroke did new opportunities arise.

Even the public, at least the respectable public, would not
necessarily have assisted the King if he had opted for the
Whigs before 1830. The Tories of the 'twenties, as has been
seen, relaxed repression, proved themselves administrative
reformers, Church reformers, reformers of the law, Free
Traders, and pursued a liberal foreign policy – all, probably,
generally popular. It was claimed in 1826 that, while His
Majesty's Government filled the offices of state, 'His Majesty's
Opposition' (the first use of the phrase) was formulating
ministerial policy. But this was not true for the greatest issues
of the day, and the Whigs remained suspect on various grounds.
They had seemed less than whole-heartedly patriotic during
the war. They were rigid defenders of property rights, and much
more inclined than the Tories to justify aristocratic patronage
in the public service. It was in fact considered a Tory characteristic to recognize the claims of talent and competence even
when they were not recommended by a long pedigree. Grey's
Cabinet was more aristocratic than Liverpool's. It was Grey
who thought Canning disqualified from becoming Prime
Minister because his mother was an actress. Many of the
prominent Tories of the 'twenties were of comparatively
humble origin: as well as Canning and Peel, Sidmouth was
the son of a physician and Huskisson the son of a very small
landowner. Further, Catholic emancipation, to which the

Whigs were committed, was unpopular outside Ireland: the General Election of 1826 registered the anti-Catholic feeling of England, strengthening the Tories. Attwood, founder of the Birmingham Political Union, saw himself as a Tory, like Cobbett. No doubt, to large sections of the public, both the old aristocratic parties seemed equally unattractive, and their disputes anachronistic; and the handful of Radicals elected to the House of Commons appeared the only acceptable politicians. But, though it was possible for Radicals to act directly on the Government or Parliament to secure particular reforms, for many purposes it was necessary to work through one or the other of the parties, and it was certainly out of the question, short of a revolution, that a Radical Government should be formed.

'Liberal Toryism' of the 1820s, it will be apparent, was the resultant of many forces whose stability was precarious. The preferences of the King and the House of Lords, and probably the electorate, were for the Tories as against the Whigs. But the major common ground they shared for this preference was Protestant feeling. The leaders of the Tories were much more liberal than most of their Parliamentary supporters, and also much more aware of public opinion. The King's wishes overtly, and party and public feeling implicitly, kept Catholic emancipation an open question within the Cabinet; though most 'Liberal Tories' supported it, they could not remain Ministers, and so could not carry out other reforms, unless they acquiesced in this situation – until 1829. Moreover, the King and the House of Lords were firm against 'fundamental' reform. By comparison with what had gone before, the measures of the Administration between 1822 and 1827 seem notably liberal and reformist. By comparison with what followed, they seem merely trivial tinkering. The only offences for which the death penalty was abolished were those for which no one had been executed for decades. The law could be 'consolidated', but not reformed. Nothing serious could be done about the Church. Slavery could not be abolished. It is significant that it was in foreign policy that liberalism seemed most pronounced. It is significant also that even here there was a greater change of style than of substance. But the respectable public was temporarily satisfied that reform could proceed without constitutional change.

The break-up of the Tory Administration in 1827, followed by Canning's death, made more rapid change unavoidable. The first put an end to the coalition between anti- reformers and moderate reformers; the second made a Government of the centre hopeless. The reactionary Ministry, Wellington's, was duly formed and, with a narrower basis of Parliamentary support, was found more, not less, amenable to popular pressure. The concession of Catholic emancipation could not have been avoided by any Government unless it was prepared for civil war; however, it was easier for a Tory Government to get the measure past the King and through Parliament. This accomplished, together with the modification of the Corn Law, domestic politics were transformed. The King's one principle had been overborne. The Tories were further divided: Wellington was now opposed by agricultural and Protestant 'Ultra' Tories as well as by Liberal Tories. He and Peel had aroused bitter feelings in their own party by going against their professions and undertaking to put through Catholic emancipation. They had also thereby removed the main cause of Whig unpopularity. One of the reasons for Wellington's emphatic rejection of Parliamentary reform in 1830 was his and Peel's unwillingness to betray again their party's principles: in the last resort there had to be some relationship between men and measures. His pronouncement brought together all the forces outside the 'Establishment' in a new conviction that constitutional reform was essential. The change of monarch made the Whigs' path to power easier, since William IV was more or less an 'Ultra' Tory Reformer. The General Election, made necessary by the death of George IV, failed to strengthen Wellington's Government. The French Revolution of 1830 helped too: it had the double effect of arousing Liberal opinion in Britain and of encouraging those who believed that change was possible without extremism.[1] It now at last became evident that the refusal of the strict Whigs to compromise with Toryism, even at the risk of ostracism dur-

---

[1] D. C. Moore, 'The Other Face of Reform', *Victorian Studies* 1961; N. Gash, 'English Reform and French Revolution in the General Election of 1830' in *Essays presented to Sir Lewis Namier* (ed. R. Pares and A. J. P. Taylor) (London, 1956); P. Fraser, 'Public Petitioning and Parliament before 1832', *History* 1961; H. Ferguson, 'The Birmingham Political Union and the Government', *Victorian Studies* 1960; C. Flick, 'The Fall of Wellington's Government', *Journal of Modern History* 1965.

ing the war and despite exclusion from office for decades, was worthwhile in the long term both from their own point of view and from that of the whole 'Establishment', as well as for the nation. They were available to reform the 'Establishment', drastically yet from within, when at last the balance of forces was overwhelmingly in favour of change.

THE REFORM ACT OF 1832

Their Bill was far more radical than any proposal hitherto made from either Front Bench. It seemed revolutionary to M.P.s, for whom the question of redistributing the handful of seats taken from the boroughs of Grampound, Penryn and East Retford (after their elections had been proved 'corrupt') had been a major issue in the 'twenties. It did not fully satisfy the political societies, but it marked such an advance that they gave it their blessing. The essence of the Whig case for their sweeping measure was this:

> The object of an extension of the Elective franchise . . . must be to give satisfaction to the people . . .; and it is conceived that this may be done by extending the Elective Franchise to those classes, who possess property and knowledge. Much more is demanded by many, but it is hoped that it is not yet too late to make a change . . ., the limit of which shall be the possession of property and intelligence; but any plan must be objectionable which, by keeping the Franchise very . . . exclusive, fails to give satisfaction to the middle and respectable ranks of society, and drives them to a union founded on dissatisfaction, with the lower orders. It is of the utmost importance to associate the middle with the higher orders of society in the love and support of the institutions and government of the country.[1]

This argument, written in specific reference to Scotland, had general application. The Whigs believed that the popular demand was so great, supported by such responsible persons, and so well-justified by social changes, that it must be met, but met in such a way as to strengthen the 'Establishment' and weaken the 'mob', by detaching from the latter and attaching to the former 'the middle classes' – in other words, the Bill was not a mere concession, it was intended also as a cure.[2] Many

---

[1] T. F. Kennedy, quoted in N. Gash, *Politics in the Age of Peel* (London, 1953), p. 15. The next three quotations come from the same chapter.
[2] D. C. Moore, 'Concession or Cure: the Sociological Premises of the First Reform Act', *Historical Journal* 1966.

claimed that the 'balance of the constitution' had been tilted against the popular element in the last two reigns, and saw the Bill as a restoration. In more detail, it was hoped to eradicate or mitigate the following abuses: the nomination of M.P.s by private individuals and their election by 'close' corporations; gross corruption among the lower class of voters; the expense of elections; the inadequate representation of the larger manufacturing and commercial towns; 'the unequal and inequitable distribution of voting power between the lower and middle classes'; and the under-representation, in terms of population, of the counties.

The following aims were explicitly disavowed: to remove all anomalies; to equalize constituencies on the basis of population; to give votes to 'mere numbers'; to assimilate borough and county constituencies; to 'take away that [legitimate] influence [of landlords] over the vote which preserves the representative system . . . from being of too democratic a character'; and to expose Parliament to more frequent General Elections. So the repeal of the Septennial Act and the introduction of the 'ballot', that is, secret voting, were not proposed. With exceptions, as long as an existing borough had a population of 2,000, it was to retain one of its M.P.s; if it had 4,000, both. A theory of the representation of 'interests', deriving in its fullest form from Burke, was used to justify the inclusion of some and the exclusion of other possible constituencies: Frome received its M.P. as the representative borough of the West Country cloth industry; and enfranchisement was accorded to the 'petty interests of the keepers of circulating libraries and vendors of oranges and lemonade at Cheltenham and Brighton'; but only a few of the populous metropolitan boroughs were given separate representation.

These various aims, adjusted by compromise and modified by less elevated political considerations, determined the shape of the Reform Act as it emerged from months of Parliamentary debate. How well it succeeded in its broader aims will be considered in the next Part. The detailed provisions were as follows. In the Act for England and Wales 56 boroughs were wholly disfranchised, 31 partly. The resulting 143 seats were redistributed as follows. In England and Wales 22 new two-member boroughs (including Manchester, Birmingham, Sheffield and Leeds) and 21 one-member boroughs were created, and 65 seats were given to counties, many of which were now divided for electoral purposes. Eight of the residue went to Scotland, the other five to Ireland. Many old boroughs were much enlarged in area. The result, if total population be taken as the true criterion, was to reduce, but not to remove, the over-representation of the South as compared with the North of England, the over-representation of borough electors as compared with county electors, the over-representation of rural as compared with genuinely urban areas and the over-representation of England by comparison with Scotland and Ireland. Anomaly survived well enough: of the boroughs left after 1832 there were a few which could not muster 200 voters for two M.P.s, while on the other hand a few had more than 7,000.

Changes in the franchise were as follows, the more minute complications ignored. A man now had first to be registered before he could exercise the franchise. In the English and Welsh counties the 40 shilling freehold remained the basic qualification for the vote. To this were added in England and Wales what may in shorthand be called £10 'copyholders',[1] £10 long leaseholders, £50 short leaseholders and £50 occupiers. These were also approximately the new qualifications for voting in the Scottish counties, where a 40 shilling freehold did not suffice either before or after the Act. In Ireland £10 freeholders were joined by £10 leaseholders. In the boroughs the basic qualification over the whole United Kingdom became the £10 occupation or household franchise, but certain ancient rights were preserved. A man could not qualify to vote in a county by virtue of a property which provided his qualification to vote in a borough, a provision which, with the 'Chandos clause' enfranchising £50 tenants, represents the direct impact on the Act of the 'Ultra' Tories. In general, the effect was to increase considerably what contemporaries thought of as middle-class representation, and slightly to reduce such working-class representation as there had been by removing anomalies in certain boroughs. In total the electorate of the United Kingdom was increased from under 500,000 to over 800,000, that is 1 in 30 of the whole population, or 1 in 7

---

[1] Copyhold was a form of land tenure which by 1832 was scarcely distinguishable in practice from freehold.

of adult males in that youthful society. The greatest proportional increase was in Scotland, from under 4,500 to over 60,000. The entire Irish electorate was under 100,000 after 1832, only 1 in 80 of the population and 1 in 20 of adult males, less than half the size of the electorate before 1829, but even so probably more than twice the size of the electorate between 1829 and 1832.

5

Culture and Society
1815-1832

MUSICAL composition is of all the arts the most difficult to relate to its social background. For the whole of the period 1815 to 1885 British composers were nonentities. A part of the explanation must be the weaknesses of musical education in Britain, which the foundation of the Royal Academy of Music in 1822 improved only slightly. Little can be said for Britain's role in musical development during the period except that she provided wealthy audiences for certain foreign composers, filling a role something like that of the United States in the early twentieth century. Before 1832 the most remarkable achievement of British connoisseurs was the Philharmonic Society's commission from Beethoven of his Ninth Symphony in 1824.

Painting is not necessarily any easier to fit into general history, and it is difficult to understand why the first half of the nineteenth century should have been the period of Britain's greatest artists, J. M. W. Turner and John Constable. Turner had been working long before 1815, and his style continued to develop well into the 'forties. His momentous first visit to Venice took place in 1819, but its fruits were delayed. Most of Constable's best-known pictures, however, date from the years between Waterloo and the First Reform Act. The appearance of some of them in the Paris salon of 1824 had a considerable impact on Delacroix and other French artists. Both Turner and Constable reflect, among other things, the Romantic delight in landscape – in Turner's case usually wild panoramas, and in Constable's peaceful Suffolk scenes. They were both ready to record the technological achievements of their time: for example, Constable painted Waterloo Bridge and the Chain Pier at Brighton, and Turner lifeboats and steamships.

Architectural monuments of these 'Regency' years are also outstanding. A last large group of aristocratic houses was being finished around 1815, for instance Ashridge and Belvoir. The most notable extension in the years 1815-32 was an enormous addition to the already huge house of the Dukes of Devonshire at Chatsworth. This, like Belvoir and the large modifications to Windsor Castle, was under the superintendence of Jeffry Wyatt, later Wyatville.

The building which is usually taken to epitomize the period is the Royal Pavilion at Brighton, completed in 1822, built for the Regent by John Nash, who indulged his master's eclectic and uncertain taste in attempting to copy Oriental palaces. Nash also began the rebuilding of Buckingham Palace for George IV in 1825. In the same year Benjamin Wyatt, Wyatville's cousin, began Lancaster House for the Duke of York.

Several of the most notable pieces of town planning in Britain were carried through in these years. 'Once, and only once, has a great plan for London, affecting the development of the capital as a whole, been projected and carried to completion.'[1] This was when Nash created Regent's Park, the terraces around it, and Regent Street between 1812 and the late 'twenties. Marble Arch was his also. Much of Grecian Edinburgh was built at this time, and a good deal of Brighton and Cheltenham. By 1815 the small 'villa' and even the semi-detached house were becoming features of the outskirts of towns.

Institutional building acquired new importance in the nineteenth century. It has been mentioned that this was the first age of museums. The great new building to house the rapidly-increasing British Museum was begun to the Greek designs of Robert Smirke in 1823. William Wilkins designed the National Gallery, begun in 1832. The Bank of England was expanding, using Sir John Soane, the eccentric architect

---

[1] J. Summerson, *Georgian London* (London, 1962), p. 177.

of the Dulwich Gallery. One of the most remarkable survivals is the offices built for the Birmingham Improvement Commissioners, 'the most striking British example of the temple paradigm',[1] designed in 1831. The churches for which Liverpool's Government advanced money are to be found in many towns, especially in London near the boundaries of the Cities – still galleried preaching-houses rather than places of sacramental worship, using Gothic forms, if at all, purely as applied ornament. The bulk of the London Clubs date from around 1830, and are particularly important in architectural history as including early examples of the revival of Renaissance styles, like the Travellers' Club of 1829. Cambridge was as active in building in the 1820s as in the 1960s. The first part of Wilkins' Grecian design for Downing College, which received its charter in 1800, was completed. In King's College his Hall and screen to King's Parade, and in St John's Thomas Rickman's New Court are among the most characteristic of Cambridge buildings. Several other Colleges built new battlemented courts or refaced old courts in what was conceived to be the 'Elizabethan' manner. If building is symptomatic, Cambridge was far livelier at this time than Oxford.

In poetry this is the age of the young Romantic rebels. About half of Byron's output comes from after 1815, including bitter attacks, not unlike Shelley's, on the 'Establishment'. He lived abroad after 1816 and had even greater influence there than at home, especially in the character of a liberal nationalist: he died fighting for Greek independence in 1824. Shelley was less well-known and well-regarded in his day, but wrote some of the best lyric poetry in the language. So did John Keats, but, without aristocratic connexions, and comparatively uninterested in politics, he was barely noticed in his lifetime. Both, like Byron, died young. All three contributed to the myth or ideal of the Romantic genius, brilliant, unstable, in ill-health, freethinking, in and out of love, scornful of the public. It is not difficult to find a plausible, though obviously incomplete, explanation for the remarkable phenomenon they represent, a brief efflorescence of Romantic poetry, in the desperate discontents of the repressive period before and after Waterloo.

---

[1] H.-R. Hitchcock, *Architecture: Nineteenth and Twentieth Centuries* (London, 1958), p. 69.

The earlier Romantic poets, Wordsworth, Coleridge, Southey and Blake, all still alive,[1] had lost the revolutionary fervour they had felt in 1789. Southey was the apologist of Liverpool's régime, ridiculed by Byron in *The Vision of Judgment*. The most notable work of any of them after 1815 was Coleridge's semi-philosophical writing. He devoted himself to study of recent German philosophy, which in many respects was concerned to revive Greek attitudes, glorification of the community, of an ideal 'reality', of myth and even inutility. Though Coleridge's thought was anything but clear, its influence on men like Carlyle, Gladstone, Newman and J. S. Mill is undoubted. Mill saw Coleridge as the antithesis of Bentham, and both as necessary to intellectual salvation: 'the one demanding the extinction of the institutions and creeds which had hitherto existed; the other that they be made a reality.'[2] Coleridge had written: 'My opinion is this: that deep thinking is attainable only by a man of deep feeling, and that all truth is a species of revelation. . . . It is *insolent* to *differ* from the public *opinion*. . . .'[3] The echoes of Burke are unmistakable.

According to Jane Austen, the young men of the 1810s were reading Lord Byron, the old Walter Scott. The reputation of the latter was fantastically high, abroad as well as in Britain. His poetry was mainly written before 1815, his novels afterwards. Some took advantage of, and strengthened, the growing cult of the Middle Ages. Many of them used themes from Scottish history, and so did much to put Scotland on the tourist map and to revive Scottish national pride. Jane Austen herself wrote her last novel, *Persuasion*, in 1815, but never attained until the late nineteenth century anything like the popularity of Scott.

Of course, polite education was still based on the Greek and Roman Classics. The standard of teaching and scholarship in these fields was rising fast. Perhaps the most characteristic single artistic manifestation of the period is the Greek Revival. It is at the back of Coleridge's thought. At length the democracy of the city-state is appreciated and glorified, and the philosophy of Aristotle restored to favour. It had taken an

---

[1] Blake died in 1827; the others survived beyond 1832.
[2] Quoted in R. Williams, *Culture and Society, 1780–1950* (London, 1961), p. 75.
[3] Ibid. p. 82.

astonishingly long time for the West to take an interest in Greek architecture as distinct from Roman. The future Prime Minister, Aberdeen, was one of the earliest serious travellers in Greece and founded the Athenian Society in 1804. The Earl of Elgin's removal to London of the Parthenon frieze, bought for the British Museum in 1816, led to much imitation of the figures on buildings of the period. The movement was not only artistic, literary and philosophical. The Philhellenes of the 'twenties, who helped those whom they supposed to be the modern representatives of the Ancient Greeks towards independence, form an important link in the history of British sympathy with nationalism abroad.

6

Britain and the Rest of the World 1815-1832

General

BRITAIN's relations with the rest of the world have to be treated in this book with presumptuous brevity. This, however, is a field in which it is notoriously easier to find a detailed narrative than a generalized survey, and so it may be useful to supply the latter.

It must first be realized, as it often is not, that relations between States differ fundamentally from relations within States. In domestic affairs the State is sovereign in the sense of giving law and commanding obedience, and often deploys its power and authority to harmonize and pacify, to achieve compromises and consensus, and to avert confrontations, within society. Over the period covered by this book the British State became increasingly successful in these aims, except in Ireland. In international affairs, at least within Europe, there seemed to be a parallel development. There was greater reluctance to engage in war, especially in Britain, than in previous periods, and fewer wars occurred than in earlier and later centuries. The Great Powers collaborated in many cases to settle international differences peacefully. But the State in its external relations remained sovereign in the sense that it was subject to no overriding control, and the factor of power and the threat of war always lurked just behind the exchanges of diplomacy. Outside Europe Britain, officially and unofficially, showed less hesitation to use force.

So great was Britain's power in the nineteenth century that, as is true only of very strong or very fortunate states, what she did domestically was scarcely affected by the actions of other Powers. Britain's interest in the rest of the world was exceptional, but for the most part outgoing. There were, it is true, a number of alarms or invasion panics, chiefly in connection with France. But their main significance was that they hastened the process, more or less continuous during the nineteenth century, of refurbishing the British navy. The fleet was usually kept at the 'two-power standard', that is, equal to the combined forces of the two largest navies other than Britain's, and never fell below the 'one-and-a-half power standard'. Britain was therefore for practical purposes immune from invasion, which every other European country experienced during the century.

Sea-power enabled and encouraged her to divide her external relations into two nearly distinct compartments, those with the Continent of Europe, and those with the rest of the world. This point must be elaborated, both in general and with particular reference to the Treaties of 1815 and the policies of the succeeding years.

British statesmen of the nineteenth century never seriously entertained the idea of annexing territory on the mainland of Europe. But they considered that Britain had interests there. They all held that the union of the Continent under one Power would be dangerous to Britain and that she must oppose, if necessary by force, any attempt to dominate Europe. They believed more particularly that Britain could not safely acquiesce in the union of France with what is now Belgium. Britain had entered on war with France in 1793 because her rulers thought that the French invasion of Belgium both constituted in itself a serious threat to British interests and security, and reflected an intention to try to dominate the whole of Europe. The Treaties of 1815 ratified the return to something like the position of before 1793, and Britain's prime concern in European politics in the period of this book was to keep France thus contained. The only other Power which sometimes seemed equally dangerous was Russia, for reasons which will appear. By extension, it was further held that it was to the advantage of Britain to preserve a 'Balance of Power' in Europe, that is, a situation in which several Great Powers were comparable with each other in strength, by supporting the weaker against the stronger. But this wider principle could be very flexibly applied, and seldom seemed to require the use of force to maintain it.

Outside Europe, on the other hand, it was the aim of Britain's statesmen that she herself should be dominant. This is not to say that they wished her to annex the whole world. Almost all of them were reluctant to take over the government of any more large territories. The history of the American colonies was regarded as an object-lesson. It appeared that the likely outcome of establishing a large settlement colony was rebellion and separation. In any case, it cost Britain a good deal to defend her Empire, and the return was uncertain, except in the case of India, where revenue exceeded expenditure. There was growing doubt that the main eighteenth-century argument for colonies, that they increased the trade of the mother-country by giving her a monopoly of their markets, was valid. British statesmen took little pride in the Empire, at least until the 1870s. But they were determined that their country's possessions and trade should be unmolested, and, though they did not forbid other Powers to acquire new territory outside Europe, they viewed the process with suspicion. In fact, as will be seen, the pressures on the home government from outside Britain, and sometimes from within, were strong in support of further annexations, and the Empire grew steadily throughout the period.

Foreign and Imperial Policy 1815-1832

In European affairs the main interest of the years after Waterloo lies in the attitude of the Great Powers to liberal, nationalist and revolutionary movements. To the rulers of Russia, Austria and Prussia, and to the Bourbon Kings restored in France when Napoleon fell, the European settlement of 1815 was sacred and indivisible, not only the frontiers between the states but also the régimes within them. Any change in either threatened the security of all governments. Reform was no better than revolution, liberalism than democracy, nationalism than expansionism: each involved all the others. The settlement, however, left the Austrian, Russian and Ottoman Empires all governing many people who felt some consciousness of nationality distinct from their rulers and from other groups within the Empire concerned.

Castlereagh considered it unpractical to try to prevent all

change; he did not think that the interests of Britain required
him to do so; and he knew that the British public would not
allow him to adopt that policy. He thought that a Power which
moved to suppress a revolution or a constitution in another
state might have expansionist intentions, and that its action
might be more likely to disturb the peace than the change of
régime against which it was directed. He was enough of a
constitutionalist to sympathize with some of the opponents of
the established order abroad. But, though he would not approve
the intervention of the Powers against the revolutions of 1820,
he would not actively oppose it. This was his version of the
policy or doctrine of 'non-intervention'.

Canning's emphasis was different. He had more sympathy
with liberal movements. He was also anxious to identify
himself with a popular foreign policy, and took to publishing
more of his despatches than his predecessors. But he did not
believe that it was in Britain's interests to support constitutionalism in all cases, and, except in Portugal, he refused to
give it active assistance. He differed from Castlereagh less in
what he wanted to happen than in his attitude to co-operation
with other Powers. Both men held that it was more important
to Britain that Europe should be at peace and that there should
be some sort of Balance of Power on the Continent than that
established régimes and boundaries should be rigidly preserved.
But Canning pursued British interests in isolation, without
regard for those of other states.

The battle of Navarino was a brilliant naval victory against
a much superior force. Yet it was described in the King's
Speech as 'an untoward event'. Canning and his successors
were torn between sympathy with the Greeks, Christians and
heirs of ancient civilization struggling against rulers who were
Moslem as well as barbarous, and reluctance to do anything
which might reduce Turkish and increase Russian power. Only
when it had become apparent that the Greeks were going to
establish themselves anyway did Canning negotiate a settlement
on this basis with Russia. Navarino was fought to put an end to
the Turks' obstruction of this settlement.

It is noticeable that even in Europe Britain was at her most
effective in questions concerning weak Powers with access to
the sea. The Mediterranean, like the oceans, was dominated
by the British navy. The use of the fleet to advance British

THE SAME TOWN IN 1840

1. St Michael's Tower rebuilt in 1750. 2. New Parsonage House & Pleasure Grounds. 3. The New Jail. 4. Gas Works. 5. Lunatic Asylum. 6. Iron Works & Socialist Hall. St Maries Abbey. 7. St Peter's Chapel. 8. Baptist Chapel. 9. Unitarian Chapel. 10. New Church. 11. New Town Hall & Concert Room. 12. Wesleyan Centenary Chapel. 13. New Christian Society. 14. Quakers Meeting. 15. Socialist Hall of Science.

Catholic town in 1440.

1. St Michaels on the Hill. 2. Queens Cross. 3. St Thomas's Chapel. 4. St Maries Abbey. 5. All Saints. 6. St Johns. 7. St Peters. 8. St Alkmunds. 9. St Maries. 10. St Edmunds. 11. Grey Friars. 12. St Cuthberts. 13. Guild hall. 14. Trinity. 15. St Olaves. 16. St Botolphs.

3 A plate from Pugin's *Contrasts* (2nd edition, 1841).

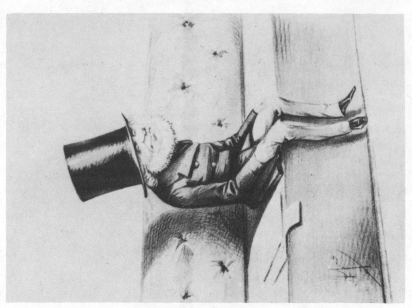

5 A caricature of Earl Russell from *Vanity Fair*, 1869.

4 The State of the Nation, a caricature of 1829.

views was considered normal, the use of the army exceptional.

Half unintentionally, Britain had much expanded her Empire during the wars with France. She had been induced, largely by a threat of French rivalry, to annex much more of India, and by 1818, through the East India Company, governed directly 553,000 square miles with an estimated population of 87,000,000, and indirectly a further 590,000 square miles and 43,000,000 people.[1] With Europe sealed off by her navy from the rest of the world, she had taken over most of the enemy French and Dutch Empires. At the end of the war she handed back some of her conquests, retaining only those which were considered necessary to her trade and to enable her navy to control the seas. But the Empires of all other Powers were crumbling. France's was almost wholly gone. The Dutch had given up Ceylon and part of Guiana, as well as the Cape, to Britain, and remained rulers of the East Indies by her permission. The Spanish and Portuguese colonies on the mainland of America, separated from the mother-countries during the wars, rebelled against them when their rule was reimposed. By 1824 the colonies were independent. Britain was the only Power in a position to fill the power-vacuum that existed in large parts of the world, and between 1815 and 1832 was sometimes tempted to annex territory in the interests of her traders or of existing colonists. In 1819 Singapore was purchased on the first ground, in 1829 the colony of Western Australia founded on the second. In general, however, it was 'informal empire' that was preferred. The South American republics owed their political independence to Britain and her navy, but they were effectively her economic colonies. Trade between Britain and South America developed much more rapidly than that between Britain and Canada, reinforcing the view that direct rule of territory overseas brought no economic advantage. The truth was that Britain was so easily the greatest industrial and commercial country of the world that no area could afford not to trade with her. She had little reason to fear foreign competition, whether in her own colonies or elsewhere. Her

---

[1] At this time the population of British North America was less than one million.

navy ensured security for commerce. Free Trade theories were peculiarly applicable to this situation.

Relations with the United States presented a special problem. Unless they were peaceful, Britain's trade and her cotton industry would be disrupted and Canada threatened, as during the war of 1812–14. There were plenty of small disputes, chiefly over the Canadian boundary, which could have led to war. But of course the American as well as the British economy would have suffered severely if it had come to that. Cotton exports to Britain made up nearly a half of total United States exports. Britain was careful not to oppose the United States' westward expansion to the Pacific, and it was with the unacknowledged assistance of British ships and policy that President Monroe was able in 1823 to proclaim his 'Doctrine' that European Powers should not interfere in the affairs of the American Continent. At various times each side avoided taking offence too readily at the actions of the other, recognizing how much it stood to lose by going to war.

In the internal affairs of the British Empire two developments of particular importance must be noticed, though they will be discussed under the next period. First, in India the arrival of Lord William Bentinck to be Governor-General in 1828 was the beginning of an era of reform. Secondly, in Canada demands became stronger for 'responsible government', that is, for the surrender of British control over the domestic affairs of the country, especially as embodied in nominated governors and executive councils, to locally-elected representatives.

PART TWO

1832-1850

The first shock of a great earthquake had, just at that period, rent the whole neighbourhood to its centre. Traces of its course were visible on every side. Houses were knocked down; streets broken through and stopped; deep pits and trenches dug in the ground; enormous heaps of earth and clay thrown up; buildings that were undermined and shaking, propped by great beams of wood. Here, a chaos of carts, overthrown and jumbled together, lay topsy-turvy at the bottom of a steep, unnatural hill; there, confused treasures of iron soaked and rusted in something that had accidentally become a pond. Everywhere were bridges that led nowhere; thoroughfares that were wholly impassable; Babel towers of chimneys, wanting half their height; temporary wooden houses and enclosures, in the most unlikely situations; carcasses of ragged tenements, and fragments of unfinished walls and arches, and piles of scaffolding, and wildernesses of bricks, and giant forms of cranes, and tripods straddling above nothing. There were a hundred thousand shapes and substances of incompleteness, wildly mingled out of their places, upside down, burrowing in the earth, aspiring in the air, mouldering in the water, and unintelligible as any dream. Hot springs and fiery eruptions, the usual attendants upon earthquakes, lent their contributions of confusion to the scene. Boiling water hissed and heaved within dilapidated walls; whence, also, the glare and roar of flames came issuing forth; and mounds of ashes blocked up rights of way, and wholly changed the law and custom of the neighbourhood.

In short, the yet unfinished and unopened Railroad was in progress; and, from the very core of all this dire disorder, trailed smoothly away, upon its mighty course of civilization and improvement.

      c. DICKENS, *Dombey and Son* (1846–8), Ch. VI.

'Our Queen [said Egremont] reigns over the greatest nation that ever existed.'

'Which nation?' asked the younger stranger, 'for she reigns over two.'

The stranger paused; Egremont was silent, but looked inquiringly.

'Yes,' resumed the younger stranger after a moment's interval.

'Two nations; between whom there is no intercourse and no sympathy; who are as ignorant of each other's habits, thoughts and feelings, as if they were dwellers in different zones, or inhabitants of different planets; who are formed by a different breeding, are fed by a different food, are ordered by different manners, and are not governed by the same laws.'

'You speak of – ' said Egremont, hesitatingly.

'THE RICH AND THE POOR.'

B. DISRAELI, *Sybil* (1845), Ch. V.

7

Narrative of Events
1832-1850

IN the midst of the domestic crisis over Parliamentary reform, Grey's Government had to deal also with a difficult international situation. The Treaty of Vienna had united the southern provinces of the Netherlands, formerly Austrian, with the old Dutch Republic, under a King of the Dutch House of Orange. This arrangement proved very unpopular in the South, and a revolution there in 1830 made it seem necessary to divide the State again. Palmerston played a great part in maintaining the independence of the area, considered a vital British interest. The new State of the southern provinces, Belgium, was securely established by the end of 1832, although the treaty settlement was not finally concluded until 1839. In the question of the disputed successions to the thrones of Spain and Portugal, Palmerston collaborated with France. The 'Quadruple Alliance' of 1834 was in effect an agreement between Britain and France to support the more liberal claimant in each country.

After the passage of the Reform Act Parliament was dissolved, and the Reformers obtained a huge majority at the General Election. The work of reforming other institutions now began. The Irish Church Temporalities Act of 1833 abolished 'church cess', the Irish equivalent of church rates, and suppressed ten Irish bishoprics. In the same year slavery was abolished in British colonies; the first effective Factory Act was passed, regulating hours and conditions of work for children in textile mills; and the State made its first, tiny, grant in aid of primary education. In 1834 the Poor Law was drastically amended.

During 1834, however, the Cabinet and its majority broke up. Four Ministers resigned in May, in order to dissociate themselves from any idea of appropriating Church property or revenues to purposes other than those of the Established Church: Richmond, the representative of the ultra-Tories of 1830; Sir James Graham, known as a good administrator; the Earl of Ripon, *alias* Goderich, *alias* Robinson; and Stanley, often described as 'dashing', who had been the Ministry's principal and very effective spokesman on Irish matters in the Commons, and had seemed destined to become their next Leader of the House. In July Grey retired, and was replaced as Prime Minister by Melbourne. Then in November Althorp succeeded to the peerage as Earl Spencer, and the King, refusing to allow Melbourne to reconstruct the Cabinet with Russell as Leader of the House of Commons, dismissed the Administration.

Peel was summoned from Rome, where he was on holiday, to form a Government. Meanwhile, for nearly a month, the Duke of Wellington transacted the necessary business of all the important departments. Peel tried to persuade Stanley and other former colleagues of Grey to join his Ministry, but he failed. In his purely Tory Cabinet Wellington was Foreign Secretary. The most important act of this Administration was to set up a body which became in 1836 the Ecclesiastical Commissioners. A General Election much increased the number of the Government's supporters in the Commons, but did not give it a majority, and in April 1835 Peel resigned.

Melbourne formed his second Government, in which Palmerston was again Foreign Secretary and Russell led the House of Commons, at first as Home Secretary. This Ministry survived until 1841. Its largest measure was the Municipal Corporations Act of 1835, which swept away the old system of government in the boroughs. The new corporations were required to create a police force for their boroughs, and in 1839 Quarter Sessions were permitted to do the same for their counties. Otherwise, this Government's main reforms were ecclesiastical.

Palmerston's chief concern during his second period at the Foreign Office was to maintain the Sultan of Turkey against a rival, Mehemet Ali, who ruled Egypt. The French were inclined to sympathize with Mehemet Ali, but Palmerston worked with the other Powers to defeat him and 'maintain the integrity of the Ottoman Empire'. In 1841 the treaty embodying the settlement of this dispute included the first international recognition that warships other than those of Turkey should not pass through the Bosporus in peacetime. In colonial affairs the Ministry took the important step of sending the Earl of Durham in 1838 to report on the tension in and between the provinces of Upper and Lower Canada. He recommended in his Report of 1839 the union of the provinces, which was carried through in 1840, and the grant of responsible government, which was effectively conceded in 1847. In 1840 New Zealand was annexed.

William IV died in 1837, and his niece, Victoria, became Queen at the age of 18. In 1840 she married the earnest Prince Albert of Saxe-Coburg.

The years 1837 to 1842 were years of serious depression, and so of working-class unrest. In 1838 working-class societies all over the country associated themselves with the demand for 'the People's Charter', whose six points were: annual parliaments, universal male suffrage, equal electoral districts, the removal of the property qualification for M.P.s, the secret ballot, and payment of M.P.s. Its supporters were called 'Chartists'. In the next year a General Convention of the Industrious Classes was elected and met first in London and then in Birmingham, some of its promoters and delegates regarding it as a superior representative assembly to Parliament; the Chartist newspaper, the *Northern Star*, achieved a circulation of almost 50,000 a week; a petition to the House of Commons for the Charter had 1,200,000 signatures; and there was an attempt at armed rebellion at Newport, Monmouthshire, in which 14 people were killed. The movement died down until 1842, when a petition for universal male suffrage and many other reforms was presented to the Commons, with over 3,000,000 signatures. Parliament took no action on any of the six points. Thereafter, until 1846, less was heard of Chartist agitation than of the campaign of the middle-class Anti-Corn Law League, founded in 1839.

A defeat by one vote on a motion of no-confidence in June 1841 forced the Whigs to dissolve Parliament, and after the General Election they were found to be in a minority by 91. Peel now formed a strong Conservative Government, including three of the four Ministers who had left Grey on the

Church question in 1834: Wellington was again in the Cabinet, the Earl of Aberdeen became Foreign Secretary, Ripon President of the Board of Trade, Stanley Colonial Secretary and Graham Home Secretary. In 1843 began the Cabinet career of W. E. Gladstone, son of a prosperous Liverpool merchant, and a brilliant student in his Oxford days, who had so far been chiefly associated with defending the Established Church against the reformers; he succeeded Ripon, who became President of the Board of Control (for India). This Ministry lasted until 1846. Its most important measures were financial. In his Budget of 1842 Peel reimposed the income tax, thus making it possible to reduce the level and number of import and export duties. The Budget of 1845 carried the process further. The Bank Charter Act of 1844 restricted the note-issues of provincial banks to existing levels, and tied the Bank of England's own issue to its gold stock. The first general Act to regulate the railways was passed in the same year. Two important reforms protecting industrial workers became law, the Mines Act of 1842, and the Factory Act of 1844, which strengthened and extended the provisions of the Act of 1833. In foreign affairs the main achievement of the Administration was to settle the dispute with the United States over the Canadian border.

Threat of famine in Ireland persuaded Peel in 1845 that the Corn Law must be suspended. The Cabinet would not at first follow him, and he resigned in December. But Russell, who in his *Edinburgh Letter* had just come out in favour of total repeal, failed to form a Whig Government. Peel resumed office before the end of the year, only Stanley of the old Cabinet refusing to serve. The bulk of the Conservatives revolted against their leaders, under the inspiration of Benjamin Disraeli, novelist as well as M.P. The measure which is generally referred to as the Repeal of the Corn Law passed in 1846, but only 112 Conservative M.P.s voted for it. Peel's Government was then brought down by a combination of Whigs and Protectionists.

Russell now formed a Whig Government dependent on the support of Peel's followers, known as the 'Peelites'. Its reforming record was remarkable, including the Act of 1846 establishing County Courts, the Education 'Minutes' of the same year, the Ten Hours Act of 1847 (improved in 1850) further restricting the working day of women and children in textile factories, the Public Health Act of 1848 and the repeal of the Navigation Acts in 1849. While revolutions were proceeding in almost every other European country, the last great Chartist demonstration passed off peacefully in 1848.

Palmerston, again Foreign Secretary, made himself progressively more conspicuous. He protested in 1846 against the marriage of the Queen of Spain's sister to a French prince, because it might lead to French rule in Spain. In the European upheaval of 1848–9 he deployed the influence of Britain to maintain peace, while expressing sympathy with some of the revolts. In 1850 he had to defend himself against a concerted attempt by his critics to censure him for his manner of conducting foreign policy, both in general and in the particular case of 'Don Pacifico', a Portuguese Jew who happened to be a British subject, whose claims on the Government of Greece for compensation Palmerston supported indiscriminately. The House of Commons, however, upheld him.

This debate, elevating Palmerston's position in his party, in Parliament and in the country, was followed by two other developments which helped to transform the political scene. The first was the death of Peel, the second Russell's *Durham Letter*, aligning himself with the feeling of Protestants against the Pope's re-establishment of a Roman Catholic hierarchy in Britain.

8

Economic and Social Change 1832-1850

Economic Development

THE four-part chronological division of this book, though appropriate for political history, is inconvenient for economic and social history. Thus within the period 1832–50 falls the crisis of 1837–42, which may reasonably be regarded as the watershed of British economic and social history between the 1780s and the 1880s. After 1832 a spell of full employment and low prices culminated in the boom of 1836. The crash came in 1837, and then a run of bad harvests led to high agricultural prices which, interacting with trading and industrial depression and consequent unemployment, reduced the mass of the people to a degree of poverty never subsequently paralleled in Britain. After 1842, while conditions in Ireland were far worse during the famine of 1845–9 than ever recorded before or known since in any part of the United Kingdom, in Britain the construction of railways and reviving trade enabled the economy to recover and embark on its most rapid phase of growth, despite a recurrence of depression in 1847–8.

To treat the years 1832–50 as a period, however, forgetting for the moment the fluctuations, does reveal the persistence of the main trends of the Industrial Revolution. The population of Britain rose from 16,000,000 to 21,000,000 between the censuses of 1831 and 1851. It was the industrial areas whose numbers grew most quickly, particularly Lancashire, Durham, Lanarkshire, Glamorgan and Monmouth. An increased influx of Irish labourers, especially into Lancashire, was important in the 1840s. At the census of 1851, 734,000 Irishmen were in Britain, about half of whom had arrived during the previous decade.[1] Sheffield, centre of the cutlery industry, joined the list of cities with over 100,000 inhabitants. Glasgow continued to draw away from Edinburgh, the Lowlands from the Highlands, the North of England from the South – except that, as always, London grew rapidly. By 1851 a third of the whole population lived in towns with more than 20,000 inhabitants.

Cotton, iron and coal remained the major fast-growing industries. The volume of raw cotton imported roughly tripled, as did the volume of iron production; coal production more than doubled. The case of iron was the most remarkable: its higher rate of growth was primarily due to the demands of the railways, mainly at home but to some extent abroad, especially in the United States. Exports increased seven times between 1830 and 1850. Scottish mines provided much of the increased production.

Mechanization, factories and the use of steam-power continued to spread, but chiefly still in the textile industry. Wool was in all these respects catching up with cotton. These were the years when handloom weaving virtually disappeared. More than half the production of cotton manufactures was exported, and cotton and wool together provided half of all British exports. But, though so important to the British economy and so advanced technologically, they were not dominant in social life. As can be shown for these years from the more thorough censuses of 1841 and 1851, in terms of the number of persons employed other occupations were more or equally notable. The textile industries had a labour force of 1 million, half of them female. Agriculture employed 2 millions, mostly male. Coal occupied 250,000, nearly all male. There were 1 million domestic servants, 500,000 persons involved in building, the same number of shopkeepers, 250,000 shoemakers and the same number making and selling beer. In assessing the importance of the new industry in the life of Britain it must be remembered also that cotton and wool factories and coal and iron mines were localized, whereas breweries, farms and shops were to be found all over the country. The typical Englishman was coming to be a townsman, but he was not an industrial worker, still less a factory hand.

---

[1] G. Kitson Clark, *The Making of Victorian England* (London, 1962), p. 77 and n.

This period, however, boasts a great economic achievement and novelty, almost a second economic revolution, in the creation of the most important part of the railway system of Britain. Railways as now understood are reckoned to date from the Liverpool and Manchester line, built by George Stephenson and completed in 1830. There existed previously considerable lengths of rails in Britain, mostly attached to some industrial concern, probably a coal-mine. But the Liverpool and Manchester was the first line which carried passengers and freight under statutory authority, solely by mechanical traction. By 1850 more than 6,000 miles of such railways had been opened in Britain. This was an astonishing feat, which it is interesting to measure against the progress of motorway building in the twentieth century, especially since over half of these lines were built in the late 'forties. It was possible by the end of this period to travel by rail from London as far as Aberdeen or Holyhead or Plymouth. Although many more miles remained to be built, the essentials of the trunk system were in operation.

In general, of course, railways were the most important application of steam power, making it possible to carry more easily and cheaply, and many times more rapidly, unprecedented numbers of people and, in the long run, also of goods. But it was the building of railways rather than their working which stimulated the economy in these years. Their construction raised problems similar to those of canal-building, but on a far greater scale. They required Acts of Parliament to authorize them. Large amounts of land had to be bought. By the standards of the day, the capital needed was enormous. The figure for paid-up railway capital and loans in 1850 was £235,000,000, equivalent to almost half the annual national income and greater than Britain's total foreign investment. In the 'thirties railways had been financed mainly by local capital, but in the 'forties the Stock Exchange mobilized investment nationally, its first large involvement in the internal economic development of the country. A huge labour force was also necessary for railway-building. In the late 'forties an average of about 200,000 men was so employed. Between two and three million tons of iron must have gone into them, more than the total annual production of 1850 and four times that of 1830. The great entrepreneurs like the engineers George

Stephenson and his son Robert, I. K. Brunel and Joseph Locke, the contractor Thomas Brassey and the company promoter George Hudson worked on a scale hitherto unknown, and abroad as well as in Britain: Brassey had railway contracts in 15 foreign countries. Fortunes were made – and, in Hudson's case, lost by over-confidence and fraud. Dickens' description, quoted at the head of this Part, conveys the force of the impact of railway-building on the landscape and on people's minds. Here was an aspect of the Industrial Revolution which directly affected the whole country.

In the 1830s, it would seem, the British Industrial Revolution was slowing down. Industrial production was still rising rapidly, but the prices of industrial products were falling to the extent that profits were low and national income *per capita* was no longer growing so fast. Overseas and domestic markets were incapable of taking the full potential output of British industry. Britain's is the only Industrial Revolution to have taken place in a country without railways. Their coming – providing employment, increasing demand for coal and iron, and offering investment opportunities which raised the level of capital formation to the 10 per cent of national income postulated by many economists, studying other national industrial revolutions, as necessary for industrial 'take-off' – gave a boost to the economy, which the operation of the new railway system repeated in the next period. Whereas in every other country railway-building was assisted by State grants of money or land, in Britain private investors supplied the entire capital required.

Railways were a British invention, no doubt because Britain had unique experience in the mining and use of coal. It was a sign of future trends that in 1850, while no other European country had yet built nearly as many miles of track, there were already more in the United States.

For British agriculture this was a decisive period, the time when it manifestly ceased to be able to supply the needs of the country for food and when it was first exposed to serious competition from abroad. Down to 1837 imports of grain were negligible in good years. In the next few years, with bad harvests, larger quantities were brought in than ever before, and by the late 'forties, after the Repeal of the Corn Law, heavy imports were made even in good years. But, although the situation of agricultural labourers remained lamentable, the industry, far from succumbing, began to advance with unusual rapidity. The reasons for this, and the significance of these developments, will be discussed later.

Social Conditions

Not only in economic, but also in social, history the years 1837–42 are a watershed. Conditions for the mass of the British people were worse than ever since, and in certain respects than ever before. This helps to account for the fact that the whole period between the passage of the First Reform Act and the death of Peel is unique for the strength and profusion of its popular movements of protest. It is also the time when 'the social question' or 'the Condition of England question' came to the fore, and when the first great pioneering attempts were made to improve matters, both by legislation and voluntary effort. The later 'forties saw considerable advance.

Down to 1842, as between 1780 and 1830, the average wage-earner's position cannot have improved much and may have worsened. The contrast with what followed is considerable, but there is no great contrast with what went before. However, the following factors rendered the period before 1842, and especially the crisis of 1837–42, particularly unhappy, or made it seem or feel even worse than it was. First, the crisis was unusually prolonged; it was the most severe depression since the Industrial Revolution had begun; and food prices were relatively higher than at any time since 1819. Secondly, the industrial and urban labour force, exposed to the full effects of fluctuations in prices and employment, was larger than ever before. Thirdly, during these years it at length became impossible for a handloom weaver, however many hours he worked, supposing he could get work, to earn a living wage. The fate of these weavers has now been fully studied.[1] Many of them evidently found other employment. Some of them were certainly unreasonably conservative in their determination to continue in the trade they had learned and to train their children in it. But for much of the period there was just not enough alternative employment. The rate at which

---

[1] D. Bythell, *The Hand-loom Weavers* (Cambridge, 1969).

in the cotton industry power looms were being installed, an average of 10,000 a year, was much the same as the rate at which handlooms went out of operation; but it was mostly women and children who were employed to mind the former, while many men had worked the latter, and one person could mind more than one power-loom. The handloom weavers were the group most involved in radical and revolutionary agitation in this period, and the group which then and subsequently has furnished the best example for those who were and are inclined to stress the sufferings occasioned by the Industrial Revolution. Another trade, framework-knitting in the hosiery industry, with about 50,000 frames mostly in the Midlands, was in somewhat the same state. Although power-knitting did not arrive until the late 'forties, there was a surplus of knitters, and wages were terribly low. Fourthly, the Poor Law Amendment Act of 1834, the 'New Poor Law', made the situation of the poor worse, as will be seen later. Fifthly, it is likely that this was the period when social provision in the new towns was at its lowest point.

In terms of the number of people to each room, the average housing of the industrial towns was probably less crowded than older housing. But houses were more concentrated, and in some parts of towns overcrowding was growing. Statistics of mortality show that urban conditions were in general worse than rural, and deteriorating. Expectation of life at birth for 'gentlefolk' was 55 years in Bath, 35 in Liverpool; for labourers 38 in Rutland, 15 in Liverpool. Death-rates in towns were rising, especially as typhus and tuberculosis were becoming commoner. The death-rate for England and Wales as a whole in the 1840s averaged between 22 and 23 per thousand, which was rather higher than earlier in the century. The provision of amenities, from churches and parks to sewers and water-closets, was not keeping pace with the growth of the towns. Further, this problem became more than proportionately greater in towns over a certain size; and, the larger the town, the worse it was for those who lived in the centre, far from open spaces and without cheap public transport to take them there.

Given this situation, it is difficult to have patience with the writers who insist on discussing living standards largely on the basis of a comparison between average wage-rates in 1800 and those in 1850, and so gloss over social factors, the difference made by the railway boom, variations by locality and trade, and the enormous fluctuations of the period. Again, those who question the concept of 'the Hungry Forties', which was indeed invented in the early twentieth century during the debate on Tariff reform, are pedantic when they insist that it is wrong to describe as 'hungry' a decade in part of which a great improvement was registered. For several years around 1840 conditions were exceptionally bad, as they were again in 1847–8; and the term is justified a thousand times over if Irish experience is taken into account.

On the other hand, it remains fair to stress, as with reference to the earlier years of the Industrial Revolution, that all the hardship was not directly caused by industrialization, and furthermore that agricultural conditions were in their own way as horrifying as industrial. The state of the poor was not worse in nineteenth-century Britain than in many other parts of the world. What seemed so appalling was that such enormous economic advance should improve conditions so little, if at all; more especially that earlier gains should be retrenched; and that it was possible for principals in that advance, the industrial workers, living in its creations, the great new towns, to suffer such squalor and misery.

It is a relief to turn to the more hopeful side of the story. During these years, especially in the 'forties, people became much more aware of the situation in industrial areas and more concerned to improve it. Cholera, a disease endemic in Asia and likely to become epidemic elsewhere if living conditions are filthy, came to England in 1832. It killed over 16,000, but it caused the establishment of a temporary Central Board of Health and some local boards. The Secretary of the Manchester Board, Dr Kay, produced a report which for the first time described the actual condition of a great urban population. There followed reports of Royal Commissions appointed by Parliament on conditions in textile factories (1833), handloom weaving (1838–41) and mines (1842), and Edwin Chadwick's Report on the Sanitary Condition of the Labouring Poor (1842). Among the forces behind these documents was the mass movement of protest in the Yorkshire woollen districts against the evils of the factory system, which from 1830 demanded a ten hours' day for all the workers involved: a notable development from merely negative riots against the introduction of machinery. Certain public figures took up these questions, most prominently Lord Ashley (after 1851 Earl of Shaftesbury), theologically a rigid Evangelical, who was active in promoting enquiries into social conditions, in introducing legislation to mitigate the situation they revealed and in running an almost inconceivably wide range of private charitable organizations.

Another approach to the problem might be regarded as a variation of the 'ancient constitution' theory, but it was religious and aesthetic rather than political in tone, strongly coloured by the twin revivals of medievalism and Catholicism. Before the Reformation, it was held, the ordinary people of Britain lived contented in a Christian community whose ideals were spiritual not materialist and which cared for the souls of individuals rather than treated them as cogs in a money-making machine. The medieval situation should be restored. In 1836 Augustus Welby Pugin published *Contrasts*. The author is best known in the history of architecture, as the designer of all the detail of the new Houses of Parliament, the passionate advocate of the virtues and beauties of Gothic art and the propounder of the view that moral standards can and should control aesthetic. *Contrasts* had an enormous impact on taste, but it also contained the germ of Christian Socialism. It depicted 'Noble Edifices of the Middle Ages and the corresponding Buildings of the Present Day'. The medieval city is dominated by spires, the modern by chimneys. Now factories and warehouses, a gas-works, Nonconformist chapels, a Socialist Hall of Science, a new jail, a lunatic asylum (but not yet a railway station) have replaced Catholic churches and abbeys. Water ran free and pure from the Gothic fountain; now it is dirty and costs money. The cruel modern workhouse is contrasted with the benevolent medieval hospital for the poor.[1] (Plate 3.)

Under these various influences many writers turned to revealing the black side of the new society and campaigning for its improvement. Disraeli's *Sybil* (1845) is especially interesting as the work of an active politician and a future Prime Minister, dealing sympathetically with Chartists, exposing evils of the factory system, stressing the gulf between rich and

---

[1] The plates mentioned appear first in the second edition of 1841.

poor, and drawing the contrast between the Middle Ages and the nineteenth century. Thomas Carlyle's tracts, particularly *Chartism* (1839) and *Past and Present* (1843), were similarly inspired, though they show an unusual readiness for State action to remedy matters, accompanied by an equally unusual distaste for representative government. Mrs Gaskell's *Mary Barton* (1848) described from personal knowledge the state of Manchester.

In the next section the principal attempts, especially Parliament's, to deal with social problems will be discussed at some length. Here it is convenient to mention some of the lesser, mostly private, efforts. One of the most important of these was the London City Mission, founded in 1835, with which Ashley soon became connected. The Labourers' Friend Society of 1842, later renamed the Society for Improving the Condition of the Labouring Classes, dealt with housing. Another was the movement to support what were called without euphemism Ragged Schools. From this decade dates the first society for the preservation of footpaths, in Sidmouth. Some industrial towns, like Preston, Derby, Birkenhead and Manchester, acquired public parks, largely by the gift of enlightened and wealthy individuals. It became lawful for municipalities to levy rates to erect baths and wash-houses (1845), museums (1845) and public libraries (1850). John Owens, who died in 1846, left a fortune to found a University in Manchester. Whether moved by religion or not, philanthropists were showing a deeper appreciation of the needs of urban societies.

Social life was much changed also by the coming of the railways. They made it possible to travel at speeds several times greater than previously. The improvement was of a different order from the modest acceleration of stage coaches in the previous century. In 1841 a rapid coach from London to Exeter took 18 hours. In 1845 the rail express took 6½. The coach fare with tips was nearly £4. The first-class railway fare was £2 10s. Far more passengers could be carried by trains than by coaches: in 1835 the Leeds and Selby Railway carried 3,500 a week, as against 400 by the displaced coaches.[1] In these decades, contrary to expectation, it was the passenger traffic which made money, not the goods traffic. The coaches

---

[1] M. Robbins, *The Railway Age* (London, 1965), pp. 15, 54 and *passim*.

were being driven off the roads, and the roads and the coaching-inns were soon neglected. Railways made it easier for the better-off to live some distance from their place of work, a practice which of course accentuated class-distinctions. But they also made possible excursions for the less well-off. To anticipate, in 1851 nearly 6,000,000 visits were made to the Great Exhibition by inhabitants of the United Kingdom, most of whom must have travelled to London by train and many of whom would not have been able to travel there at all but for the railways. In 1840, partly as a result of railway-building, the penny post was established. The number of letters carried by the Post Office more than quadrupled between 1839 and 1849. As well as much-improved communication, the railways brought standardization. For example, it proved impossible to maintain local times, which had hitherto varied by a quarter-of-an-hour or more from one part of the country to another. The next period saw the social impact of the railways further extended.

9

Politics and Reform
1832-1850

THE largest batch of pioneering reforms of the nineteenth century was passed during this period. It could reasonably be maintained that even in the twentieth century the legislature has never overhauled institutions so thoroughly or taken such important initiatives as in these years. Each of these reforms has now been the subject of much study, directed particularly at discovering why it was passed. Special interest attaches to the question how influential were popular movements or public opinion on the one hand, and the work of Jeremy Bentham on the other. In this section the main reforms will be reviewed and an attempt made to establish their significance as well as their origins. Chartism, the great unsuccessful campaign, will also be considered.

The Structure of Politics
An essential part of the explanation for all of them, in their strengths as well as their limitations, is to be sought in the structure of politics after the passage of the First Reform Act.[1] As was shown earlier, Grey's Government had intended the Act to remove the 'illegitimate', but not the 'legitimate', influence of the aristocracy; to enfranchise 'property' and 'intelligence', or 'the middle classes', but certainly not to create a democracy or even to give the new voters more than a share of power with the aristocracy; and to restore or modify, but by no means to destroy, the 'balance of the constitution'. Even within the framework of these aims the Act had a less radical effect than many had expected. Though the most rotten boroughs were destroyed, aristocratic influence in the

---

[1] See for much of this section Gash, *Politics in the Age of Peel* (Oxford, 1963).

Commons remained strong, to the point that there were still about 60 English and Welsh M.P.s who were nominated by individuals, mostly peers. In the House of Commons elected in 1832 sat 217 baronets or sons of peers, and the figure fell only to 180 by 1865. The Whig Cabinet formed by Melbourne in 1834 was the first to contain more members of the Lower than of the Upper House, but its 'commoners' included Palmerston the Irish peer, a baronet and several close relatives of peers. Not until 1858 did a Tory Cabinet have more members of the House of Commons than of the Lords. If the grosser forms of corruption at elections declined, and the enormous expenses exceptionally incurred before 1832 are not paralleled afterwards, abuses like the bribery and 'treating' of voters, the creation of voting qualifications and the impersonation of electors remained common. A contest in a specially expensive borough like Yarmouth might cost each side £10,000, and £2,000 to £5,000 for each side was not abnormal in a borough. County contests could cost even more. Between 1832 and 1850 a total of 69 results of elections in individual constituencies were set aside because of proved corruption.

In terms of the balance of the constitution the Act did not at first seem to have reduced royal power. As Professor Gash puts it:

> By contrast [to George IV] William IV was a cauldron of energy. In his short reign of seven years, he twice dismissed a Ministry; twice dissolved Parliament for political purposes before its time; three times made formal proposals to his Ministers for a coalition with their political opponents; and on one celebrated occasion allowed his name to be used, independently of his political advisers, to influence a crucial vote in the House of Lords.[1]

In 1839 Victoria, by making difficulties about appointing Ladies of the Bedchamber acceptable to Peel, prolonged the life of the Whig Government. The Upper House, though chastened immediately after the passage of the Act, soon became obstreperous again, rejecting some Whig measures and drastically amending others; and by its mere existence it discouraged and moderated proposals of reform.

However, it is not right to lay the chief stress on the continuity between unreformed and half-reformed politics. The

---

[1] N. Gash, *Reaction and Reconstruction in English Politics 1832–1852* (Oxford, 1965), p. 5.

contrast was in fact very great, partly as a result of the actual provisions of the Act, more because the Act was the outward sign of important shifts and changes of attitude. One specific and quantifiable effect of the Act was particularly significant: the increase in the number of constituencies contested at General Elections. At least twice as many more than ever before, and over two-thirds of the total, 277 out of 401, were fought in the first Election after the passage of the Act. Though the figure declined pretty steadily thereafter down to and including the Election of 1859, it never again fell as low as before Reform. This change reflects both the political enthusiasm of the 'thirties and the fact that more constituencies were now uncertain in their allegiance, because more electors were free either to choose between 'influences' or to follow their opinions. The Reform Act for Scotland contributed much in this connexion, giving that country, hitherto one vast rotten borough, 'a political constitution for the first time'. In Ireland also, by the combination of Catholic emancipation and Parliamentary reform, however grudging, the independence of the electorate was notably increased. The effect of these changes was considerable. Under the unreformed system Commons majorities would scarcely have been returned, as in the General Elections of 1835 and 1841, against a Ministry supported by the monarch. In the second case the conversion of a majority of 1 into a majority of 91 was achieved by an impressive swing of public opinion.

Another important development to which the Act directly contributed was the growth of party organization. The requirement that voters be registered brought into existence 'registration societies', in each constituency one Whig and one Tory. There had previously existed in many places at election times unofficial committees of notabilities backed by a paid agent, but it was a novelty, outside advanced constituencies like Westminster, for any permanent organization to be set up to concern itself in any way with the mass of electors. However, these new societies had no voice at all in the choice of candidates or in prescribing policy. Their existence contributed in turn to the formation of new political clubs in London, the Carlton for the Tories in 1832 and the Reform for the Whigs in 1836, supplementing for political purposes White's and Brooks', too exclusive and social for the years after Reform. The increase in the number of constituencies where traditional local influences did not dominate gave greater opportunities for intervention by the party leaders in elections. It became usual in the more open constituencies for the Carlton and the Reform Clubs to have some say in the choice of candidates and to form the channel by which contributions to the expenses of electioneering were made from party funds, money entrusted by wealthy supporters to the discretion of the leaders and their agents.

Parties, however, developed more in this period than can be explained by the operation of the Reform Act. The importance of party divisions in Parliament was growing. It has already been pointed out that during the debates on Reform the 'non-political' M.P. virtually disappeared. From 1835 to 1845 political groupings in Parliament were further simplified: apart from a handful of Radicals, all M.P.s were attached either to the Whig or the Tory Front Bench. After 1845 there was a greater number of Parliamentary parties, Peelites and Protectionists as well as Whigs, rather than a reversion to the situation where many Members were truly 'independent'. These parties displayed a degree of solidarity remarkable in view of the fact that many M.P.s still owed their seats to their local position regardless of their party affiliation. This development can only be understood by taking into account other factors of more general importance: the growth of the organs of public opinion, associated with the improvement of communications, and a fundamental change of attitude to politics.

In sheer circulation figures the Press prospered greatly between about 1832 and about 1850. *The Times*, easily the largest daily, sold nearly 40,000 copies a day in 1850. The total number of stamped newspapers sold in the British Isles in 1829 was 33,000,000; in 1850, in England alone, the figure was just double. Some semi-political weeklies of an original character founded in the 1840s did particularly well: by 1850 *Punch* (1841) was selling 30,000, the *Illustrated London News* (1842) 100,000, the *News of the World* (1843) 56,000 a week. Of the hundreds of stamped provincial newspapers, none of which were dailies until the late 1840s, a few like the *Leeds Mercury*, the *Stamford Mercury* and the *Manchester Guardian* sold as many as 10,000 copies a week. The *Northern Star*'s unstamped 50,000 was astonishing, and did not last. The impact of the Press is notoriously difficult to gauge. It is clear that each copy of a newspaper was usually read by many people, partly because the cost was so high, even after the stamp duty had been reduced from 4d. to 1d. in 1836. No contemporary seems to have doubted that *The Times*, with exceptional circulation, exceptional coverage and exceptionally good sources of information, was uniquely influential. Its great period runs from the 1820s to the 1850s. Other newspapers copied much that it wrote. Great men competed for the Editor's ear, and provided him with confidential information. Its 'leaders' were treated with enormous respect. It was common for politicians to remark that *The Times* (or, as Macaulay first used the phrase in 1828, the Press Gallery) amounted to a fourth estate of the realm. But no satisfactory conclusion was ever reached on the question whether the Press formed public opinion or reflected it. Obviously, it did both. But most conspicuously it informed people. The knowledge of public affairs which a reader of *The Times* could have in this period was greater, though less up-to-date, than any reader could now acquire from English newspapers. Parliamentary debates were printed in full, whole 'Blue Books' (Parliamentary Papers) were published, detailed despatches from abroad appeared unaltered. As compared with previous periods, the reader of *The Times* was in most respects better-informed than the Prime Minister himself could have been a few years earlier.

Parliamentary leaders were ambivalent in their attitude to the Press and to other forms of public expression of opinion. The early years of Grey's Ministry were a period when on the one hand Whig politicians publicly associated themselves with the Birmingham Political Union, though only with great trepidation, and on the other hand prosecuted with vigour those who published unstamped newspapers. Just as the extension of the franchise to the middle classes had been coupled with its withdrawal from the working classes, so the reduction of the stamp duty in 1836 was partly intended to separate an enlarged respectable legal Press from a better-controlled gutter Press. In 1839 the Commons abandoned discussion on petitions, which before 1831 had had priority over other business and had enabled popular opinion to be expressed in the House. Yet the rise of the Press could not be resisted without unacceptable measures of repression. The only recourse was to compete in publicity. The House of Commons published its own division lists from 1836, in order that they should be accurate. Publication of Parliamentary Papers grew rapidly. There was a more modest increase in the numbers of speeches made outside Parliament by politicians, especially Brougham and Peel.

As it happened, although the Septennial Act was not repealed, two royal deaths and the Reform Bill crisis made five General Elections necessary between 1830 and 1837, inclusive. Although the precedent set by the 1831 Election, a national appeal on a single issue, was not followed up, Peel's 'Tamworth Manifesto' of 1834, putting a programme before the whole electorate, marked a recognition by Conservatives that electioneering was now less localized, and more concerned with issues and prospects of legislation, than before. And politicians felt and responded to the pressure of opinion more than was strictly necessary for the sake of electioneering. Joseph Parkes, who as the Whigs' party organizer knew as much as anyone about the mechanics of registration, 'influence' and corruption, nonetheless urged supporters of the Municipal Corporations Bill to agitate. Nothing, he said, was more effective in persuading the Cabinet to live up to its declared intentions and the Lords to give way. While almost the same sort of people were returned to Parliament in 1832 as previously, they tended now to think of their role as M.P.s in a new way, partly because constituents could in more cases call them to account for their sins of omission and commission, and partly because of a change in the general public attitude to politics. It now seemed natural and necessary for the Government to put forward large measures of reform. General legislating came to be regarded as the principal function of Parliament. Its sovereignty was now applied to great ends. A symptom of this development was the supersession of Select Committees of the House by more specialist and powerful Royal Commissions, on whose often sweeping recommendations many of the principal measures of the period were based. Signs of such a shift of approach had been evident before the Reform Act, and had contributed to its passing; the fact of its passage in its turn encouraged demands for other reforms.

This greater concern with issues and legislation would

seem, incidentally, to have intensified party feeling. But the current of reform carried all parties with it. Whigs adopted the name 'Liberals', as their party became a progressive coalition between the old aristocratic Whigs who continued to dominate Cabinets, men of similar views but lower social position, and genuine Radicals. And Tories became 'Conservatives', promoters, in the words of the Tamworth Manifesto, of 'a careful review of institutions, civil and ecclesiastical, undertaken in a friendly temper, combining, with the firm maintenance of established rights, the correction of proved abuses and the redress of real grievances'. Peel and Wellington called off the House of Lords when it seemed to be compromising their position as moderate reformers.

Obstreperous though they could still be, most peers recognized that the manner of the passage of the Reform Act made it a victory for the Commons over the Lords. The use of the threat to create peers was never forgotten, nor the King's dramatic drive to Westminster, the ceremonial guns booming, dissolve Parliament in 1831 before the Lords could pass a motion of protest. It was pointed out, of course, that the country could not have a revolution every year. But that consideration was as likely to make the Lords give way as the Commons. Before 1831 a defeat in the Upper House had been more certain to bring a Ministry down than a defeat in the Lower. After 1831 defeats in the Lords never caused a Government to resign. The balance of the constitution had decisively shifted, and the Upper House did not attempt to restore it until after 1886.

As regards the monarchy, the initiatives of William IV and Victoria were incautious in that they served to demonstrate its weakness. The Governments installed by William IV in 1832 and 1834, and that prolonged by Victoria in 1839, failed to survive against the wishes of the Commons and the electorate. The strength of parties was such that their leaders could reject suggestions for coalition and maintain themselves in office even with only a small majority. The Conservative Peel proved less sympathetic to royal interventions than the Whigs. After the Election of 1841 the Queen, under the tutelage of Prince Albert, decided for the future to act impartially between the parties. In 1845 she abandoned the exercise of the monarch's personal electoral patronage. Perhaps, if these decisions had not been taken, the confusion of parties in the 1850s would have permitted effective royal initiatives. But, as with the Lords, it was not until after the end of the period covered by this book that the Queen again became an active partisan, and then in circumstances in which she could achieve little.

Each of the reforms of 1832–50 was the result of a particular balance of forces. Among the strongest of the forces there remained the House of Lords, the Church, the Tory party and the landed interest, almost as closely-related as before. But all these elements were subtly changed during the struggle over the Reform Bill and after its passage. They became more aware of other forces of society and more willing to compromise with them. In extending the electorate and redistributing the constituencies, the Act expanded the 'Establishment'. But more notable than this physical broadening was the mental broadening brought about by the crisis. The essential change that took place between 1827 and 1832 was the weakening of inertia. Reform acquired momentum.

The Churches and Education

Between the First Reform Act and the Repeal of the Corn Law ecclesiastical matters were the most hotly-contested of all. In particular, the well-disciplined, nearly inclusive Parliamentary parties of 1835–45 aligned themselves on the question of the appropriation to secular purposes of the surplus revenues of the Established Church. The Ministers who resigned from Grey's Government in 1834 because they opposed such appropriation carried with them many of his former supporters, who after a period of uncertainty joined the Conservatives, while the narrow majority of Melbourne's second Ministry depended on an alliance in favour of appropriation between Whigs, Liberals, Radicals and the Irish Roman Catholic M.P.s led by O'Connell, an alliance which lasted in a weakened form until 1850. The Conservatives remained the party concerned to preserve so far as possible the privileges of the Established Church of England and Ireland; while the Liberals, though most of those in Parliament were members of the Church and supporters of its Establishment at least in England, sympathized with the demands of Dissenters for religious, political and social equality with Anglicans.

For many of its advocates Parliamentary reform had been

desirable not so much for itself, but as the necessary first step to some other change; and prominent among these ulterior motives was the wish for drastic reform of the Church. Around 1830 the abuses of the Church were being laid bare, not without exaggeration, by radical, often secularist, critics, such as the author of the *Extraordinary Black Book* of 1831. The Bishops, notorious as enemies of change in many spheres, feared, with most of their clergy, for the fate of the Church at the hands of a reformed Parliament, and made matters worse by voting against the Bill of 1832. The riots of that year were as much anti-episcopal as anti-aristocratic. Within the Church, in this atmosphere of crisis, respected laymen put forward proposals for the redistribution of its wealth and other reforms. Dr Thomas Arnold, for instance, Headmaster of Rugby School since 1828, ruined his prospects of an ecclesiastical career by advocating that a reformed Church Establishment should broaden its scope to embrace Nonconformity. The Bishop and Chapter of Durham, to anticipate the expected spoliation, used some of their wealth to found in 1832 a small, poor, Anglican University in their Cathedral close.

Long before this time the claim of the Church of England to be the Church of all Englishmen had ceased to be even nearly realistic. But those who moved in landed and aristocratic circles and were educated at the great historic institutions might be pardoned if they had failed to appreciate the fact. The changes of 1828–36 rubbed it in. It was made legally possible, and some thought it politically likely, that the Government should be dominated by non-Anglicans. In 1832 the final court of appeal in ecclesiastical causes, including matters of doctrine, the Archbishop of Canterbury's High Court of Delegates, was replaced by a secular body, the Judicial Committee of the Privy Council. The Irish Church Temporalities Act of 1833 might be read as a first essay in lay reorganization of the Church, perhaps in confiscation. The Municipal Corporations Act drew out the implications of the Repeal of the Test and Corporation Acts, turning many towns over to the rule of Dissenters. In 1836 the establishment of civil marriage and the chartering of London University breached two more Anglican monopolies.

However, the lay 'Establishment' rallied to the clerical. Peel's Ecclesiastical Commission was composed of friends to the Church, though reformers. By the Established Church Act of 1836 Parliament entrusted to an enlarged version of the same body the preparation of detailed schemes of reform. The revenues of the Church were not confiscated, but redistributed internally. Cathedral establishments were much cut down, Bishops' incomes equalized, diocesan boundaries redrawn, new parishes created for ill-provided areas, stipends of ill-paid clergy increased, tithe commuted into a money payment. By the Pluralities Act of 1838 strict residence requirements were imposed on beneficed clergy, and they were forbidden, among other things, to engage in most forms of trade and to farm much land. The Bishops, safe after all in the House of Lords, presided over the process. Progress was slow, as it was necessary to wait for existing beneficiaries to die off. Reform did not reach Trollope's Barchester until the 1850s. But it was now certain to come in the end. By co-operating in its own reform, the Church warded off further attacks on its privileges. The House of Lords rejected the Whigs' Bills to abolish church rates in England, and ensured that Oxford and Cambridge remained Anglican preserves. It was Peel who had made the opportunity for the Establishment to save itself. The opportunity was used by

> one who accomplished much in time of drought and desolation:
> Blomfield Bishop of London
> Builder of many Churches
> One who was usually right
> And never intimidated, never disheartened,[1]

the most influential of the Ecclesiastical Commissioners.

On the other hand, the Church received no more grants of public money, and it became impossible for the State to accord it new favours. While in 1839–40 it was strong enough to impose important modifications of the Whigs' education proposals, in 1843–4 the Conservatives' attempt to establish a national educational system staffed by Anglican schoolmasters had to be abandoned because of furious Nonconformist opposition. The Church retained most of the privileges it had been granted in the past, but for the future it had to be regarded as one denomination among many, all to be treated

---

[1] T. S. Eliot, 'The Rock', quoted in O. J. Brose, *Church and Parliament* (London, 1959), p. 67.

alike. The historic trappings of Establishment remained attached to an effectively secularized State.

Outside the sphere of legislation the crisis of Reform provoked various reactions in the Churches. Within the Establishment, it strengthened the case of the Evangelicals and their friends, and the standard and standards of the clergy rose generally. Theological colleges date from this period, neatly illustrating several points: that there was genuine concern within the Church for improvement; that people would subscribe money generously in the cause of reform; that the old Universities, even with the assistance of Durham and the Anglican King's College of London University, founded in 1831, could not be counted on to produce sufficient or satisfactory clergy unaided; and that even the most respected and ancient of all corporations, thought by some to be properly the First Estate of the realm, saw advantages in assimilating itself to the middle-class professions. It should not be supposed that the Church lost its aristocratic associations during this period, or that clergymen ceased to be prominent in local government. In the 1860s over a thousand clergy were county magistrates, a quarter of the total. But the nearly 20,000 clergy of the time were now much more fully occupied than their predecessors in what seem to the twentieth century tasks appropriate to their calling. Nearly all incumbents helped to run and pay for local schools. Anglican clergy became known for their concern about factory and slum conditions. 'We believe the Anglican clergy to be the most pernicious men of all within the compass of the Church;' wrote a Dissenter in 1851, 'but also the most sincere, the most learned, the most self-denying.'[1] As the State became more secular, the Church became more religious.

The most famous reaction was the Oxford Movement. It is dated from the sermon on 'National Apostasy' preached by John Keble in the University Church at Oxford on Bastille Day, 1833. What roused him was the Irish Church Temporalities Act in particular; in general, not the irreligion of the masses, but the treason of their rulers. In the Oxford of the late 1830s the Vicar of the University Church, J. H. Newman, became a magnet for able undergraduates; and he and E. B.

---

[1] James Martineau, quoted in Chadwick, *The Victorian Church*, vol. I, pp. 230-1.

Pusey, Regius Professor of Hebrew, came to be regarded by them and by many of the clergy as the leaders of a great religious movement. In a series of *Tracts for the Times* they and others combated the idea that the Church is a mere utility with the assertion that it is a divinely-inspired repository of doctrine and wisdom, authenticated by the Apostolic Succession from Christ by way of St Peter through the episcopate down the ages. The clergy are set over the laity in matters of faith. Material 'progress' is worthless. Narrow rationalism is wholly insufficient. It is necessary both to salvation and in order to know the truth that one should accept the doctrines of the Church, however improbable they may seem. And the confession of faith of the Church of England, the 39 Articles of 1571, is reconcilable with much Roman Catholic doctrine.

Associated with the movement were other important tendencies. One was the Gothic Revival. Another was a glorification of the potentialities of Establishment, which was expressed in its most extreme and unrealistic form by Gladstone, then 'the rising hope of those stern unbending Tories', in *The State in its Relations with the Church* (1838). The State and the Church ought to be co-extensive, the Church hallowing the State, the State supporting the Church. Yet another – and this no doubt is a large part of the explanation for the appeal of Newman to the Oxford undergraduates of the day – was the movement, in which he was also prominent, for the reform of the University and its education. He had won his Fellowship by merit and examination at one of the few Colleges, Oriel, where this was yet possible. He resigned his Tutorship because he took more seriously than the Head of his College the phrase 'in loco parentis'. It was not that he wanted to reform the system as liberals proposed, by including modern subjects and laicizing the teachers. Precisely the opposite. He had a vision of the glories of the old methods, if duly renovated. The learning of facts, or explicit preparation for a specific career, especially part-time and on one's own, were not education. A body of gentlemen teaching each other by example and conversation under the personal guidance of clergy and the spiritual sway of theology, Queen of the Sciences: this was the ideal of education presented in his *Idea of a University*, to which Oxford, even half-reformed, corresponded better than any other place of learning.

Few people swallowed Newman's views whole. His conversion to Rome in 1845, followed by others' among the more devoted of his followers, reduced the influence of the movement. But many people with widely-varying careers acknowledged that it had made a great impact on them as undergraduates. Though most laymen and many clergy were hostile, others who did not abandon the Church of England accepted some of the movement's insights. Its most obvious result was, by reviving interest in theological questions, to provoke doctrinal quarrels within the Establishment. However, although 'High Churchmen', those who avowed the influence of the movement, became contrasted with 'Evangelicals' who rejected it (a debasement of the latter term), the assertion of Catholic values in fact worked together with the older campaign for moral reformation in imposing stricter codes of behaviour on both clergy and laity. In general history perhaps the chief importance of the movement is as the most extreme of the protests against what was usually regarded as the spirit of the age, contributing to the counter-attack on a broad front which older values, suitably redefined, and older institutions, temperately reformed, launched immediately after the apparent triumph of the proponents of radical change in 1832.

As between Anglicans and Nonconformists, sectarian disputes were embittered not only by the Romanizing tendencies of the Oxford Movement but also by the Dissenters' and their Deputies' adoption, at the moment of what seemed to be victory, in 1833, of the cry of Disestablishment. From this time onwards a good proportion of Nonconformists, though not necessarily of Methodists, worked to disrupt the union between Church and State. The Liberation Society, with this aim, though not at first under that title, dates from the education affair of 1844. Many Dissenters became militant opponents of the 'Establishment' in all its aspects.

Roman Catholicism gained in Newman one of its great thinkers, though it was some time before he was fully accepted in the Church he had joined, especially in England. The conversion in 1850 of the Archdeacon of Chichester, H. E. Manning, unable to accept a doctrinal decision of the Judicial Committee, was more quickly appreciated, because he was a man of great pastoral and administrative ability. But the immediate effect of these accessions on English opinion generally was to increase the traditional animus against Rome, especially as the large increase in the number of Roman Catholics in Britain was mainly due to Irish immigration. In 1850 the Pope thought it opportune to establish a normal hierarchy of bishops in England, hitherto treated as a schismatic country requiring special arrangements. This step was taken in Britain as a declaration of war on Protestantism. In revenge, the Government promoted an Act to limit the range of titles that Roman Catholic dignitaries might use. While this Ecclesiastical Titles Act, like most of the remaining provisions on the Statute Book directed against the spread of Roman Catholicism, soon became inoperative, the bitter feeling persisted.

No Church in the British Isles failed to reappraise its relationship with the State in this period. But the most radical attitude of all was taken up by the Church of Scotland. This other Established Church was Calvinist in origin; though English Low Churchmen were prepared to worship in its churches, the theology of the Oxford Movement was quite alien to it. Most of its members thought that each of its congregations should elect a minister to serve it. However, the law gave to landlords the right of patronage to livings in the English manner. The claim of a congregation to elect their minister, or at least to veto a 'presentation', was revived in the 1830s in the midst of a movement of general reform analogous in some respects to the Evangelical Movement. The General Assembly of the Church of Scotland, a representative body which no English Church could match and which was the nearest thing to a Scottish Parliament, supported the claim for a veto in 1834. Successive Governments refused to alter the law, and in 1843 the majority of the Church seceded, leaving the whole endowment in the hands of the minority. To maintain the new Church, of course, required a great outlay of money on the part of the seceders, and that sufficient money was forthcoming is remarkable evidence of the strength of feeling involved. This example commended itself to some English High Churchmen, who wondered whether the spiritual advantages which the Church of England could hope to derive from independence of the State might not outweigh the material and other benefits of Establishment. But this question troubled few Anglicans. A more important outcome of the new situation in Scotland was to create a political opportunity for opponents of the Church of

England and of Conservatism. Here was another country like Ireland, in which the Established Church in possession of the endowments was the Church of a minority.

For nearly all denominations, finally, this was a period of expansion. As well as fighting the State and each other, all were increasing their provision of churches. In particular, they were becoming ever more conscious that new urban areas were especially short of places of worship and that a large part of the working classes had no contact with any sect. Dissenters might have the edge over Anglicans in industrial areas, but 'a sadly formidable portion of the English people are habitual neglecters of the public ordinances of religion'. As the following table shows, the situation was improving overall. But it is probable that most of the new churches were used mainly by middle-class persons, since they were generally built by local public subscription and therefore were rarely in poor districts, and since they generally contained a good proportion of pews reserved for people who could afford to pay rent for them.

Church of England

	Churches built	
1801–31	500
1831–51	2029

Dissenters

Number of places of worship

	Methodists	*Independents*	*Baptists*
1801	825	914	652
1831	4622	1999	1613
1851	11007	3244	2789

(*from the Ecclesiastical Census of 1851*)

Education was inseparable in this period from the Churches. True, a State grant of £20,000 was made annually from 1833 to assist in the building of schools. In 1839 it was raised to £30,000 a year, a Committee of the Privy Council was established to administer it, with Dr Kay as its Secretary, and inspectors were appointed to inspect schools which had received grants. The annual grant had reached £125,000 by 1850, because by the Education Minutes of 1846 grants might be used to increase the salaries of teachers in schools pronounced efficient by the inspectors, and to support training colleges for teachers. But as yet there was little sympathy with the idea of secular education; it was generally accepted that most of the provision for education must be made by Churches, and with their own financial resources; and the State grants were mostly administered by the two 'approved' Societies, the National, and the British and Foreign, both religious. The State seemed to Nonconformists too bound up with the Church of England to deal impartially with them, especially after the inept proposals of 1843, and they espoused as a matter of principle 'voluntaryism', which the Congregationalists carried to the extreme of refusing all State aid. So in this period the history of education is primarily a history of 'voluntary' effort.

Secondary education will be considered in the next Part. The amounts of money subscribed to the various denominational societies for promoting primary education are moderately impressive: by 1859, for example, £750,000 to the National Society, £175,000 to the Congregational Board of Education, £157,000 to the British and Foreign Society.[1] By the same date illiteracy was declining fast. In 1839 a third of males and a half of females marrying put their mark to the register, not their signature; in 1861 only a quarter of males and a third of females. In the Report of the Newcastle Commission on Popular Education of 1861 it was claimed that, of 2,600,000 children who ought to have been receiving education, all but 120,000 were doing so. This was optimistic, and the education in question was often very primitive in these cheap schools. But there is no doubt that a great deal had been achieved, though much of it only in the 'fifties.

Municipal, Police and Law Reforms
It was hardly possible to reform Parliament without reforming borough corporations. This was done for Scotland in 1833, England and Wales in 1835. In the latter case, Radical and Nonconformist demands for better representation interacted with the growing fear and disgust felt by the Government and the landed gentry at the disorder endemic in towns. The preparatory Royal Commission was biased but persuasive. This was the classic instance when wrecking amendments made by the House of Lords were disowned by Peel for the Conservative party in the Commons and the country, and abandoned. The measures were drastic. Almost every old corporation was swept

---

[1] D. Owen, *English Philanthropy, 1660-1960* (Cambridge, Mass., 1964), p. 119.

away. The only notable exception, and that of course of great
symbolic importance, was the City of London, which remains
to the present day unreformed. In all the boroughs concerned,
wholly new elective councils were set up. The franchise was in
appearance much more liberal than the Parliamentary, since
all householders might qualify, but the additional requirement
of three years' payment of poor rates was so restrictive that in
some places fewer people could vote for their town council than
for their M.P. Women were explicitly excluded. There was a
property qualification for membership. A third of the council
was to be elected each year, and in addition aldermen were to
be co-opted by the council. The Act required each council to
appoint two salaried officials, a town clerk and a treasurer, and
permitted it to appoint stipendiary magistrates. The measure
allowed room for development. Councils, subject to the control
of the Privy Council, might 'make such Bye Laws as to them
shall seem meet for the good Rule and Government of the
Borough'; they could levy a rate; provision was included for the
councils to take over, by agreement, the powers of improvement
commissioners; and it was made comparatively easy for the Act
to be extended to towns previously unincorporated. Manchester
and Birmingham soon had their charters and corporations.

By 1850 a reasonably efficient system of police was established
in London, the towns and half the counties. In so far as there
was a public demand for this reform, it came from the propertied
classes, and there survived even among them a good deal of
distrust of the police. However, no one doubts that standards of
public order and behaviour were raised as a result of the change.
It was partly the institution of the police which made contemporaries willing to stomach the mitigation of the law's severity.
In the period covered by this book the highest figure for death
sentences passed was reached in 1831: 1,549 in England and
Wales. For death sentences inflicted the worst years were 1816–
1822, when the average was over 100. In the next decade the
average was 58, and in 1831 it was 52, that is, 1 in 30 of the sentences. In 1832 the penalty was abolished for a number of
offences like forgery and cattle-stealing, and in 1837 for several
more, so that few crimes other than murder remained capital.
In 1838 the total number of death sentences was 116, of which
6 were carried out. After that year no one was hanged in nineteenth-century England except for murder. The accepted alter-

native punishment for serious crime was transportation to Australia. It was used so freely that in 1836 about 52,000 persons were serving terms. By 1850 objections from other Australians, together with revelations of the conditions in which the convicts worked, had much restricted the practice. In consequence, it was more necessary to build prisons in England, and in the late 'thirties and 'forties about forty were erected. Prison inspectors were first appointed in 1835. Other enormities of the unreformed period were being eradicated. The pillory was abolished in 1837. Flogging in the armed services was still considered necessary, but at least the number and permitted severity of floggings was much reduced between 1830 and 1846. Bear-baiting and similar sports were made illegal in 1835. These reforms are among many which rendered the country more civilized.

It is hard to discover what are the precise significance and effects of changes in legal procedure. But much effort was devoted in these years, largely through Brougham's initiative, to speeding up litigation and rationalizing the legal system. Many of the worst absurdities and the longest delays had been eliminated before 1850. In civil cases obvious benefits accrued from the establishment of County Courts with jurisdiction where the amount at issue was less than £20. Previously almost all civil cases had to be heard in London.

Factory Reform
Children had always been put to work, in agriculture as in other industries. It was to the advantage of their parents, and was usually held to be to the public benefit. But the Industrial Revolution created conditions of child labour in many respects worse than had existed before. Tiny children employed in factories and mines might be away from their parents, at night, for more than twelve hours on end, minding machinery under brutal discipline. Even if the machinery did not mangle them, their health was likely to be ruined before they reached maturity.

More remarkable, though, than the change in the conditions was the change in the public attitude to them. It became widely accepted that young children should not be employed in factories and mines at all, and that the hours of work of older children should be restricted. But it was equally the common view that adults must be treated as responsible individuals capable of making a contract about their working conditions without assistance. Compromise legislation was made difficult by the fact that children, as mills were usually organized, seemed essential to the industry, and so limitation of their hours might in effect limit those of adults. It was, on the other hand, still believed by many, understandably, given the vicissitudes of industry and the novelty of a fast rate of growth, that any restrictions placed on the recruitment of labour might make the difference between profit and loss to the manufacturer. In places like Manchester, after all, the number of labourers over the age of 20 was hardly greater than the number of those aged between 10 and 20.

What carried the laws controlling employment in factories and mines was a combination of many forces: the Ten Hours movement; humanitarian feeling, voiced by Evangelicals like Ashley, using comparisons with the conditions of West Indian slaves of whom Parliament took such care, and refusing to put profit before welfare; the ideas and experience of the more enlightened factory-owners, who themselves dispensed with child labour and found long hours unprofitable; and the willingness of the landed interest, especially the Tories, to put down upstart Radical manufacturers. What made the laws more effective than earlier attempts, and progressively better, was the introduction in the 1833 Act of inspection of factories by professionals, and the successive recommendations of the inspectorate, once established. This was the proposal of one of the members of the Royal Commission, Edwin Chadwick, formerly Bentham's secretary.

By 1850 a 10 hour day, or a 58 hour week, for women and for children under 18 had been imposed in textile factories, indirectly affecting many adult men also. Children under 8 might not work there at all. In the mines the employment underground of women and of children under 10 was absolutely prohibited by the Act of 1842. Other industries and trades were as yet virtually unregulated.

Poor Law Reform

What made it imperative to reform the Poor Law, from the point of view of Ministers, was the pressure of the landed interest to reduce the poor rates. It was the problem of the South and agriculture which dominated their thinking. Opinion generally concentrated on condemning the 'Speenhamland

system' as the great abuse of the old law. It was strongly held
that employers should not be encouraged to pay low wages by
the subventions available to their employees under the Poor
Law, that it was 'demoralizing' to the labourer to have to
depend on this charity, and that in order to ensure an adequate
supply of labour in areas of economic advance there should be a
free labour market. To change the system it came to be accepted
that centralization of Poor Law administration was necessary.
This was largely as a result of the report of the Royal Commission on the Poor Laws, set up in 1832, the first of the great
Royal Commissions, which was very much influenced by
Chadwick and other Benthamites.

The Poor Law Amendment Act set up a body of three Poor
Law Commissioners, with Chadwick as Secretary, who were
independent of Parliament, whose tenure had to be renewed
after five years, but who in the meantime had very large powers
to control the administration of relief. In particular they were
required to divide the country into unions of parishes, like those
few formed under Gilbert's Act, in each of which the ratepayers were to elect boards of guardians who must provide
adequate workhouses and administer relief through paid
officials under the directions of the Commission. Thus for the
first time, though for specified purposes only, an elective system
of local government was established over the whole country,
divided up on a fairly rationalist basis; the authority of the J.P.s
was displaced; and Parliament delegated powers of interference
in the localities unmatched since the days of Star Chamber.

It is important to realize that certain things which had been
much canvassed were not done. The Royal Commission did not
accept that the Poor Law should be altogether abolished, as
had been proposed by Thomas Malthus in his influential *Essay
on the Principle of Population* (1798). The law of settlement was
only modified, and still acted as a discouragement to migration.
Liability to rates was unaltered.

How relief should be administered was left to the Commission
to decide. Its first object was to eradicate supplementation of
wages from the poor rates, but it hoped also to dispense with all
'outdoor relief' for the able-bodied and to restore the workhouses to their true function. Necessarily, as the problem was
viewed, the workhouse had to be made unattractive, 'less
eligible' than the miserable working conditions outside. The

intention was to deal with children, the sick and the aged in a different way in different buildings. The Commissioners failed to make provision of allotments for the poor, one of the obvious ways of relieving agricultural distress.

The Act, and the efforts of the Commissioners, were partially successful. Unions were established and built their workhouses. The 'Speenhamland system' was perhaps destroyed as far as official expenditure was concerned. The poor rates fell, and expenditure on poor relief was lower in every year between 1835 and 1850, except for 1848–9, than it had ever been between 1816 and 1834. The administration was considered to have justified itself, and was very soon saddled with other tasks like registration of births, marriages and deaths, and vaccination. The guardians were more professional than their rivals, the J.P.s and the clergy, or their predecessors, the overseers, and better capable of collecting information and attending to detail.

On the other hand, the Commissioners found that they could not get all they wanted done. Even when what the Commissioners wanted was sensible, local boards of guardians might refuse to co-operate. Hence, special provision for children, the sick and the aged was seldom made. Moreover, the Commissioners' wishes were not always grounded in a realistic appreciation of the situation. 'Outdoor relief', it was found, was indispensable if the poor were to be kept alive and the country quiet. In the industrial districts it was the only possible means of coping with cyclical unemployment. Here troops sometimes had to be called in to give effect to the Commissioners' regulations even in modified form. In agricultural areas unemployment, if less severe, was more continuous and no more tractable. The wages of agricultural workers did not at first rise to offset the loss of the 'Speenhamland' subsidies. More general opposition arose because the new authority was enforcing a callous law, insisting for instance on separating husbands from wives and parents from children in the workhouses. Many people simply resented centralization, system, uniformity and efficiency.

The opposition won a token triumph in 1847, when Chadwick was dropped from the Commission, which was replaced by a Board, headed by a Minister in Parliament.[1]

---

[1] The best general discussion is in S. E. Finer, *The Life and Times of Sir Edwin Chadwick* (London, 1952). See also U. Henriques, 'How Cruel was the Victorian Poor Law?', *Historical Journal* 1968, and the articles there cited.

6 Crimple Valley Viaduct. A lithograph by G. Gibson of York, August 1847. The viaduct was 120 feet high and 1,873 feet long. The York and North Midland Railway, Harrogate branch, ran over it; the Leeds-Thirsk line under it.

7 (*overleaf*) The construction of Holborn Viaduct, London, in 1869.

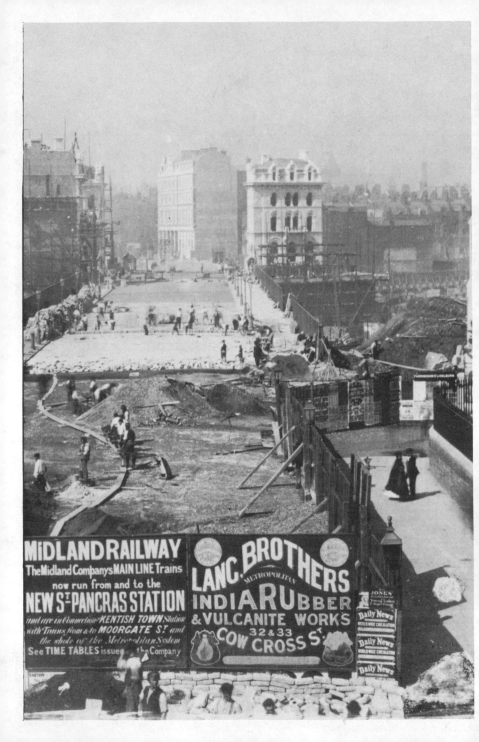

8 Tavistock Workhouse, Devon, by Gilbert Scott, built in the late 1830s.

9 Society of Friends' Soup Kitchen in Manchester during the Cotton Famine. It could prepare up to 1,000 gallons of soup a day. From the *Illustrated London News*, 22 November, 1862.

Sanitary Reform

While he was still nominally Secretary to the Commissioners, Chadwick was actually working on health questions. His Sanitary Report of 1842 revealed the full horror of British urban life. He argued that the high incidence of disease and the high mortality in towns were due not so much to destitution as to squalor. His remedy was not, as might have been expected, medical, but engineering: a continuous and adequate water supply, combined with an efficient system of sewers. This Report leaned heavily on Kay's earlier work, and on the contribution of doctors trained in the Edinburgh medical school. But it was incomparably more thorough. It became a best-seller and, reinforced by subsequent enquiries, both of Royal Commissions and private bodies, created a strong body of opinion, well placed rather than widespread, in support of a measure under which local authorities could be compelled to take proper action in this field.[1] In 1848, with another cholera epidemic threatening, the Public Health Act was passed. It set up a General Board of Health, of which the members appointed were Ashley (unpaid), Chadwick (paid) and Viscount Morpeth (in his capacity as a member of the Government). This Board was to supervise the establishment and operation of local boards of health. Such boards were to be created either if one-tenth of the inhabitants of a locality petitioned to that effect, or if the death-rate in a locality exceeded 23 per 1,000. In corporate towns the council was to be the board. Otherwise a special board was to be elected by ratepayers. The act did not apply to Scotland and the City of London. Under the instructions and inspection of the General Board, the local boards

> were given powers to enforce drainage, provide and maintain sewers, and compel the provision of privies. They could pave and cleanse streets, and provide a scavenging service. They dealt with nuisances, offensive trades, and meat inspection. They were empowered to inspect and regulate common lodging-houses. Under certain limitations they could close burial grounds, provide or control water supplies, and provide public parks. They could raise a rate, and were given borrowing powers for the construction of works.[2]

---

[1] There is a modern edition, by M. W. Flinn (Edinburgh, 1965), with a first-rate introduction.

[2] G. M. Young and W. D. Handcock (ed.), *English Historical Documents*, vol. XII (1), 1833–1874 (London, 1956), p. 757; and *passim* for this whole section.

These powers, constituting a vast infringement on the liberty of individuals, were not wholly unprecedented, but they now became much more general and much more fully-used than before. Up to the end of 1853 182 towns had taken advantage of the Act.

Chartism

Some of the signatures on the Chartist petitions were spurious, but the number that were genuine must be easily great enough to qualify the movement as the most widely-supported in history before the twentieth century. Yet it failed. Though five of its six points have now become law, three of them within the period covered by this book, this outcome had little to do with Chartism. The effects that it did have were indirect, and for the most part unintended: encouraging the Government and the upper classes to promote public education, increase provision of churches, improve living and working conditions, and found county police forces. In this case, with greater truth than of the agitation of 1830–2, it can be said that the 'Establishment' decided to cure the social disease rather than concede the political demand. Only after the failure of Chartism was further Parliamentary reform advocated by any of the leaders of the traditional parties.

A movement of such dimensions, however, is of enormous interest to the historian from all manner of points of view. Its essential precondition, or at least the precondition of its receiving mass support, was distress. Only during the economic crises of 1837–42 and 1847–8 were monster petitions procurable. Unequal distribution of property was cited in the Charter as a root cause of the movement. But it is most significant that it was not direct remedies for distress or inequality that the Charter proposed. The fact was that the participants could not find adequate remedies, and in any case their social and economic grievances were so varied that they could not agree on a pro-gramme to meet them. The one explicit proposal for social reform associated with a wing of the movement, the campaign for land nationalization or redistribution, remained a minority demand. Some few Chartists placed most stress on amendment of the Factory Act of 1833. A much larger group was strongest against the New Poor Law. For some Chartism was another attempt to realize the Utopian socialist aims of the Grand

National Consolidated Trades Union, a body which for a few months in 1834 claimed the support of a million working men and proposed by a General Strike to establish the reign of co-operation and virtue. Only discontent with the limited concessions of the First Reform Act united them all, and Parliamentary reform was the only generally acceptable remedy. The political programme was considered extreme, and was a reversion to Paine's ideas. But the striking fact is that the programme was political, a fact which helps to illuminate the whole of nine-teenth-century working-class history. The race of the 1820s to harness economic discontent to political aims had been won. Further, for the great majority of the supporters of Chartism the movement was constitutionalist. The 'physical force' Chartists, advocates of rebellion or general strike, never attracted a large following. Even the Newport 'rising' was intended only as a mass demonstration.

Chartism's relation with the Industrial Revolution is of great interest too. It was mostly a movement of people involved in trade and industry rather than agriculture, and it came near to embracing the whole of the urban working classes. Only an industrialized society could have produced it. But it was patronized less keenly by factory workers than by the representatives of earlier stages of industrial development, handloom-weavers and framework-knitters threatened by the advance of steam-power and large-scale production. Though primarily a northern and midland movement, it was strong also in the West Country and East Anglia, where old industries were being driven out of existence by the competition of the North, and quite well-supported in London. For some it was a revolt against too little, for others against too much, industrialization.

Many reasons for its failure may be advanced. For the fact that it did not impose its programme by force the explanation is simple. Most of the participants did not wish to use force. The Government, especially when the Whigs were in power, was moderate and tactful in dealing with Chartists, by comparison with its attitude to the agricultural labourers who rebelled in the early 'thirties or with the repression of earlier decades. But it was also firm in using the army and the police, and railways to transport them about. The Chartists, geographically divided, with inferior weapons and means of communication, would have had little hope even if they had intended a general rising.

There was little sign of disaffection in the army. In any case, Government apart, the concessions of the First Reform Act had done their work. The 'Establishment' was united against the threat of rebellion, and its power in most localities was too well-grounded to be overthrown.

As for the fact that the Chartists' demands were not carried peacefully, the solidarity of the 'Establishment' and its control of Parliament accounted for it. The union of the working classes called forth a union of the middle classes. To nearly all those qualified to vote or to sit in Parliament, the Charter was absurd, the rhetoric of the *Northern Star* vulgar and irrelevant. Constitutional reform was still conceived as a matter of balancing forces and powers. Further, where anything approaching democracy reigned, as in the government of London outside the City, corruption, parsimony and limited views seemed to dominate. The example of the United States in the age of Jackson did nothing to persuade the British upper classes in favour of democracy. Many of the privileged displayed great ignorance of the achievements of some of their social inferiors. There was preposterous snobbery and condescension, exaggerated fear of revolution. But at least the 'Establishment' of the 'forties showed real concern at the state of the poor, and took some action to improve it. This helped to reduce the appeal of Chartism after 1842.

Though Chartism failed in the sense that its programme was not at once enacted, and though its mass support disappeared after 1848, it did not vanish. A smaller, more explicitly socialist Chartism survived into the next period. But this had little importance at the time.

Free Trade and the Repeal of the Corn Law

The question 'why was the Corn Law repealed?' (strictly, at first, suspended only) has aroused almost as much controversy as the question 'why was Parliament reformed?' At the time and since, people have believed that with Repeal the voice of public opinion, particularly that of the industrialized provinces, institutionalized in the Anti-Corn Law League, triumphed over the landed interest, hitherto secure in its control of Parliament. But this view is too simple.

The League was founded to bring together the hitherto scattered elements of an agitation of some years' standing. Its headquarters were at Manchester, its leader was Richard Cobden. It campaigned for universal Free Trade, but with special reference to the Corn Law. Its formation marked the abandonment by most industrialists of claims to protection for themselves. It also represented a deliberate diversion of agitation away from Chartism, the promotion of a middle-class alternative to the chimerical programme of the working classes. Its organization was most efficient, using lectures, petitions, pamphlets, newspapers like the *Economist* (1843), and buying up freeholds in order to win by-elections. Its petitions obtained nearly as many signatures as the Chartists'. Its funds, at least £250,000 altogether, were vastly greater.

This was the core of its arguments. Britain now depended on imports of food to support her population adequately. Since, by the operation of the Corn Law, food imports were not so large as desirable and so cheap as possible, some people starved and many went short in agricultural as well as industrial areas, while the home market for manufactures was reduced because unnecessarily high prices had to be paid for food, with consequent loss to manufacturers and additional hardship to their employees. Again, with food imports limited, Britain's total trade was diminished, because many countries could not pay for British goods unless Britain was paying them for food, among other products – hence a further reduction of her industrial output, profit and employment. Agriculture must now take third place behind trade and industry, in the interests of the country as a whole, as a consequence of the Industrial Revolution. However, farming would not in fact suffer seriously, because of the built-in protection afforded to it by transport costs and the general shortage of grain in Europe.

After the split in his party, Peel himself attributed Repeal to Cobden and the League. But this was to minimize his own role and that of others not connected with the League. It must first be realized that much greater contributions to Free Trade than Repeal were made by the Budgets of 1842 and 1845, with which the League had little to do. These were to a large extent Peel's own work, in line with the report of the Select Committee on Import Duties of 1840 and based on the proposals of civil servants, reinforced by the general conviction of almost all those who had studied the matter that tariffs did harm rather than good. Successive Governments since Liverpool's time had taken this view, and reductions in import duties had been made by the Whigs in the 'thirties as well as by the Tories in the 'twenties. Deficit led to reversal of this policy in 1840. In order to resume advance in the direction of general Free Trade, what was needed was the reimposition of the income tax, to provide an alternative source of revenue. This was what Peel carried through in 1842, with an exceptionally strong Cabinet and an exceptionally solid party behind him, and against the background of the economic crisis of 1837–42 and the deficit. In return for an income tax of 7d. in the £ on incomes of over £150 per annum, he reduced 750 of the 1,200 duties. More drastically, in 1845 450 duties were repealed, and many others lowered. In 1842, before the Budget, customs duties yielded an average of over 30 per cent on all imports, as against over 60 per cent in 1822. The change over twenty years was partly due to remissions of duty, more to the great growth of imports of articles which carried less heavy duties, like cotton. But in 1842 customs revenue formed 46 per cent of total revenue, a higher proportion than at any time since before the wars with France. The poor, that is, paid relatively more of the taxes than previously. After Peel's reforms the average import duty was 25 per cent, and the proportion of the revenue derived from customs around 40 per cent. Among the duties repealed were many on raw materials, including meat; among those reduced were those on tea and sugar, hitherto very heavy. These changes must have contributed much to the revival of trade after 1842. They must also have improved the standard of living of the working classes. The most striking development for which they must be largely responsible was a very rapid increase in sugar consumption. Per capita consumption of sugar in the 'thirties and early 'forties was visibly lower even than in previous decades. From 1839 to 1844 it never reached 17 lb. The average from 1800 to 1809 had been 19 lb. In 1845 it was 19 lb. again, and thereafter rose almost uninterruptedly. In 1853 it reached 30 lb., and fell below that figure in only two later years.[1] Peel was very conscious of the social implications of his policies. 'Whatever be your financial difficulties and necessities,' he said in introducing the Budget of 1842, 'you must so adapt your measures . . . as not to bear on the comforts of the labouring classes of society.'[2] The

---

[1] It is now over 100 lb.
[2] Young and Handcock, *English Historical Documents, 1833–1874*, p. 426.

Budgets of 1842 and 1845 are Peel's greatest achievement, and the principal contribution of Governments to the better economic and social situation of the later 'forties.[1]

By comparison with the whole range of tariffs modified in these Budgets, the Corn Law was of lesser economic importance. But it was of enormous political importance. This had been true ever since its first enactment, but the League directed still more attention to it. Though its lecturers, pamphleteers and orators could argue a most convincing logical case for Repeal, they also indulged in unreasonable demagogy against the aristocracy, the 'Establishment' and politicians of the old parties. The League succeeded in making the Corn Law the symbol of landed and aristocratic dominance of Parliament. Hence it provoked a bitter and organized reaction. The Reform Act had much increased the number of county constituencies, and thereby strengthened the direct representation in the Commons of the agricultural interest, of the farmers as against the landowners. In the Election of 1841, while Peel himself remained silent on the Corn Law, the Conservatives had won most of the counties because they were believed to be the party of agricultural Protection. Russell had made this certain by supporting publicly in 1839 the replacement of the sliding scale of 1828 by a fixed duty on corn, a policy to which the Whig Cabinet had finally agreed as an electioneering gambit in 1841. As Peel unfolded his liberal policies, discontent grew within his party. He overcame it in modifying the sliding scale in 1842, on the sugar duties in 1844 as well as in 1845, and in 1845 on the increase in the grant to the Roman Catholic seminary at Maynooth in Ireland. But the same combination was building up as in 1829–30, of Protestant agriculturalist Tories, suspecting betrayal by their leaders. In 1844 an Anti-League was founded.

Peel was privately convinced that Repeal was the right policy some years before 1845. What persuaded him to act was the outbreak of potato blight in Ireland in the autumn of that year, which threatened catastrophic famine. As Peel saw it, the Government must procure additional food for Ireland, and in order to do so must suspend the Corn Law. There seems to have

---

[1] See A. H. Imlah, *Economic Elements in the Pax Britannica* (Cambridge, Mass., 1958).

been no dissent from the view that suspension, in the political climate created by the League, meant effective Repeal. Russell's *Edinburgh Letter* was based on the same calculation. But when Peel actually proposed the suspension he linked it with other measures: a further reduction of duties, this time on foreign manufactures; and drainage loans for farmers. Again, he showed a broader grasp than the League or the Whigs.

In order to understand how these decisions could be made and succeed, many factors have to be considered. Until the 1830s there was a large surplus of grain in Europe, more of which, but for the Corn Law, would have found its way into Britain, doubtless lowering prices. There were difficulties, of course: the shipping was not always available, and bad harvests in Britain were often matched by bad harvests in Europe. But the main provision of the Corn Law was that excluding entry of cheap corn altogether.

British agriculture had been adapting itself to the post-war situation. The output of wheat was evidently rising, the output of meat more rapidly. But it is a matter of dispute whether the growth of wheat output kept pace with the rise of population before the 1830s. To me it seems unlikely that it did, since it is known that the acreage of wheat grew little, if at all, and that the improvement in yields was only slight.[1] In Britain as well as in Ireland, though to a lesser extent, increased cultivation of the potato must have been a necessary compensation for a lesser supply of grain. Not until 1837–42, however, was the insufficiency clearly revealed. But by this time the European surplus was dwindling, at least outside Russia. A Corn Law was no longer necessary to ensure that all the grain produced by British farmers in a good year could be sold at reasonable prices. Further, what is called 'high farming', larger-scale and more scientific, had been developing in Britain, and areas ill-suited to arable had been turned over to pasture. The 1840s were a period of notable development in agricultural techniques: the Rothamsted experimental station was founded in 1843, large imports were made of guano for manure, wheat-yields rose much more rapidly. Peel's drainage loans were designed to assist the transition to 'high farming'. The larger farmers felt

---

[1] M. J. R. Healy and E. L. Jones, 'Wheat Yields in England, 1815–1859', *Journal of the Royal Statistical Society* 1962.

some confidence that they would prosper even against overseas competition.[1]

No doubt these changes helped to account for the acquiescence of some landlords and great farmers in Repeal. They entered Peel's calculations, which were primarily economic. But political considerations predominated with most men. The majorities for Repeal in both Houses were composed of some Tories and most Whigs, responding to the initiatives of their party leaders and often suppressing their own doubts because of the common assessment of the political situation, that public opinion, largely formed by the League, would accept nothing less and, if baulked, would turn to more revolutionary demands. As in 1829 and 1832, enough members of the 'Establishment' recalled that their position rested on opinion, not on force, and adopted the Whig attitude that concession to the views of the respectable was the only security against the violence of the masses. Incidentally, they preferred to give way without forcing a constitutional crisis like that of 1831–2, and avoided a General Election or a threat to create peers on the issue of the Corn Law.

Repeal is often said to have made little difference. It did not affect the Irish situation much. It was certainly less important in economic terms than the total of the rest of Peel's tariff changes. Perhaps, in the same terms, it was less important even than the other reductions of 1846. But it did lead to a much-increased import of grain into Britain. Taking the total quantities of grain and flour imported, in 1846 itself a little more was brought in than in any previous year, in 1847 nearly three times as much, and from 1848 to 1859 inclusive an average of twice as much each year as ever before. As for prices, they did not fall. Rather, Continental prices rose. But corn must have been cheaper in Britain because of Repeal than it would have been under the Corn Law. Most important, economic fluctuations became less violent. As the best-informed had predicted, British agriculture did not at first suffer. As yet, the prairies had not been opened up, and the railways and shipping scarcely existed to transport grain in bulk from so far away.

Politically, the crisis over Repeal was enormously important. Disraeli, whom Peel had refused to consider seriously for office, seized the opportunity to carve himself a political position. He

---

[1] See articles by D. C. Moore and S. Fairlie in *Econ.H.R.* 1965 and F. M. L. Thompson, ibid. 1968.

did not lay much stress on the merits of the case. He argued rather that Peel had no business to defy the majority of his party and its convictions. The Protectionists were led by Stanley in the Lords and Lord George Bentinck in the Commons. In 1848 Bentinck died, and Disraeli soon became, by default, effective Leader in the Lower House. By 1850 no progress had been made towards reuniting Protectionists and Peelites, and the repercussions of the split were felt until at least the 1870s. The bitterness generated was very great, and helps to account for the Liberals' long tenancy of office between 1846 and 1885. In a wider sense, Repeal had a great impact on popular politics. It was very generally accepted that in agreeing to the measure the 'Establishment' had committed itself to a more benevolent and disinterested policy all round. Throughout the rest of the period covered by this book many popular leaders held that Repeal proved the goodwill of the upper classes and demonstrated the possibilities of peaceful reform.

General Considerations

This mass of reforms, it has already been pointed out, remodelled, more or less drastically, most of Britain's historic institutions, and included also some remarkable initiatives. Each Act, however, dealt with a particular matter and was the product of a particular balance of forces. What generalizations, then, can be made about the measures and their origins?

In the cases of Parliament and the municipalities the 'Establishment' explicitly broadened itself. The same tendency was evident in the recognition given in 1828–9 and later to Roman Catholics and Nonconformists, although they remained in some ways outsiders. Further, when new administrative machinery was established, the elective principle was usually extended to it, providing, however, for the representation of property, not numbers. Though the House of Lords lost none of its theoretical power and was not changed except in spirit and by considerable creations of Whig peers, the aristocracy was weakened. The Church lost much of its privileged position, and contracted towards the status of a mere denomination. From each remodelling of an old institution there emerged a closer approach to rationality, uniformity and system. Some of the more obvious anomalies were removed, some norms were laid down. In the special cases of the Poor Law, factory and health measures, the central administration acquired new powers. Together with the Municipal Reform Act these constituted the chief statutory encouragements to professionalism and also the main delegations by Parliament of detailed legislative power. On the other hand, the reforms had many limitations. All of them were unoriginal either in that they generalized detailed precedents, as in the case of Free Trade, or made old measures more effective, as with the Factory Act of 1833, or in that they aimed at applying more widely the practice of certain areas or groups, for instance progressive Gilbert Act Unions which had rejected the ideas behind the Speenhamland decision, good unreformed corporations like Liverpool, improvement commissioners, humane and intelligent factory masters, or model clergymen. Many of the measures used local government machinery, new or old, much more than central administration. They were all very economical. The New Poor Law was explicitly designed to save money; the motive was present behind many of the others. The total number of inspectors appointed was under 100, the professionals in the localities remained few, the census of 1851 found less than 75,000 people engaged in public administration, of whom most were revenue or Post Office officials and 'only 1,628 engaged in the civil departments of the government' for general administrative purposes'.[1] Even local government expenditure hardly rose in the aggregate. The revenue of English and Welsh counties doubled between 1830 and 1850, from about £700,000 p.a. to £1,500,000 p.a., but the reduction in poor rate compensated for this increase. The Church was still the principal social service, and the Poor Law the next.

No doubt many of these limitations arose from the fact that the power of the landed and more precisely the agricultural interest was maintained by the Reform Act, even strengthened, at least against the aristocracy. It remained much easier to score off manufacturers than off squires. The law of 'real' or landed property was scarcely altered, and the Game Laws only in the interests of farmers; county administration was hardly touched, except in the case of the Poor Law, passed almost purely to meet the complaints of the gentry. Their only real defeat was over the Corn Law.

More generally, though, all the measures were strong asser-

---

[1] M. Abramovitz and V. F. Eliasberg, *The Growth of Public Employment in Great Britain* (Princeton, 1957), p. 17.

tions of the power of the State and of the legislative sovereignty of Parliament. After nearly two centuries almost barren of general legislation, it was revived. True, the legislation cost very little and employed few people. But it was extraordinarily effective. By repealing many pointless and unpopular laws, by creating a tolerable police force, and by relying on the growth of 'Evangelical' morality, all of which tended to increase respect for law, Parliament was able to make great changes with slight expenditure and a tiny administration. The period saw a remarkable demonstration of the power of law, backed by little but opinion.

To discuss the origins of the reforms is to enter an area of acute controversy. In the remaining paragraphs of this sub-section I shall try to take into account all the main points that have been made against the simple view that the measures were the result of the pressure of enlightened and humanitarian public opinion, led by Bentham and his followers.[1]

All the reforms discussed in this section were, in part, responses to the great economic and social changes of the late eighteenth and early nineteenth centuries, attempts to take account of the rise of population or the growth of towns, the development of communications, of factory industry, of the middle class or of Nonconformity. It has been suggested that they can be regarded in this light as inevitable. There is more force to this contention in regard to some reforms than to others. The economic and social changes made some sort of Reform Act inescapable. No doubt industrialization makes it necessary to improve primary education above the level it had reached in Britain in 1800. But those very instances recall that the nature of the response and its timing are far from being determined by the progress of economic and social change, except in a sense different from that just used, and so wide as to cover all history. Reform of all kinds was delayed by the wars with France and the reaction associated with them. The struggles of the seventeenth century had a profound influence in the nineteenth, both because of the way people thought about them and because of their historic legacy. Educational reformers advocated State education in the 1830s using the example and experience of

---

[1] The latest article in the controversy, which gives all the references, is by L. J. Hume, 'Jeremy Bentham and the Nineteenth-Century Revolution in Government', *Historical Journal* 1967.

Prussia, which had adopted the measure for military reasons as much as any, and certainly not in response to industrialization. And the progress of industrialization does not explain why it was introduced in Britain only in 1870, and then unsystematically, having been imposed by a British Government on Ireland in 1831. Public Health legislation might seem the clearest case of a direct response to economic and social change. But, insofar as it was, the response was long delayed. Further, the exact nature of the sanitary problem deserves thought. It was not that mortality rates and social conditions in industrial Britain were worse than in the rest of the world. They were, astoundingly, at every point in the nineteenth century on average better than almost everywhere else. It was the internal contrasts that were so striking. Again, the United States, for a variety of reasons, was much slower than Britain to enact legislation controlling commercial and industrial practice, even allowing for the fact that America's Industrial Revolution occurred later.

In no case does it appear that 'public opinion' simply extorted a measure. But a moment's reflection shows that to write in these terms is absurd. Short of a revolution a reform could only be carried with the support of some of the 'Establishment'. In the preceding sub-sections instances have been given of various relationships between forces 'outside' and 'inside'. Peel's Free Trade convictions owed little to public opinion, except in the very restricted sense of the opinion of those who had studied the question. But he acknowledged the effectiveness of the League and reckoned that it had made mere suspension of the Corn Law impossible by 1845. Russell was much more directly influenced by outside opinion on these matters. Wellington and many other peers of both parties, though reluctant, felt the pressure. In the case of factory reform the earliest measures owed little to opinion, but Ashley was converted by the agitation of the early 'thirties, and so progressively were more and more M.P.s, though of course other motives operated. It has been claimed that much of the progress of factory legislation after 1833 was inspired by the inspectorate and other officials who tried to work the early Acts. This influence should be acknowledged, but it was not they who promoted the Act of 1847. On Parliamentary reform, the Act that was passed in 1832 was not what opinion 'outside' wanted. But it would never have been proposed and carried if there had not been a massive movement of opinion, both respectable which might be won over, and 'mob', fear of which made the attempt at winning over the 'middle classes' politically feasible. On law and health reform there was only a narrow range of interested opinion, but it was nonetheless important. In general, feeling both inside and outside the 'Establishment' moved during the 'twenties in favour of general legislation to effect reforms in the interests of economy, efficiency, uniformity, order, better representation and religious equality.

Both Peel and Russell deserve much individual credit for their support of reforming measures, so helping to convert their parties. Recently Peel's role has been much overstated. With all the contribution he made by his Free Trade legislation of the 1840s, to the compromise over Church reform, to criminal law, police and prison reform, and by controlling his party and the House of Lords over the Municipal Corporations Act and other Whig Acts, it must not be forgotten that he opposed many of the extensions of criminal law reform in the 1830s and the limitation of factory working hours throughout, that he backed the educational measure of 1843, which betrayed an Anglican bias, and that he encouraged the House of Lords in its rejection and amendment of many reasonable reforms, especially connected with the Church and the Universities. Peel had a mind of great power, capable of devising large schemes on its own; he showed a remarkable willingness to admit previous error; he was unequalled in economic matters; and he cared desperately about the condition of the people. But Russell too was a great leader in this period. His later career was overshadowed by Palmerston's; his reforming initiatives aroused little interest in the 'fifties and 'sixties. In the 'twenties, however, it had been mainly he who had kept the Whigs bound to the support of Parliamentary reform. In the 'thirties he kept them, often against the opposition of Melbourne, working for further reform, of the Church, in Ireland, of municipal corporations, of the law. In the 'forties he had much to do with making them help repeal the Corn Law. He supported the Ten Hours Act, and was personally much involved in the advance of State education. If he was too doctrinaire, he was sufficiently advanced to be able to be tolerably consistent. He was small of stature, he could be small-minded where questions of patronage were concerned, but he had a broad outlook on large matters and took great risks as leader.

It has been suggested by Professor Gash that, while the Whig case for Parliamentary reform was appropriate to the political situation of 1831–2, the Tory case against it was more cogent: that is, that the settlement was inconsistent and could not be final, that it would lead on to democracy and so to debasement of public standards. But in this matter and in general many Whigs had to be content to go less far than they would have liked, and to defend an unhappy compromise, partly because of the strength of the Tories, especially in the House of Lords. It is significant that, whereas Peel's Government of 1841 was frightened of the Chartists and comparatively restrictive in its dealings with them, Russell in 1839 refused to be alarmed and to take special powers. The difference symbolizes the wider difference that the Whigs were more prepared to trust the people as a whole, to take risks, to 'follow the argument wherever it led'. The Tories could never have proposed the Acts of 1832 and 1835, and, if a majority of politicians had accepted their case against them, Revolution could hardly have been avoided, leading presumably to no less 'debasement'. In this period, when the mass of backbenchers took their cue from the small, slowly-changing group of Front Benchers, distinguished by ability, industry and experience as much as by social position, the role of the latter was of exceptional significance in reconciling the 'Establishment' and opinion.

The detailed question remains: how influential were Bentham and his followers? The recent tendency of historians has been to play down their contribution, and there is a clear limit to the amount of influence that can be exerted by an individual, still more perhaps by an abstract thinker and a recluse like Bentham, on a varied mass of legislation passed by a representative Parliament susceptible to numerous pressures. All the same, no other theoretical reformer was nearly so important as Bentham was. It has already been indicated that in the 1820s he and his associates had direct influence on public opinion and on some politicians. After his death in 1832 the story is somewhat different. There seems to have occurred a reaction against his kind of radicalism during the 'thirties, both outside and inside Parliament. His own proposals for reform were in many cases superseded as more thorough enquiries were made into the existing situation. But two areas were particularly affected by his ideas.

The first was that of 'new administration' as a whole. His

associates constituted a high proportion of those who could be considered experts in fields where the existing Civil Service had little experience, or in the matter of general administrative reform. They were experts partly by previous study, partly because they were apostles of professionalism and scientific enquiry. Hence they were prominent in Royal Commissions. Later they were also to the fore in drafting and administering the measures for which the Commissions had prepared the way. Chadwick of course was the most famous and effective. He did not owe his detailed proposals to Bentham, but he derived from him his general attitude, that after thorough enquiry into a particular problem a perfect solution to it should be discoverable, and enforceable by law and efficient administration. The solutions he propounded were always modified in the process of law-making, but his contribution to the final measure remained significant and unmistakable. It has been suggested that reform waited on the advance of knowledge. But it is not clear that the remedies applied were the most correct ones. What Chadwick and others of the school supplied were solutions which they believed to be scientifically supported, and the faith and will to seek and carry them out. This was enough. It is easier to credit that their contribution should be so important if it is recalled how small was the range of candidates for work of this kind, and how small the whole élite of politicians and students of politics.

The second sphere of Bentham's special influence was, as was to expected from the emphasis of his own interests, the reform of the law itself. In detail, he had made proposals for radical reform of many branches of the law. These were by no means adopted as they stood. But the resistance of the profession and of conservatism could not eliminate all his proposals. In general, his faith in the power of law and his unclouded assertion of the sovereignty of Parliament communicated themselves to the public and, with important assistance from the work of a disciple, John Austin, a widely-studied legal writer, to the profession itself. It could still be truly said of the Benthamites in 1936:

> They came down into a world where medieval prejudice, Tudor Law, Stuart economics, and Hanoverian patronage still luxuriated in wild confusion, and by the straight and narrow paths they cut we are walking still.[1]

---

[1] Young, *Portrait of an Age*, p. 10.

10

Culture and Society
1832-1850

'WE are not now called upon to prove,' says the Camden Society's *Few Words to Church-Builders* of 1844, 'that Gothick is the only true Christian Architecture.' That the Society could make this claim at that date witnesses to an astoundingly rapid shift of taste and outlook. The Camden Society, founded in 1839, was Cambridge's contribution to the Oxford Movement. While 'Romanism is taught *Analytically* at Oxford,' wrote a critic, 'it is taught *Artistically* at Cambridge.' The Society had to change its name during the crisis of Tractarianism, in 1845, to the Ecclesiological Society, but its teaching continued to flourish, capturing Evangelicals and even Nonconformists at a time when, doctrinally and ritualistically, the High Church was under a cloud. The Webbs called the years 1832 to 1836 'the iconoclastic years'. They had in mind constitutional and legal changes. But the epithet was apt on a broader front. Nothing better signalizes the end of iconoclasm than the Gothic Revival, and 1836 marks its serious beginning. Its ideas as well as their execution owed most to Pugin, who first propounded the views that artistic style is organically connected with the state of society, that the choice of style is a moral question and that Gothic is the most natural and the true Christian style. Pugin himself in 1834, when his vision was fully developed, followed his opinions to a logical conclusion and joined the Roman Catholic Church. His outlook, however, proved acceptable in some degree to most denominations.[1]

The story of the Gothic Revival continues into the twentieth century. Progressively from the 1840s churches in its style, either

---

[1] See K. Clark, *The Gothic Revival* (London, 1964). Quotations from pp. 154, 150.

new buildings or old buildings 'restored', became more numerous; if they were Anglican, surpliced choirs were put into their chancels, there to be screened in so that they could hardly be heard by the congregation; organs, now considered indispensable, joined the choirs, deafening them without sustaining the singing of the people. J. M. Neale, one of the founders of the Camden Society, additionally rediscovered something of medieval symbolism and translated dozens of Latin hymns of the Dark and Middle Ages, which, associated with insipid tunes, formed the core of *Hymns Ancient and Modern*, published in its first complete form in 1861. A memorial window in stained glass was considered a novelty in 1842. Not thereafter.

Before 1850 the Revival produced few of its greater monuments. It was still fighting for acceptance. This was the period of Grey Street in Newcastle-upon-Tyne, Greek and greatly admired. When the Fitzwilliam Museum came to be built in the 'thirties, it was in a classical style. So was St George's Hall, Liverpool, in the 'forties. In Edinburgh and Glasgow Greek Revival building continued to predominate into the 'fifties at least. Pugin's own churches were, through no fault of his own, generally mean. Not until the late 'forties did the full programme of the Ecclesiological Society, which demanded the use of the Decorated style, attain dominance. The most characteristic Gothic buildings of the period are secular and less than pure, the Scott Monument at Edinburgh and the Houses of Parliament at Westminster. But the latter was of immense importance. After the destruction of most of the old Palace of Westminster by fire in 1834, the decision was taken to rebuild in the Gothic style. The reasons were partly special to the site, namely, the style of the surviving Abbey and Hall. But 'ethical' arguments supervened. Gothic, it was claimed, was the English style *par excellence*, the style most appropriate to constitutionalism, the only natural style. Starting in 1836, Charles Barry designed the building's plan, Pugin all the ornament and detail. Barry had been the architect of the Travellers' Club and preferred other styles to Gothic. The plan, in consequence, is a compromise: the design seemed to Pugin Palladian, but it is asymmetrical. The detail, on the other hand, down to the inkstands, is Gothic. The House of Lords was ready for occupation in 1847, Big Ben was completed only in 1858 and the Victoria Tower in 1860. The result commanded admiration from the first. It is a proper testimony to the faith and pride of the Victorians in their representative institutions. But it marks also the triumph of the Gothic Revival, and so the defeat of iconoclasm.

It was not a total victory, though. The greatest investment of the 'forties was in the railways, and to some extent they were insulated from the battle of the styles. Though Euston Station was given a classical portico and at Temple Meads in Bristol the roof was based on the hammerbeam at Westminster Hall, iron and glass structures more commonly covered the platforms. One of the greatest and simplest of road bridges, Clifton Suspension Bridge, designed by the railway engineer, Brunel, was begun in 1836, though not completed until 1864. An oddly important building was the large new conservatory required by the Duke of Devonshire, 277 feet long, 132 feet wide and 67 feet high, using a glass vault with an iron framework, designed by his gardener, Joseph Paxton. These structures have been regarded as forerunners of modern functionalism, a new type of architecture, using the materials made available by the Industrial Revolution. Pugin repudiated them, however, and so did John Ruskin, whose *Seven Lamps of Architecture*, published in 1849, developed the notion that art was bound to morality, which, he thought, led to the view that art was opposed to utility and negated the possibility of beauty in iron and true architecture in railway stations.

In the 'thirties and 'forties Turner painted what are now regarded as his masterpieces, including the Venetian oil-paintings, the fiercest of his horror seascapes and *Rain, Steam and Speed* of 1844. At the time they were scarcely understood. But here again Ruskin in *Modern Painters*, the first volume of which appeared in 1843, transmuted aesthetic criticism, taking Turner as his hero and arguing that art is not a matter of faithful realist representation, but of expression of thought. Five years later, in the excitement of the last Chartist demonstration, Holman Hunt and John Millais, two art-students, founded the 'Pre-Raphaelite Brotherhood', rather vaguely concerned to go behind Raphael for their inspiration, more precisely devoted to the most exact realism in the painting of poetic, religious and allegorical subjects. Dante Gabriel Rossetti joined them almost at once. With glorious inconsistency Ruskin found it in his heart and mind to fight for them as well as for Turner.

An invention of this period, photography, which became a

practical proposition in 1839, makes it possible to illustrate ninteenth-century history more fully than that of earlier centuries. It also totally changed the situation of painters, who, if interested in realism, now faced competition from an infallible machine.

It is remarkable how quickly some of the greatest writers of the nineteenth-century conquered the widening public. Tennyson's *Poems 1842* established his reputation, and by around 1860, when he had thirty more years to live, he was to all classes The Poet. Dickens made his name with *The Pickwick Papers* in 1836–7. It appeared in monthly parts, and the later ones sold 40,000 copies each. This figure surpassed even Scott's sales. *Nicholas Nickleby* in 1838–9 sold 50,000 a part. *The Old Curiosity Shop* reached 100,000 a part in 1841. The first two volumes of Macaulay's *History of England*, which came out in 1848, sold about 20,000 in a year. Further, it seems that the popularity of some of the writings of this period was unusually tenacious. From 1870 to 1882 Dickens' works sold over 4,000,000 volumes in England alone. Macaulay remained the best-known historian, and Tennyson's poetry was rivalled only by Martin Tupper's *Proverbial Philosophy* (1838–42), 'common-place maxims and reflections couched in a rhythmical form,'[1] and, later, by the American Longfellow's. A new edition of Carlyle's *Sartor Resartus* in 1882 sold 70,000.[2] With government encouragement of libraries, and with railway book-stalls, perhaps the writers of these years had special advantages. But it must be remembered that, for whatever reasons, for the rest of the period covered by this book, and beyond, it was the authors who made their name in the 'thirties and 'forties who exerted the widest influence. Add to those already mentioned in this paragraph Mill, Spencer and Ruskin, and the dominant writers of the second half of the century have been named.

To summarize the significance of the literature published between 1832 and 1850 is impossible in a short space. Among the famous works of that period which have yet to be noticed are Disraeli's major political novel, *Coningsby* (1844); Dickens' *Oliver Twist* (1837–8) and other novels; Carlyle's *French Revolution* (1837) and *Cromwell* (1845); Macaulay's *Lays of Ancient Rome* (1842); W. M. Thackeray's *Vanity Fair* (1847–8); *Jane Eyre*

---

[1] So the *Oxford Companion to English Literature*.
[2] Statistics from R. D. Altick, *The English Common Reader* (Chicago, 1963).

and *Wuthering Heights* (1847) by Charlotte and Emily Brontë respectively; and James Mill's son, J. S. Mill's *Political Economy* (1848). The list is so tremendous that it can only be a list.

Certain observations, however, on four of these works contribute to the general argument of this book. Macaulay's *History* is the *locus classicus* of Victorian optimism and pride. The famous third chapter of the first volume inaugurated worthy social history, and its theme is that progress has been immense and that there is no reason why it should not continue. It is tempting to relate this conviction to the change of mood from the anxieties of the early 'forties to the confidence of the 'fifties. For Macaulay personally this is scarcely just: he was always sanguine. For the book and its vogue it is more reasonable. It presented to the public a renovated Whiggism, justifying the 1688 Revolution by subsequent material prosperity as much as by the constitutional blessings it secured.

Dickens' novels, it was said, contributed greatly to concern for improvement of social conditions. This claim requires definition. *The Pickwick Papers*, of course, is partly historical, and glorifies the days of coaching, which were soon to pass. *Oliver Twist* often appears to be about the unreformed Poor Law, not the New. Dickens knew little about the North and its industry. Further, he was not an advocate of State action in principle nor in many particular cases. He trusted in individuals, not institutions. But he exposed certain evils, especially abuses of the Poor Law and in Chancery, and squalid housing conditions; he was humanitarian; and he was absolutely without 'deference'. If he was not good at portraying the very poor, his message was that rank and wealth were in no way correlated with goodness or worth. Though anything but a revolutionary, he was, politically and socially, though not economically, an egalitarian. The combination of attitudes is characteristic of much Radicalism throughout the period, in all classes.[1]

Mill's *Political Economy* became the stock textbook of economics as soon as it was published. Its interest is that, while asserting the iron laws of supply and demand, wages and so on, it showed distaste for them. Progressively in its later editions it became more sympathetic to what was called socialism. Mill came to support restrictions and taxes on inheritances, taxes on

---

[1] Cf. H. House, *The Dickens World* (London, 1942).

rent from land, and co-operation in industry. In these attitudes he joins the Christian Socialists, who also date from 1848, and anticipates much later discussion and legislation, for example the Irish Land Acts.

Tennyson was working during the 'forties on what is regarded as his greatest poem, *In Memoriam*, for his friend Arthur Hallam, who had died in 1833. It was published in 1850. What is so striking about it is its reflection of the spiritual questionings of the period. It confides in an after-life, guaranteed no doubt by the Incarnation. It accepts, or is compatible with, the Christian stress on personal responsibility and fulfilment. But it is anything but dogmatic. Tennyson was thoroughly aware of scientific thought. In Charles Lyell's *Principles of Geology* (1830–3) and, vulgarized, in Robert Chambers' *Vestiges of Creation* (1844), the evidence had been set out which made it impossible to maintain any longer the literal truth of the Bible in its account of the Creation and the Flood. *In Memoriam*'s burden is that there is ground for faith in Man and the development of the human race, though 'the implied metaphysic will be in detail shadowy – a philosophy of Somehow, wavering between a hopeful doubt and a doubtful hope'.[1] It was this conviction which was adopted by those who, unable to accept Catholic or Evangelical dogma, clung to elements of Christian faith, ideals and ethics. After the débâcle of the Oxford Movement in 1845, this was the dominant attitude of intellectuals to philosophy and religion.

---

[1] G. M. Young, 'The Age of Tennyson' in his *Today and Yesterday* (London, 1948), p. 62.

I I

Britain and the Rest of the World 1832-1850

DURING these years Britain took decisive action in relation to all her principal dependencies. The effects on world history have been enormous, greater possibly than those of her domestic development, certainly than those of her foreign policy, over the same period. The most important instances concern Ireland, India and the struggle over 'responsible government' in the settlement colonies.

Ireland

The Act of 1800 had made Ireland legally part of the United Kingdom. But she never became integrated with England, even to the degree that Scotland did. Irish nationalism was to develop further later in the century, but it had been maturing already before the Union. The Irish were thought of, and thought of themselves, as a distinct people. Already relations between them and the British had been poisoned by a long history of unhappy incidents. Matters were made worse by the fact that the two nations were both established in both countries, and by the grave domestic problems of Ireland.

Most of the land of Ireland was owned by persons of English origin. Many of these landlords were absentee. Those who worked the land were mostly Irish, mere tenants under English law, but conceiving of themselves as part-owners. Most landlords were Protestant, most tenants Roman Catholic, yet the tenants had to pay tithe to the Protestant Established Church. Thus there was a clash of nationality, religion and attitude to law, in addition to the normal tension between the receiver and the payer of rent. Further, the situation was radically different in one small area of Ireland, Ulster. There landlords accepted that tenants had some rights in their holdings, and many of the tenants, being of Scottish origin, were Protestant. Land was all-important in Ireland. The linen industry flourished, especially round Belfast, but general industrial development was stifled by British competition and lack of mineral resources. Irish agriculture was prosperous in a sense. It produced a good deal of corn, which was mostly exported to Britain, and an ever-increasing amount of potatoes, on which the mass of the inhabitants lived. Enclosure had not occurred as in Britain. Rather, the number of small tenanted plots was allowed to grow fast. The population was rising rapidly, and by the census of 1841 had reached at least 8,000,000, twice the modern level and equal to over half the population of England and Wales at that date. Standards of living were far lower than in Britain, and there was no general Poor Law until 1838, when a stricter version of the English Act of 1834 was enacted for Ireland. For most Irishmen a smallholding and the food it produced offered the only prospect of survival, except perhaps for emigration. It has already been pointed out that large numbers of Irishmen swelled the population of Britain by the 1840s, especially in the Glasgow and Liverpool areas. Their primitive and ostentatious Catholicism heightened Protestant sentiment, and their poverty and tolerance of squalor intensified distaste for them, in Britain.

Doubtless Ireland's problems would have been better treated separately from Britain's, and in fact special measures were usually passed for the island. But the constitutional relationship made it necessary for Ireland's affairs to be discussed at length by Parliament at Westminster, rather than treated like those of a straightforward colony. The presence of many Irish land-owners in the House of Lords made certain kinds of legislation very difficult to pass, and the addition of 100 odd Irish M.P.s to the House of Commons not only bedevilled British politics and delayed British business but also, in the state of the electoral system both before and after the changes of 1829 and 1832, gave publicity and authority to unrepresentative views on Irish questions. Moreover, Irish conditions bred so much violence that the army rather than the civil power was employed to enforce order, and the ordinary liberties of the subject were abridged more often than not.

In the field of education in particular, Parliament showed itself prepared between 1831 and 1850 to enact measures for Ireland far more drastic than would have been entertained for Britain: an undenominational State education system was imposed in 1831; new Universities, intended to be secular, were chartered in 1845. The Irish Church Temporalities Act was nearer to confiscation of Church property than anything applied in Britain during these years. But the reforms of Parliamentary representation and of municipal corporations (1840) were decidedly restrictive. Tithe, though its collection had been rendered impossible by concerted violence by 1832, was not made a charge on landlords and commuted until 1838, two years later than for Britain. An attempt to modify the land law in the interests of the tenants was defeated in the Lords in 1845.

Ireland in the 'forties supplies another example, like Chartism in Britain, of a great popular movement which had no direct influence on Parliament. O'Connell, the victor of Catholic emancipation, was the effective spokesman of Ireland in the 'thirties and 'forties, until his death in 1847. He worked with the Whig Government of 1835–41 in the hope of procuring Irish reforms, and with some success. In 1840, however, he took up the cause of Repeal of the Union, which commanded wide and enthusiastic support in Ireland but was anathema in England. By 1843 the movement seemed to some as strong as the Catholic Association had ever been. But Peel's Government defeated it in that year by measures of coercion, by forbidding at the last moment a monster meeting arranged at Clontarf, and by securing the imprisonment of O'Connell. The reasons for the failure of the movement are similar to those for the failure of Chartism. O'Connell insisted on legality and order among his followers. He successfully advised them to acquiesce in the prohibition of the Clontarf meeting. So there was in reality much less reason to fear civil war in Ireland in 1843 than in 1829. Repeal was a less meaningful programme even than the Charter; it was quite unclear what was supposed to be substituted for the Act of Union. Although the House of Commons contained some 30 Irish M.P.s who supported it, there were more opposed to it. Ireland in fact was less united in favour of Repeal than it had been in favour of Emancipation. Britain was virtually unanimous on the question, whereas she had been divided in 1829. Peel's answer to the movement, like his answer to Chartism, was social legislation: better security for Roman Catholic endowments, an increased grant for the seminary at Maynooth and attempted land reform. Castastrophe intervened. With successive seasons of potato blight, perhaps a million Irishmen died of starvation and associated disease between 1845 and 1849. Roughly the same number emigrated. Peel's Government tried to ease the situation by distributing cheaply specially-imported maize and by a programme of public works. In March 1847 the number employed on relief works reached its maximum of 734,792. This policy was then abandoned by Russell's Government in favour of compelling the Irish upper classes to organize and pay for adequate provision against starvation, both individually and through the Poor Law. It soon became evident that this could not suffice. The Treasury had to assist, though technically only with loans. In August 1847 3,000,000 Irishmen were being fed at the public expense. While, throughout the period of the famine, grain was leaving the country for consumption in Britain, between September 1846 and July 1847 cereal imports were four times as high as exports.[1]

It will always be disputed how much Governments could and should have done to relieve the situation. Considering their attitudes in other matters, their beliefs that the State should not normally interfere in the workings of the economy and that it was the business of the local propertied classes, in Ireland as in Britain, to support the poor, and bearing in mind the pressure of British taxpayers and economists against relief expenditure by the Treasury, the remarkable fact seems to be that they did so much. The scale of the calamity was without recent precedent and contemporary parallel in Western Europe. On the other hand, while it is said that during Peel's Ministry no one actually died of starvation in Ireland, during Russell's the story was very different. It has been implied that Peel, if he had remained in office, might have carried out policies better-calculated to preserve lives, but, if so, he never indicated what they would have been. The problem became more difficult after he resigned. However, an indictment lies against the whole framework of the age's economic ideas. More specifically, for the Irish it was

---

[1] R. D. Edwards and T. D. Williams (ed.), *The Great Famine* (Dublin, 1956), p. 244. I am grateful to Dr E. R. Norman for drawing my attention to this point.

another, and the greatest, count against Britain that hundreds of thousands should die while their produce was being shipped to feed other parts of the United Kingdom. In result, the population of Ireland fell, and continued to do so well into the present century. It was 6,500,000 in 1851, 5,800,000 ten years later. The average age of marriage climbed into the thirties, as men waited for the opportunity to obtain a holding of reasonable size. Emigration continued on a large scale. Subdivision of land ceased, and by the Encumbered Estates Act of 1849 the British Government applied a new remedy to Ireland, encouragement to Free Trade in land and so, it was hoped, to enclosures and the development of 'high farming'. This enactment, attempting to establish in Ireland a system which had proved successful in Britain, was another instance of an Irish measure more drastic than could have been passed for the United Kingdom as a whole. Characteristically too, it failed. Recipes applicable in Britain did not succeed in Ireland.

India

When Lord William Bentinck went to India as Governor-General in 1828, he wrote to Bentham: 'I shall govern in name, but it will be you who will govern in fact'.[1] With Benthamite influence came more general radical attitudes. Bentinck and his assistants despised the old culture, languages, laws, customs and religions of India, and wanted to introduce progressive Western ideas and institutions into the country. Associated with Radical administrators came Christian missionaries, first allowed into India in 1813, equally critical of much that they found there. Bentinck legislated for India in the ruthless manner Bentham recommended for all countries. Ritual murders and suicides were forbidden. The codification of the law began, based on English notions, and for the first time some Indian judges were appointed to administer it. There already existed provision by the Company, under the Charter of 1813, for an annual subvention to Indian education. Bentinck, relying on an Education Minute written by Macaulay, declared in 1835 that 'the content of higher education should be Western learning, including science, and that the language of instruction should be

---

[1] Quoted in T. G. P. Spear, *India* (Ann Arbor, 1961), p. 256.

English'.[1] English was made the official language of government business. By these measures Bentinck forcibly exposed India to the ideas of the West, especially of his own country, to Christianity, individualism, egalitarianism and nationalism. The effects are never likely to be wholly effaced.

Responsible Government in the Settlement Colonies

In nearly all settlement colonies there existed legislatures, but they were unable to act with freedom, because their resolutions were subject to the veto of the governors, which was often used, and to overriding control from Britain. Further, the electorates were not able to impose ministers on the governor even when a party won a majority of seats in the legislature. In one such area the home government between 1832 and 1850 asserted its authority anew against the settlers: in the West Indies the emancipation of slaves was forced on reluctant white electorates and legislatures. But in Canada this is the period when the mother-country first significantly relaxed her control.

Canada, apart from the maritime provinces, was divided into Upper and Lower, the latter being predominantly French. Rebellions in both colonies in 1837 were the culmination of many years of disputes between the elected assemblies on the one hand and the nominated governors and legislative councils on the other. Although the Government accepted immediately only one of Durham's two main recommendations, for the union of the provinces, in 1847 the Earl of Elgin went out as governor and conceded the other, 'responsible government', that is, he took his Ministers from the majority party in the assembly and followed their advice, carrying the Whig conception of monarchy, very soon after its final adoption in Britain, to Canada. However, there remained, technically at least, a superior power in the Parliament at Westminster; laws made in the colonies could still be disallowed if they conflicted with the law of England; and the British Government maintained control over foreign policy.

Formal and Informal Empire

Of the annexations of this period, the most important was that of New Zealand. The balance of forces here was complex.

---

[1] Spear, *India*, p. 260.

Missionaries were at odds with promoters of systematic colonization. The Government stepped in finally in order to retain some control of the situation, partly in the interests of the native Maoris, partly to forestall French intervention. The expansion of the territory under British control in India continued. On the other hand, the Colonial Office declined to take over Sarawak, where James Brooke, a former officer of the Indian Army, had become the effective ruler in 1841.

South Africa presented a special problem. In Cape Colony, settled originally by the Dutch and only recently annexed by Britain, conflicts between the 'Boers' of Dutch origin and the Government were aggravated by the attitude of British humanitarians and missionaries, whose Protestantism, unlike that of the Boers, led them to campaign for the emancipation of African slaves. In 1835–7 about 5,000 Boers left the Colony and established themselves under republican governments, effectively independent of Britain, in the Transvaal and Natal. This emigration is known as the 'Great Trek'. The motives behind it included land-hunger, general dissatisfaction with British government, and particular discontent over the favorable treatment accorded to non-whites in the Colony and over the refusal of the Colonial Office to ratify the annexation of an area called Queen Adelaide Province. Not only this district but also in 1843 Natal was brought under British control, and in 1848 the Orange River Sovereignty as well. These annexations were chiefly to counterbalance the influence of the Boers. Not until 1852 did Britain actually recognize the independence of the Transvaal. (See Map p. 286.)

Informally, or half formally, the war with China in 1839–42 was the symbol of Britain's penetration into a huge market and of the West's impact on a civilization of vast antiquity and, until recently, superior achievement. By the peace China ceded Hong Kong to Britain.

Perhaps the most striking development of all was the enormous increase in emigration from the United Kingdom, from Britain as well as from Ireland. The famine largely explains the exodus of Irishmen. But now more were emigrating West than into Britain, and Englishmen, Welshmen, Scotsmen and most other European nationalities, especially Germans, were joining

them. Before 1846 there were only three years in which more
than 100,000 persons left the United Kingdom for extra-European countries, 1832 and 1841–2. Thereafter there was only one
year in the nineteenth century when fewer than 100,000 did so,
1861. The figures for the late 'forties are: 1846, 130,000; 1847,
258,000; 1848, 248,000; 1849, 299,000. In the early 'fifties the
average was over 300,000 a year. Of the total, 70 per cent went
to the United States and virtually all the rest to some part of the
Empire, chiefly to Canada, especially before 1851. Nearly two
million Irishmen, all told, left Europe between 1845 and 1854,
and probably something like 400,000 from other parts of the
United Kingdom. The discoveries of gold in California and
Australia in 1849 and 1851 helped to maintain and re-direct
the flow.

It is significant for discussion of the impact of the Industrial
Revolution that, even in the case of Britain, it was from the
rural rather than from the urban areas that emigrants usually
came. Free or cheap land was available to settlers in America.
But most Irish immigrants settled in towns. The appeal of
a more democratic constitution was important, but it was
decisive that the United States offered the best opportunities of
employment and that Irishmen already there paid the cost of
their relatives' and friends' passages. To emigrants as to traders,
the formal Empire proved comparatively unattractive.[1]

Foreign Policy

Palmerston dominated British foreign policy in this period. He
was Foreign Secretary for 15 of the 21 years after 1830. He
exerted exceptional influence in the Cabinet. The combination
against Mehemet Ali, largely his own achievement, was imposed on reluctant colleagues. In the late 'forties he often
ignored ordinary processes of consultation. At first his authority
rested on his unrivalled industry and knowledge, his assurance
and clear head. Later his position with the public and in
Parliament made Russell as Prime Minister fear to discipline
him.

He could be as doctrinaire, and as sharp, as Russell. 'Her
Majesty's Government,' he wrote, 'do not happen to recollect
any Country in which a Constitutional system of Government

---

[1] W. A. Carrothers, *Emigration from the British Isles* (London, 1965).

has been established that has not on the whole been better off in consequence of that system than it had been before'.[1] He thought the despotic régimes of Europe ought to change their ways. In particular he condemned Russian rule in Poland and Austrian in Italy. He gave his blessing to an 'unofficial' expedition in support of the Spanish Liberals in 1836. He supported rebels in the Kingdom of the Two Sicilies, again semi-officially.[2] He publicly criticized what he saw as tyranny, and praised its opponents. But he put British interests as he understood them before ideological considerations. He was clear that Austria must be maintained as a major Power, offsetting the influence of Russia in Eastern Europe. Throughout the crisis of the 1848 Revolutions he worked to preserve peace before all else. He refused to protest against Russia's intervention to crush the Hungarian Revolution on behalf of Austria in 1849. When he thought either France or Russia was challenging for hegemony he acted decisively.

By his dominance of the Cabinets in which he served he made their foreign policy, and therefore that of the Liberal party, individual. His methods and manner, however, were more unusual than his aims. Like a handful of other great Ministers concerned with foreign policy, Castlereagh, Canning, Gladstone and Salisbury in this period, but unlike the lesser fry, he believed that Britain should exert her influence continuously, to direct events to her advantage, perhaps to the general advantage, not shirking threats of force. He was exceptional among these, though, in that he deliberately aired his views to foreign representatives even when he knew the Cabinet did not share them; he conceived, further, that it was Britain's positive duty to offer advice even if she had no intention of acting to enforce it; he was ready to use dubious methods, as with Spain and Naples; and he was the most publicity-minded of all Foreign Secretaries, having copious Blue Books printed and identifying himself with certain public prejudices. Accidentally, the Conservatives were exceptionally pacific in this period, and there was a clearer contrast than is usual between party foreign policies. During these years also, a more fundamental dispute

---

[1] To Guizot, 19 March 1841 (quoted in H. W. V. Temperley and L. M. Penson, *Foundations of British Foreign Policy* (Cambridge, 1938), p. 112).

[2] G. B. Henderson, 'Palmerston and the Secret Service Fund', *English Historical Review* 1938.

arose: the ultimate aim of many of the supporters of Free Trade
was peace between nations, and Cobden gave wide currency to
criticisms of secret diplomacy, interventionism and the pursuit
of the Balance of Power. The Don Pacifico debate, however,
showed clearly where majority support lay.

The Eastern Question was the area of chief development in
foreign policy in these years, and Palmerston was again much
involved. The Greek revolt had alarmed the Powers by showing
the weakness of the Ottoman Empire. In 1833, after a brief war
in which Russia crushed Turkey, the former acquired by the
Treaty of Unkiar-Skelessi a virtual protectorate over the latter.
This state of affairs Palmerston set out tó modify. He acted
against Mehemet Ali because he considered it essential that the
Turkish Empire be weakened no further, and in the settlement
he secured, on paper, the surrender by Russia of her pretensions
to protect and advise the Turks. Fear of Russia in Britain increased markedly in this period, partly because of her expansion
towards India. Between 1839 and 1842 the Russian and British
Empires almost clashed on the North-West Frontier of India,
as Britain sought to intervene in Afghanistan and Russia
infiltrated Persia.

PART THREE

Since the abolition of the corn laws we have given up political agitation; we felt we might place confidence in parliament; instead of political action, we tried to spend our evenings in the improvement of our minds.

A TRADE UNION DELEGATION, to Gladstone, 1863.

The years of Palmerston's last Cabinet, 1859 to 1865, were avowedly years of truce – of arrested development. The British system like the French, was in its last stage of decomposition. Never had the British mind shown itself so *décousu* – so unravelled, at sea, floundering in every sort of historical shipwreck. Eccentricities had a free field. Contradictions swarmed in State and Church. England devoted thirty years of arduous labor to clearing away only a part of the *débris*.

The Education of Henry Adams, 1906.

12

Narrative of Events 1850-1868

BOTH the death of Peel and Russell's Protestant stand weakened the Whig Government: Peel had been its steady supporter, the *Durham Letter* alienated Irish Roman Catholic M.P.s. In February 1851 the Ministry took an opportunity to resign, but had to carry on because no alternative Administration could be found. In December Palmerston was dismissed. He had repeatedly angered the Queen and Prince by failing to follow the accepted practice of submitting despatches for royal approval before sending them off. Russell felt strong enough to drop his Foreign Secretary on this occasion, because his particular offence was to welcome, without consulting the Cabinet, the *coup d'état* by which Louis Napoleon, the future Napoleon III, established his position as ruler of France. Earl Granville, notoriously deferential, became Foreign Secretary. In February 1852 Palmerston joined with the Protectionists to defeat the Government in the Commons.

This time the Earl of Derby (formerly Lord Stanley) agreed to form a Ministry, though he was unable to induce any but Protectionists to join it. Disraeli became Chancellor of the Exchequer and Leader of the House of Commons. There followed an inconclusive General Election. The Government was brought down in December after a devastating assault on Disraeli's Budget by Gladstone.

Lord Aberdeen, after Peel's death the recognized leader of the Peelites, an ageing and rather gloomy man, succeeded in form-ing an Administration of Whigs and Peelites. On paper it was very powerful. Russell was Leader of the Commons; he was also at first Foreign Secretary, then 'Minister without Portfolio', then Lord President of the Council. The courtly Earl of Claren-don succeeded him as Foreign Secretary in 1853. Gladstone was Chancellor of the Exchequer, Palmerston Home Secretary, and

The Balkans, the Eastern Mediterranean and the Crimea
Boundaries of c. 1860

Russia

Austrian Empire

R Danube

Budapest

Moldavia

Bessarabia

Crimea

Sebastopol

Wallachia

Serbia

Sinope

Montenegro

Ottoman Empire

Constantinople

Ionian
Islands
(British)

Greece

Athens

Navarino Bay

Crete
(Ottoman)

Cyprus
(Ottoman)

Suez Canal

Egypt

Ottoman Empire

------- Allied Expeditionary Force 1854-6

Graham First Lord of the Admiralty. Gladstone vindicated his attitude to Disraeli's Budget by producing the first of his own masterpieces in 1853. In the next year the Ministry became involved in the Crimean War, fought in alliance with France to defend the Ottoman Empire against Russia. An army was sent to the Crimea, arriving in September. The allied forces failed to take the fortress of Sebastopol, and spent the bitter winter outside it, lacking adequate clothing, supplies and medical services. *The Times* publicized the facts, and in January 1855 the Commons carried by 305 to 148 a motion to set up a committee to enquire into the situation. Russell had resigned to support the motion. After it had been passed, the Ministry left office.

Derby refused to form a Government without assistance from other parties than his own, and so Palmerston constructed an Administration which was at first very like Aberdeen's, but soon lost Russell and the Peelites. Sebastopol did not fall until September 1855. The Government and British opinion wished to continue the war, but Napoleon III wanted an early settlement. Peace was made at Paris in March 1856.

Palmerston's Ministry was defeated in the Commons in February 1857 over the conduct of hostilities with China. Parliament was dissolved, and the Government won a large majority. Soon afterwards the first news arrived of the Indian 'Mutiny'. By the end of the year it was under control. In February 1858 Palmerston was defeated again in the Commons, and this time resigned. The question at issue was a Conspiracy to Murder Bill, brought in by the Ministry to meet Napoleon's protests that under the existing law of England preparations such as those recently made there to assassinate him could not be restrained.

Derby formed his second Ministry, with Disraeli in the same offices as before. It maintained itself long enough to carry the measure to transfer the powers of the East India Company to the Crown, but was defeated in the Commons on its Parliamentary Reform Bill in March 1859. A General Election failed to give it a clear majority, and in June a vote of no-confidence was passed against it by 323 to 310.

Palmerston returned to power, and formed a strong Administration which lasted for over six years, until his death. Throughout, Russell was Foreign Secretary and Gladstone Chancellor of the Exchequer. The main problems the Government had to face were in foreign affairs. War had broken out in April 1859 between France, as the ally of Piedmont-Sardinia, and Austria. Britain remained neutral while Lombardy was conquered by Napoleon. When peace was made in July, she campaigned against Austria's legitimist claims in Central Italy and in favour of the self-determination of the area. This policy was a compromise between the strongly pro-'Italian' views of Palmerston, Russell and Gladstone on the one hand, and the pro-Austrian attitude of the Queen and some of the Cabinet on the other. Chiefly by pressure on France, Britain helped to make possible between May and October 1860 the success of Garibaldi's expedition to Sicily and Naples, which enabled Cavour, the Piedmontese Prime Minister, to unite almost the whole Italian peninsula into one Kingdom. From 1861 to 1865 the Ministry had to deal with the dangerous situation created by the American Civil War. In the early stages of the war Britain nearly became involved on the side of the South, first by reacting too violently to the seizure by the North of the British ship *Trent*, carrying envoys from the South to Britain, secondly by allowing the *Florida* and the *Alabama* to be built on Merseyside for service as privateers on behalf of the South. But the Cabinet succeeded in its intention to remain neutral. Attempts to assist by diplomatic action the Poles' revolt against the Russians in 1863, and Denmark against Austria and Prussia in the war of 1864, failed completely.

In 1861 Prince Albert died, and the Queen became for some years a recluse. She remained, however, a shrewd, persistent and opinionated adviser and critic of her Governments, especially on foreign questions.

At the age of 80 Palmerston won an increased majority at the General Election of 1865, but before meeting the new Parliament he died. He was succeeded by Russell, since 1861 an Earl. Gladstone became Leader in the Commons, Clarendon Foreign Secretary. The Government proposed a Parliamentary Reform Bill, was defeated in June 1866 and resigned. Derby formed his third Ministry, in which Disraeli again held his old offices. The great achievement of this Administration was to pass the Second Reform Act in 1867. In February 1868 Derby retired, and Disraeli became Prime Minister. A General Election increased the Liberal majority, and in December Disraeli gave way to Gladstone as Prime Minister.

13

The High Victorian Economy

IF we take the period 1842 to 1873, the natural division in economic history, we can better appreciate the full extent of high Victorian 'growth'. Between those dates the volume of British exports rose by 350 per cent, about 11 per cent a year, as compared with 7 per cent a year from 1816 to 1842. The United States and the advanced countries of the Continent were making great industrial progress, but in the early 'seventies Britain still possessed two-thirds of the world's capacity for cotton factory production and accounted for half the world's output of coal and iron. It was a degree of pre-eminence no country matches today.

Population was growing as fast as before, and the manner of its continuing redistribution remained much the same. Three shifts of emphasis reflected important economic changes. First, as mechanization proceeded further, the woollen industry was noticeably more prosperous. Between 1851 and 1871 exports of woollen manufacture doubled, and imports of raw material from Australia and New Zealand increased four times. Hence Bradford joined the list of British towns with more than 100,000 inhabitants. Secondly, the iron industry continued to grow fast. Whereas in the previous period it was in Scottish ironfields that the greatest increase of output occurred, now it was in those of the far North of England: Cumberland and North Lancashire, Durham and the North Riding of Yorkshire. From these years date the boom-towns of Barrow-in-Furness and Middlesbrough. In 1856 the Bessemer process was invented, and steel production made much cheaper. Thirdly, the most obvious movement revealed by the figures of urban population increase is that to the ports. Not only did the growth of London become more rapid again, but five ports reached 100,000 inhabitants in this period: Dundee, with a large jute industry; Newcastle-upon-Tyne, port for the ironfields and coalfields of Tyneside, and also a centre of the chemical industry; Hull, now the third port of Britain after London and Liverpool, with Yorkshire industry behind it and with its own fishing fleet; and the naval ports of Portsmouth and Plymouth, marking the replacement of wooden by an iron navy. Two other towns attained this size by 1871: Salford, effectively part of one conurbation with Manchester, and Stoke-on-Trent, capital of the pottery industry and centre of the coal and iron district of Staffordshire.

After 1851 the absolute number of persons employed in agriculture declined. So, paradoxically, did the labour force of the textile industries, as machines displaced men. The notable increases were registered in mining, metalwork and transport. That in metalwork reflects the development of the engineering and machine-tool industries, essential accessories of general mechanization.

Growing ports, and an increasing labour force concerned with transport, point to the fact that this was a period of great development in railways and in shipping. The length of railway open in Britain in 1868 was twice that in 1850, and still the greatest of any country in Europe. Between the same years receipts from passenger traffic nearly trebled, receipts from goods traffic more than trebled. Railway towns, such as Crewe, were built. During this period the canals lost the bulk of their custom to the railways. Producers of perishable goods benefited particularly. It was the railways which made it worthwhile to expand the North Sea fishing fleets, since their catch could now be delivered fresh to distant cities. In general, towns could derive food supplies from further away than before. Hence, partly, London could resume more rapid growth, and hence, partly, agriculture flourished. Seaside holidays became more common: Brighton, Southport, Torquay and Margate were growing fast. The continuing development of railways contributed to unify the country further. An outward and visible sign of this process was the standardization of building materials. Local stone or brick, slate or tile ceased to impress their character on a district. Everywhere now, there were cheap and nasty bricks to be had; and everywhere a little money and a little taste, good or bad, could diversify stark red bricks with bright blue bricks and harsh white bricks, and so on.

More remarkable was the growth of British shipping. Between Waterloo and 1837 the tonnage of British shipping remained almost the same, about 2¼ million. Over that period earnings from shipping increased in real terms, but not in absolute terms. Britain retained her primacy in the sense that she still had the largest merchant fleet in the world. But the United States' was superior in quality and catching up in tonnage. From the late 'thirties the British marine grew absolutely, and from the 'sixties even relatively to other nations'. Its tonnage of sailing ships more than doubled between 1837 and 1865 – the peak, at almost 5,000,000. Steam tonnage increased twelve times, though as yet to less than 1,000,000. Shipping earnings increased about four times over the same period. How important this growth was will be evident from the fact that these earnings were the largest item in Britain's invisible trade until the 'seventies, when interest on foreign investment came to rival them, and that they roughly equalled in amount the surplus on the balance of payments. The growth of Britain's merchant fleet was associated with a large expansion of British shipbuilding. Britain became dominant in the construction of iron ships especially. In the 1820s about 80,000 tons altogether were built each year in the United Kingdom; in the 1830s an average of 100,000; in the 1840s 130,000; in the 1850s 210,000; in the 1860s 310,000. By the late 'sixties about half the sailing ships and almost all the steamships were iron ships. Much of this construction was carried out on Clydeside, and by this time the industry used larger concentrations of workpeople than any other. It was investment in ships and railways, including railways overseas, which maintained the high rate of capital formation first achieved in the previous period. A principal benefit arising was a lowering of transport costs generally.

Between 1850 and 1868 the fluctuations of the economy were less wild than previously. There were exceptionally high food prices in 1853-4, partly because of bad harvests, partly because the Crimean War cut off Russian supplies of corn. The cotton famine, caused by the American Civil War, led to great hardship in Lancashire from 1862-5. There were commercial crises in 1857 and 1866. But there was nothing like the accumulation of calamities of 1837-42 in Britain or 1845-9 in Ireland. Prices in general rose, by about 20-30 per cent from the low point of

1851 – the only break in the secular fall from 1815 to 1896. There is a consensus that conditions improved for the working classes. However, although the volume of exports was rising so quickly, real national income and real national income per capita increased at much the same rate as before. It is believed, then, that the gains were better distributed in this period. Average real wages rose slightly, because the number of people employed in the more highly-paid occupations was growing more rapidly than the population.[1] It was a very great benefit to the poor that Free Trade policies reduced the cost of food and also steadied the fluctuations in food prices. Much more marked, though, was the advance of the middle classes, which will be discussed in the Conclusion.

Investment, especially domestic, was made safer by the Acts of 1855, 1856 and 1862 providing for the registration of companies and the easy adoption of 'limited liability', previously available only in special cases. However, it was to be remarkable for a long time yet how small were British firms by comparison with the great American combines and German trusts. The Stock Exchange continued to be chiefly concerned with government stocks, foreign and British, and railway shares of all countries, rather than with industrial securities. But all the same there was a marked increase in the number of public and limited liability companies, and in the number of shareholders. This development of course carried one stage further the capitalist division between owners and workers, making a new separation between shareholders and managers. The operation of the Bank Charter Act, by slowly reducing the number of provincial note-issuing banks, was increasing the control of the Bank of England over the currency, thus contributing further to the security of investment. Banking facilities were of course being extended to meet growing demand.

At some point the question must be put: how were these spectacular rates of growth maintained? The obvious answer would be: by scientific and technological discovery, in which Britain's pre-eminence was exalted in the Great Exhibition of 1851. But this would be correct only to a certain extent and in a special way. First, it must be realized that there were exceedingly few scientists and not very many technologists in any

---

[1] Cf. pp. 196–7.

professional sense. As for scientists, there was a growing but small group of theoreticians and experimenters, some of whom were associated with an old University, more likely Cambridge than Oxford, but more with London University or some other London technical institution. The most famous of these men in the field of the physical sciences was Michael Faraday, who made great advances in the study of electromagnetism. Faraday was essentially an experimenter; his ideas were put into mathematical form by James Clerk Maxwell, who also contributed much to thermodynamics and other areas of physics. But there was no scientific course for undergraduates at either old University until 1850, though Cambridge was strong in mathematics. Moreover, the need was not as yet apparent for large-scale scientific study, undertaken for itself but nonetheless with a view to making possible technological change in the long run. Nor was there much recognition of a need for technological courses at a University level. There was a lot of technical education to be had at a modest level. But what was being trained, and what at this stage was most obviously required, was a body of skilled workmen and practical engineers capable of making comparatively small improvements not generally calling in aid any deep theoretical knowledge. The potentialities for this sort of change that were inherent in the general process of applying steam power and coal heating to a variety of industries, or in making iron a better substitute for wood in building, or in improving machine-tools, were enormous. This approach was dangerously empirical and untheoretical in relation to future developments, but it served very well for the period. There could still be vast developments in chemical industry without synthesis of artificial materials – though they were just beginning to matter, with superphosphates being manufactured for manure and aniline substitutes for natural dyes. There was no call yet for the commercial use of electricity, no thought of atomic power.

Further, a good part of the growth was not directly due to any improvement or discovery of this kind. Population was increasing very rapidly in most parts of the world, providing a largely unexploited market. Some regions remained to be explored, and their inhabitants exposed to Western civilization. The first of the United States West of the Mississippi date from the 1840s; China was being brutally 'opened up' to British

trade from around 1840; large parts of Africa were still un-
visited by white men. Railways and steamships combined with
the expansion of the market to lower costs, regardless of technological development in industry. Both forms of transport were
not only faster for each journey, they made possible many more
journeys. With the telegraph, first used commercially in 1844
and brought into wide use in this period, not only was the pace
of diplomacy quickened to the point of loss of dignity, but trade
and investment became far less of a gamble. The Atlantic
cable was at last laid in 1866. Knowledge of the rest of the world
increased rapidly and immensely.

It is important to appreciate that nineteenth-century
economic growth proceeded under different conditions and
assumptions from those of the twentieth century, especially in
Britain. World trade since 1914 has grown less fast than world
production. The greatest modern economies concentrate on
production for the domestic market, and insulate themselves
from the economies of other countries. International travel and
contact is physically easier and more common now than a
century ago, but governments exercise stricter control over it.
Passports and currency restrictions were barely known in the
nineteenth century. Emigration was absolutely much greater
then than now. There was something near to a world economy
operating from the mid-nineteenth century, presided over by
Britain, with sterling as its currency and London as its capital.
In this climate Karl Marx, seeing the world becoming ever more
homogeneous, discounted the power of nationalism. Even
Giuseppe Mazzini, the prophet of Italian unification, like
Marx an exile in England, saw nationalism as tending towards
international co-operation. World trade was growing substantially faster than world production from 1815 to 1885. 'Trade
was an "engine of growth" in the nineteenth century . . ., a
means whereby a vigorous process of economic growth came to
be transmitted from the centre to the outlying areas of the
world.'[1] Alfred Marshall could write in 1890: 'The dominant
economic fact of our own age is the development not of the
manufacturing but of the transport industries.'

Against this background the significance of the Free Trade
policy becomes clearer. In opting for it, Britain not only placed

---

[1] R. Nurkse, *Patterns of Trade and Development* (Oxford, 1962), p. 14.

agriculture behind industry in importance, in the last analysis she placed industry behind trade. This did not at first harm British agriculture. American grain was not yet available cheaply enough and in sufficient quantity to make British arable farming largely unprofitable; there was an overall shortage of grain in Europe. Though imports of grain and other food rose, heavy investment in drainage and fertilizers, and some shift from arable to pasture, maintained, even increased, the prosperity of British farming in the 1850s and 1860s. As for British industry, in 1846 and until the 1870s it could for almost all purposes ignore the competition of the rest of the world. The shipbuilding industry and the merchant marine apparently benefited from the loss of their protection. The silk industry was one of the few to suffer. It seemed unreasonable to hope for still more rapid development in cotton, coal and iron, making allowance for the distortions of wars. If exports could grow so fast, so much faster than production and national income, concentration of investment in transport, regardless of whether it was foreign or domestic, seemed natural. There was less reason than modern economists postulate to feel concern at the shortage of scientists and technologists, and at the small amount of capital flowing into industry, or to press for restrictions on the export of machinery and skilled workmen and on the import of goods competing with British products. Britain was most obviously 'the workshop of the world', but as importantly its universal carrier and banker. Free Trade had not been adopted out of pure calculation. It was for some a gamble, for some an ideal. But it was taken to be so successful in material terms that it became an economic dogma. In this period it was adopted even in some other countries. Men did not realize how unusual were the circumstances which made it such a spectacular success.

> The industrial revolution [had] happened to originate on a small island with a limited range of natural resources, at a time when synthetic materials were as yet unknown. In these circumstances economic expansion was transmitted to less developed areas by a steep and steady increase in Britain's demand for primary commodities which those areas were well suited to produce. Local factors of production overseas, whose growth may in part have been induced by trade, were thus largely absorbed by the expansion of profitable primary production for export. On top of this, the centre's increasing demand for raw materials and foodstuffs created incentives for capital and labour to move from the

centre to the outlying areas, accelerating the process of growth-trans-mission from the former to the latter.[1]

Britain's economy, then, was developing its late Victorian and early twentieth century characteristics: 'high specialization, a high import ratio, great dependence on manufactured exports, . . . diminishing dependence on indigenous raw materials and diminishing dependence on home food supplies'.

By 1870 the ratio of retained imports to net national income . . . had risen to about 28 per cent – a figure surpassed only for a short time in the 1880s. . . . The pattern of imports was changing. About 35 per cent of all imports were now food, of which grain was 9 per cent, and about 50 per cent raw materials; manufactures accounted for about 15 per cent. But . . . home agricultural produce accounted for about 82 per cent of total supplies of the main staple foodstuffs, and probably about three-quarters of the whole when allowance is made for imports of sugar and other tropical produce. Exports of textiles accounted for about 56 per cent of the whole; cotton now 35 per cent, wool 13 per cent. But exports of metals and metal manufactures were beginning to mount; now they represented 21 per cent of the whole. . . . Between 1851 and 1871 the proportion engaged in manufacturing . . . slightly de-clined, . . . while the proportion engaged in transport and commerce rose . . . [2]

These characteristics, which were to prove dangerous in a period of world wars, were in general appropriate to the age of the Pax Britannica.

---

[1] Nurkse, op. cit., p. 15.
[2] E. A. G. Robinson, 'The Changing Structure of the British Economy', *Economic Journal* 1954, p. 448.

14

Society and Politics
1850-1868

Governmental Action

'WE live in anti-reforming times', wrote Gladstone in 1860.[1] There is certainly a contrast between the heroic legislating of 1832–50 and the quiet consolidation of 1850–68. But there was no area in which the reforms of the previous period were not somewhat extended.

Law reform continued, though, as usual, the landmarks in the process are difficult to pick out. As for the police, at length it was made compulsory in 1856 for counties to establish forces, to be run with the aid of a grant of part of the cost from the central government, provided that inspectors declared them to be efficient. The building of prisons proceeded, and in 1865 they were placed under the more direct supervision of the Home Office instead of the local authorities. This was the period when the lawlessness of the early nineteenth century was effectively tamed. Although the range of indictable offences grew, as legislation invaded new fields, the number of trials in relation to population fell after the early 'sixties. In 1867 transportation, and in 1868 public executions, were abolished, marking a further stage in the advance of humanitarianism and civilization.

In Public Health legislation there was considerable development. It used to be thought that the lapse of the original General Board of Health in 1854 marked a withdrawal of central, or any, control, and that only the Public Health Act of 1875 restored the situation. In fact the work of the Board was

---

[1] Quoted in W. E. Williams, *The Rise of Gladstone to the Leadership of the Liberal Party, 1859–1868* (Cambridge, 1934), p. 35.

well continued after 1854 under a Committee of the Privy Council, and the extension of regulation proceeded up to the important Act of 1866, in which much that had previously been permissive became compulsory and additional powers were given to health boards. The Act of 1875, it emerges, was little more than a measure of consolidation. In 1853 vaccination was made compulsory. With all this activity mortality rates scarcely fell. It was presumably an achievement that they did not rise further.[1] In 1860 was passed the first significant measure directed against the adulteration of food.

Factory legislation was steadily widened also. The most important Act was one of 1867, covering all workshops employing more than fifty people and a large variety of named occupations. The Poor Law was significantly modified in 1865, when the pauper's need to have a parish of settlement in order to qualify for relief was abolished. The State's education grant rose to around £1,000,000 per annum as the purposes for which it could be given were extended.

Municipalities, too, slowly extended their sphere of operations. Seven towns owned their gas supply in 1850, 49 in 1870. Many more water companies than that were publicly owned, and there was a growing number of public libraries, baths, washhouses and parks. The greatest changes were being carried through in London, largely by the Metropolitan Board of Works, the first local authority for the Capital as a whole, set up in 1855. In the 'sixties the construction of the Victoria Embankment was in progress, reclaiming land from the Thames, at once improving the drainage, creating a thoroughfare and providing parks additional to those purchased in other parts of London. An Act of 1866 made it possible to preserve the remaining commons in the metropolitan area. The City of London, with Liverpool and Glasgow, was making small beginnings in compulsory slum clearance and the provision of model working-class dwellings. Local government expenditure per annum (excluding poor relief) rose, as more amenities were provided, by £8,000,000 between 1840 and 1870, of which £5,000,000 represented town improvements. The confusion of authorities increased almost as fast. After the Education Act of 1870 there were in England and Wales:

---

[1] See R. J. Lambert, *Sir John Simon* (London, 1963).

52 counties, 239 municipal boroughs, 70 Improvement Act districts; 1,006 urban sanitary districts, 41 port sanitary authorities, and 577 rural sanitary districts; 2,051 school board districts, 424 highway districts, 853 burial board districts, 649 unions, 194 lighting and watching districts, 14,946 poor law parishes, 5,064 highway parishes not included in urban or highway districts, and about 13,000 ecclesiastical parishes. The total number of local authorities who taxed the English taxpayer was 27,069, and they taxed him by means of 18 different kinds of rates.[1]

Further, they were elected or appointed in a variety of ways. Britain was a much-governed country by this time, but the administrative system was far from rational. Benthamite models had been applied in certain fields, but not over the whole area of government.

The Church of England lost during this period a few more of its privileges and powers as an Establishment. In 1857, after debates of inordinate length in which Gladstone spoke a hundred times against the measure, an Act was passed to make civil divorce a generally available process. In the same year jurisdiction over wills and marriages was withdrawn from the ecclesiastical courts. A magnificent series of legal battles over the making and levying of church rate in Braintree, in which over a period of sixteen years twenty-six judges and eight courts considered the question, four deciding one way and four the other, culminated in the judgment of the House of Lords in 1853 that, while it was a parish's duty to repair its church, a rate for that purpose could not be levied if opposed by a majority of the vestry. This made it almost impossible to impose church rates over most of the country. Finally, in 1868, the new alliance of Whigs, Liberals, Radicals, Irish and Nonconformists in the House of Commons, under the leadership of Gladstone, carried a Bill abolishing compulsory church rates, which the House of Lords accepted. The State asserted its dominance over the Church in ecclesiastical appointments also. With the exception of a few ardent supporters like Gladstone, the Oxford Movement, strong among the clergy, was unpopular among laymen inside and outside the Church, the more so as it became more ritualistic in this period. The Prime Ministers of the day, especially Palmerston, who was a relative and close friend of Shaftesbury, virtually debarred High Churchmen from preferment. The only gain made by clericalism in these years was the

---

[1] Quoted in Young and Handcock, *English Historical Documents, 1833–1874*, p. 615.

revival of Convocation, strictly of the two Convocations of Canterbury and York. These clerical assemblies had met only formally since 1717. Year by year through the 'fifties the meetings became less purely formal, and from 1861 both Convocations met regularly and transacted business. The achievement, however, was more symbolic than material.

At length the two ancient Universities were reformed, though most moderately. The Oxford Act was passed in 1854, the Cambridge Act in 1856. Practically all the teaching posts remained restricted to unmarried priests of the Church of England, but within this limit they were opened for competition. Dissenters were to be admitted to first degrees. These changes helped to make possible a notable improvement of standards, particularly at Balliol College, Oxford, and some broadening of the curriculum. In both Universities the establishment of courses in science was accompanied by the introduction of courses in Arts subjects other than classics and theology, such as philosophy and history.

In 1855 the Civil Service was partially reformed. The body of government servants was already clearly divided into Parliamentary and party-political on the one hand, and non-Parliamentary and non-partisan on the other. But it was as yet undecided that a Civil Servant must refrain from all public, as well as strictly political, advocacy: Chadwick was only one of many who have been called 'Statesmen in Disguise' since their activities included much public campaigning.[1] The body of government servants outside Parliament was ill-organized. It was not under the control of one authority. The pay was poor. There was little or no division of labour within each office. Many of the appointments were made by patronage. It could be said that 'Admission into the Civil Service is indeed eagerly sought after, but it is for the unambitious, and the indolent or incapable, that it is chiefly desired.'[2] The most effective and best-recruited group of government servants were technically not part of the central administration until 1858, namely the servants of the East India Company. There talent was genuinely sought, as witness the careers of James Mill, Macaulay and Grote, the historian of ancient Greece, but even so it was not

---

[1] See the article of this title by G. Kitson Clark in *Historical Journal* 1959.
[2] Quoted in G. A. Campbell, *The Civil Service in Britain* (London, 1955), pp. 29, 21.

until 1853 that the Company decided to restrict all its posts to successful competitors in written examinations.

Home government departments had improved in efficiency during the century. A Treasury circular of 1833 had boldly declared that 'My Lords deem it important that all offices under the Crown should be filled by persons competent to perform the duties of these situations.' Individual political heads had proved reformers, like Graham at the Admiralty. The great surviving sinecures had been abolished by the Whigs of the 'thirties. But general measures of reform were not officially proposed until 1853. In that year two Civil Servants, Northcote and Trevelyan, reported that the Service should be reformed in the following way: it should be placed under Treasury control, be recruited by competitive examination, be better paid and pensioned; promotion should be by merit, and the Service should be divided into administrative, executive and clerical grades, in order to separate the most from the least responsible duties. In 1855, under the stress of public indignation at the incompetence revealed during the Crimean War, the Government made some concessions. There were to be examinations for entry to all departments, run by a Civil Service Commission, but they were not to be fully competitive. Within the Cabinet Peelite concern for efficiency, inherited from Pitt and Liverpool, was largely overborne by Whig love of patronage.

Until the Second Reform Act of 1867, which will be treated later, constitutional change was slight. But a serious attempt was made to limit corrupt practices at elections in 1854, though without much success; practising Jews were admitted to the House of Commons in 1858; and in the same year the first and least important of the Chartists' demands was met, the abolition of the property qualification for M.P.s.

When Gladstone said that the times were against reform, he was in the midst of battles over finance. As Chancellor of the Exchequer from 1852–5 and from 1859–66, he fought to prevent war and defence expenditure stopping progress towards Free Trade. He won. In order to pay for the Crimean War without incurring large debts, he raised income tax to 1s. 2d. in the £. His successor took it to 1s. 4d. in 1855–6, the highest figure it reached between 1816 and 1915. In the Budgets of 1853 and 1860 Gladstone was able to reduce tariffs to the point that only 16 articles continued to make an important contribution to the revenue. The Budget of 1860 was associated with an Anglo-French commercial treaty, negotiated by Cobden, seen by both him and Gladstone as a contribution to peace as much as to Free Trade, under which British duties on French wines and French duties on British manufactures were reduced. One of Gladstone's proposals for 1860, the repeal of the paper duty, had to be deferred because of the opposition of the House of Lords, but was carried in 1861, the Commons denying the Lords a right to amend budgetary details. This completed the repeal of the 'taxes on knowledge'; the advertisement duty had gone in 1853, the stamp duty in 1855. In this field the shade of Peel continued to conquer.

Social Development
H. T. Buckle, in his *History of Civilization in England,* published in 1859, wrote: 'The whole scope and tendency of modern legislation is, to restore things to that natural channel from which the ignorance of preceding legislation has driven them.'[1] In the face of the achievements just surveyed and of those of the previous period, this claim seems preposterous. Buckle could make it, however, because public attention was concentrated on certain types of reform other than social legislation: those that increased the opportunities of Nonconformists and the middle classes and reduced the privileges of Anglicans and the aristocracy, destroyed anomalies, or freed trade and the Press. It no doubt helped that the cost of the changes, small in any case, was borne largely by local government agencies, and that the central administration withdrew from overt control of their work. Central government expenditure in this period rose, but almost wholly because of war and defence costs. Anyhow, even though false, it was a common belief in the mid-nineteenth century that *laissez-faire* had triumphed in social as well as economic matters. This view was important for the future, in discouraging new breaches in the principle. That it was widely held at this time is symptomatic of the overall weakening of the reforming drive of the 1830s and 1840s.

Other writers, while appreciating that not all recent legislation had tended to give the individual greater freedom, thought that it should have done. In 1851 Herbert Spencer published his

---

[1] Quoted in House, *The Dickens World,* p. 174.

Social Statics, exalting the rights of the individual against governmental interference of all kinds, claiming by way of supporting evidence that the whole tendency of the biological development of the human species is towards greater individuation. In 1859 J. S. Mill's *On Liberty*, though much readier to accept State action, mounted another criticism of Benthamite attitudes: urging that the individual ought not to be reckoned as just one of millions of persons with similar attributes and aims, whose 'greatest happiness' can be secured by legislation based on numerical calculations of the sum of pain and pleasure; rather, that exceptional individuals must be protected and cherished by the State against legal and social pressures to conformity; and that law is not of universal efficacy. The cult of the individual is especially characteristic of this period, but the ideas of Mill and Spencer exerted great influence from this time until at least the First World War.

These intellectual reactions were reinforced by a broad change of mood. Basic to the explanation of this change, and of the consequent slackening in the pace of reform, is the improvement, however modest, in the prosperity and security of the mass of the population. The heart of the change is this: the likelihood, and with it the fear, of revolution dwindled. No doubt they had been often exaggerated previously, but they had been a serious factor in political calculation since the 1790s. Now there suddenly seemed little reason for alarm.

Broadly, the middle classes had been won to the 'Establishment', or at least to faith in gradualism, by the reforms of the 1830s and 1840s. The solidarity of the special constables against the Chartist petitioners of 1848 was accepted as proof of the fact. In 1859, when an invasion panic led to the foundation of the 'Volunteer Movement', it was considered safe to allow all patriotic persons who could afford it to provide themselves with rifles.

Working-class radicalism had been much influenced by the Repeal of the Corn Law as well as by economic betterment. Plans for Grand National Unions, with generalized programmes, now gave way to steady pressure, by small unions of skilled workmen, for specific improvements in working conditions. Schemes for land nationalization developed into building societies. William Lovett turned from Chartist agitation to advocacy of popular education and self-improvement among the working classes. Reformers lamented in the 'fifties and early 'sixties that they could no longer arouse public enthusiasm. Here is Cobden in 1863:

> Bright's powers of eloquence . . . [have] been most unsparingly used since the repeal of the Corn Laws – now going on for nearly twenty years – in advocating financial economy and parliamentary reform, and in every possible way for the abatement of privilege and the elevation of the masses. If he could talk till doomsday he would never surpass the strains of eloquence with which he has expounded the right and demolished the wrong cause. Yet see with what absolute lack of success![1]

This change had been brought about partly by deliberate efforts on the part of the Church and the aristocracy, broadening their conception of social duty and submitting to measures contrary to their own immediate interest for the sake of social peace. Just as 'deference' is exceptionally conspicuous among the lower orders in these years, so is 'condescension' at the top of the social scale. The Queen for the first time visited industrial towns, Manchester in 1851 and Birmingham in 1858, finding the inhabitants gratifyingly loyal. Her domestic and private life, said an avowed democrat in 1860, was 'worthy of all praise'. From this time dates the monarchy's recovery of respect, as it abandoned power. Dukes expressed themselves honoured to become mayors of industrial towns. This is the highpoint of public aristocratic piety. Archbishops preached in the open air. 'Deference' to the aristocracy continued to be enforced as well as earned, by the use of 'influence' more or less 'legitimate': by careful selection of tenants in 'closed' villages, by lavish expenditure with tradesmen, and by entertainment of employees. The law of Master and Servant still gave large powers to employers to discipline their workmen. But there was a genuine rapprochement between classes in this period, based on acceptance of the established order of society, with the understanding that old privilege would not bar the way to all change, that the poor man in theory had an opportunity to become rich and great, and that a peer as well as a workman had to prove his title to public respect. Capitalists and labourers found common ground in the principle of 'self-help', extolled by Samuel Smiles in another of the famous books of 1859. The fact was glossed over that the aristocracy retained

---

[1] J. Morley, *The Life of Richard Cobden* (London, 1903), p. 881.

enormous social and political power and showed little dis-
position to share it, and that unskilled or unlucky workmen
remained at the mercy of the Poor Law.

Both rulers and ruled, then, saw their problems as less
desperate than before. The drastic proposals of Radicals commanded less sympathy. Minor rather than major reforms
were passed. Palmerston could even say 'We cannot go on
adding to the Statute Book *ad infinitum*.'[1] Events abroad,
intrinsically more interesting in this period, stole the stage
from domestic politics: Louis Napoleon's *coup d'état* and
imperialism; the Crimean War; the China War; the Mutiny;
war and revolution in Italy; and the American Civil War.

This generalized picture needs elaborating. First, in various
ways the 'Establishment', while reforming itself and adjusting
itself to change, was acquiring new strength. The history of
education best illustrates the point. Under 'the voluntary
system', the pet of Nonconformity, the Established Church in
fact extended its influence. Reform had made it more effective.
The number and quality of its clergy continued to increase.
In the third quarter of the nineteenth century it made the
largest absolute contribution in church building, though other
denominations made greater relative contributions. In educational provision it easily outstripped its rivals. Around 1860
the Church of England claimed about nine-tenths of the
elementary schools in the country and three-quarters of the
children, and of course the revival of interest in theology had
ensured that Church schools taught both more specific and
more varied doctrines by this time than they would have
done earlier in the century. The ancient Universities, reformed,
though with clergy still virtually monopolizing teaching posts,
deployed their prestige and endowments more effectively.
Their chief courses of study remained classics and mathematics,
but these were better taught than before, and now offered, it
was held with some reason, the best education available in the
country. The Civil Service Commission examined candidates
in their University subjects. It was the special emphasis of
Gladstone's arguments in favour of the recommendations of
the Northcote-Trevelyan report that competitive examination
would open the Civil Service to the best products of the old

---

[1] Quoted in E. L. Woodward, *The Age of Reform, 1815–1870* (Oxford, 1962),
p. 169.

public schools and Universities, humanely educated under Anglican guidance. Thus the gentlemanly, amateur tradition of British administration was perpetuated into a bureaucratic age, with these modifications, that future Civil Servants had to be better at classics than their predecessors, and that brilliant middle-class boys were allowed to qualify as gentlemen by competitive examination.

Similar tendencies are to be observed in the history of the public schools. In the early nineteenth century something corresponding to secondary education, preparing for the University, could be had either in one of a handful of schools properly called 'public', such as Eton, Harrow and Westminster, or in a large number of old grammar schools, or in new, often Dissenting, academies. The public schools, brutal, ill-organized, dominated by classical studies, were as anomalous as other parts of the Anglican, aristocratic 'Establishment', yet they were gaining in social prestige and drew boys from all over the country. The grammar schools, also Anglican, served their localities, had very variable standards and resources, and as a group were losing reputation. The academies, more modern in outlook, supplied some of the deficiencies of the traditional schools.

Classical teaching in the ancient public schools, as in the ancient Universities, was being improved from around 1800. Arnold, as Headmaster of Rugby from 1828 to 1842, provided a model for a more fundamental transformation of these schools. He improved both discipline and teaching, using the senior boys as prefects and treating them as mature students in the Sixth Form. He also placed the Chapel at the centre of the life of the school, claiming that it was with the formation of a manly and godly Christian character rather than with academic success that he was primarily concerned. This example and ideal inspired the foundation of many new schools, and the remodelling of many existing schools, which annexed the title 'public': Liverpool College in 1840, Cheltenham 1841, Eltham 1842, Marlborough 1843, Rossall 1844, Radley 1847, Lancing 1848, Bradfield 1850, Wellington College and Epsom 1853, Clifton and Haileybury 1862, and so on. The case of Liverpool College is interesting as being early and urban. The occasion of the movement to found the school was an attempt by the new Corporation elected under the Municipal Reform Act to support

10 Steep Street, Bristol. A photograph taken in the 1860s of a street that was
the main road to Gloucester until 1871. The signs depict climbing boys, still
employed to sweep chimneys until at least 1875.

11 A Trade Union Membership Certificate, 1852.

undenominational education. A demand arose for the establishment of a school which would not expose 'the children of the middle classes . . . to the risk of imbibing latitudinarian, if not infidel opinions'. 'Sound religion' must be associated with 'useful learning.' Mere 'instruction', especially in science, must not be accepted as true 'education'.[1] The same arguments appear in almost all instances.

In these schools as in the old Universities, religion, and particularly Anglicanism, triumphed over secularism, and classics over science. The production of gentlemen, not of scholars or of entrepreneurs, remained the aim. The Oxford Movement, successful only to a limited extent within the Church, won a great victory in education. Most schools, it is true, were not Anglo-Catholic, but they were Anglican, more specifically so than Arnold wanted. By the end of this period Dissenting academies scarcely existed, and wealthy Nonconformists were sending their children to Anglican public schools. There had been some attempt made to found Nonconformist public schools, for example Taunton in 1847 and Bishop's Stortford in 1868, an endeavour which illustrates the pervasiveness of an ideal of primarily Anglican inspiration.

The public school movement had important effects on social relationships. It was the extension of an aristocratic system to the upper middle classes, but only after that system had been purified. As by the Reform Act and Civil Service Reform, the élite was extended and the old 'Establishment' made some concessions, winning wider approval in the process. Further, in all these instances the chances of the less prosperous would seem to have been reduced. A growing proportion of the upper classes declined to educate their sons locally. Without their support the cheap local grammar schools withered away like the Dissenting academies. In the classic case of a refoundation, the Headmaster of Uppingham, Edward Thring, finally removed his school from the town, although it had been nothing more than the local grammar school when he first took the post, because the sanitation was inadequate. The inhabitants improved the drainage. In return they received back the opportunities for trade and employment which the school's, the masters' and the boys' money provided. But

---

[1] D. Wainwright, *Liverpool Gentlemen* (London, 1960).

Uppingham School no longer educated the children of the town.

Most public schools were boarding schools. Soon after their foundation, often in spite of their founders, organized games came to overshadow for many of the boys and for some of the teachers the academic side of their education, and also to receive undue recognition as character-building agencies on a level with the Chapel and religion. This development emerged strongly in Thomas Hughes' *Tom Brown's Schooldays*, published in 1858. As Professor Briggs says, 'Although Hughes exaggerated in reading back a cult of games into his days at Rugby, he did not exaggerate the trend in many of the new and some of the old public schools.'[1] The codification in 1846 of the rules of football as played at Rugby was an earlier landmark. Traditional disorder and violence were tamed, to be replaced by organized competition, elevated into a cult.

This was a phenomenon not confined to the public schools. Such violent or traditional sports as remained legal were moderated into respectability. Lord George Bentinck cleaned up racing scandals in the late 'forties. The Queensberry Rules for boxing date from 1867, seven years after the last, legendary, illegal prize-fight. Other games acquired codes and networks of clubs and national controlling bodies. The first All-England Cricket XI dates from 1846, the first M.C.C. overseas cricket tour from 1858, though so little had the Empire grown that the destination was the United States and Canada. The traditional association of the game with betting was frowned on. The status of the amateur, that is, the gentleman, was glorified. Batsmen came to be admired for the beauty of their style rather than the strength of their arms. The Oxford and Cambridge Boat Race, first rowed in 1829, became an annual event from 1856. The first association football clubs for adults date from 1858; athletics appeared at Oxford in 1850; the Open Golf Championship was first played in 1861; croquet was introduced in the early 'fifties, and the All-England Club was established in 1868. A telling illustration of the change of attitude to sport is the following comparison. Here is the inscription on a tombstone in the churchyard at Cranbrook, for a man called Clark, who died in 1836: 'He was

---

[1] A. Briggs, *Victorian People* (London, 1954), p. 162.

one of the few enterprising travellers who have succeeded in ascending to the summit of Mont Blanc.' Here is an account of Huxley and Tyndall, climbing with the Alpine Club in 1857, the year of its foundation:

> We were about to try our strength under unknown conditions, and as the various possibilities of the enterprise crowded upon the imagination, a sense of responsibility for the moment oppressed me. But as I looked aloft, my heart lightened, and I remarked cheerily to Hirst that Nature seemed to smile upon our work. 'Yes,' he replied, 'and, God willing, we shall accomplish it.'[1]

Sport has become earnest, not to say religious and spiritual. Spontaneity and heedlessness have gone. So Victorian Britain disciplined herself.

In many particular ways society was becoming more complex, more technical and so in a sense more civilized. Trams first appeared in 1860 in Birkenhead, the underground railway in London in 1863. Modern hotel life began with the great railway hotels. In the 1850s the Singer sewing-machine company pioneered hire purchase and (with W. H. Smith's railway bookstalls) multiple shops. Department stores in Britain stem from the foundation of the middle-class co-operative enterprises, the Civil Service Stores in 1864, the Army and Navy in 1871. Not only Civil Service examinations, but many other kinds of examination were started. The College of Preceptors, a body awarding certificates on the results of examinations, was founded in the 1840s; Oxford established Local Examinations for schoolboys in 1857, Cambridge in 1858. The most important landmark in the development of the professions over those years was the creation by statute in 1858 of the General Medical Council and the register of qualified practitioners.

I have represented this period so far as one of ordered development, consensus, moderation, even conservatism, a time of increasing social discipline when the 'Establishment' grew in strength. Certainly, the area as well as the violence of dispute seems diminished by comparison with the 'forties. But there were fundamental critics and opponents of the *status quo*, who asserted themselves during the 'sixties, especially after the death of Palmerston in 1865.

---

[1] Quoted in N. Annan, *Leslie Stephen.*

To set against Buckle, Spencer and the individualists, there were more upper-class sympathizers with socialism than before. A group of Anglican clergy, led by F. D. Maurice, calling themselves Christian Socialists, began in 1848 to make a serious effort to associate the Church with the aspirations of working men for social reforms. They worked for causes such as sanitary reform and 'co-operation', that is, in its less idealistic form, profit-sharing between consumers and producers. Dickens' *Hard Times* (1854), among other things, is an attack on the crude doctrine of *laissez-faire*. John Ruskin, with *The Political Economy of Art* (1857) and *Unto This Last* (1860), developed the tradition of Pugin, linking admiration for medieval architecture and society with condemnation of Victorian technology and materialism. Mill himself, with all his concern for the individual's intellectual and moral freedom, believed, as has been seen, that the distribution of goods should be made more equal by the State.

Working-class activity was much less violent, political and Utopian than in the days of the Chartists. It was therefore the better calculated to impress many members of the 'Establishment'. In some industries skilled workers succeeded in creating Trade Unions of a new character, embracing members from all over the country, run by a national organization based in London and boasting considerable funds; not so wide and visionary as the ephemeral Grand National Union of the 1830s, but larger and better-managed than any previous Unions which had achieved a measure of permanence. The chief exemplar of this type of Unionism was the Amalgamated Society of Engineers, founded in 1851. This and similar bodies concerned themselves to some extent with general politics, especially in this period with foreign affairs, particularly the American Civil War. But they campaigned also for improved working conditions and the relaxation of the law of Master and Servant. In 1866–7 they were prominent in the agitation for Parliamentary Reform, in alliance with the more radical Liberals. They are the principal illustration of the growing strength and power of the 'labour aristocracy', which increased much more rapidly in these years than the population as a whole.

Between 1851 and 1871 the number of 'engine makers' in the census returns more than doubled, the number of 'shipwrights' almost doubled,

while the 'puddlers, forgers and moulders' engaged in the iron industries rose from 80,000 to 180,000. The 29,000 'railway servants', exclusive of labourers, became 84,000 in an industry which offered comparatively secure and regular employment. In these years... the title 'artisan'
and 'workingman' took on the specific meaning of 'skilled, respectable
workingman' to differentiate its holder from the more casually employed, unskilled 'labourer'. The number of respectable tradesmen
was also swelled by the increase in those occupations which ministered
to a prosperous consumer society: 'plumbers, painters and glaziers'
increased from 62,805 to 103,382, while 'cabinet makers and uphol-
sterers' and 'printers' both nearly doubled.[1]

In 1867 the development of these unions was threatened by a
decision of the courts. In *Hornby v. Close* it was declared, contrary to what had been supposed, that Union funds were not
protected by law against the default of officials, the judge
asserting that Unions were still illegal. During the next period
they had to renew efforts to achieve recognition.

Nonconformity seemed to have been tamed during the
'fifties, and Methodism was divided and in decline. No doubt
the Low Church policy of the Government had helped to
calm Dissent. But during the 'sixties widespread revival
movements were associated with a return to militancy. This
kind of movement is in its nature difficult to describe adequately. Here it is possible only to mention certain landmarks
in the story and to give a general appraisal. The Liberation
Society intensified its agitation in the middle 'fifties. It now
had the unequivocal support of Congregationalists, who
positively refused all State aid and became the core of Voluntaryism. In 1853 the United Kingdom Alliance was formed
as a national temperance organization. The campaign against
drunkenness was a vital aspect of evangelism in the nineteenth
century. The Primitive Methodists, the largest of the dissident
Methodist groups, were especially strict on this question.
The Alliance and the Liberation Society demanded pledges
from candidates at Parliamentary elections, with growing
success in the 'sixties. In the late 'fifties C. H. Spurgeon, whose
chief ties were with the Baptists, began to draw thousands to
hear his sermons at the Surrey Gardens and Exeter Hall in
London. The beginning of the great revivals, affecting most
denominations, is dated to 1859. Their most striking results were
achieved in Wales, where resentment against the dominance

---

[1] F. B. Smith, *The Making of the Second Reform Bill* (Cambridge, 1966), pp. 8–9.

of an alien aristocracy and an alien church was enhanced and exploited by missionary activity, by a growing Welsh-language Press and by the Liberation Society. From 1864 a National Association in Ireland agitated for the disestablishment of the Anglican Church there. The National Education League was founded in Birmingham in 1868 to bring together those, including some Nonconformists, who had begun to work for free, unsectarian, universal primary education. Altogether, these new organizations and this increased revivalist activity represented a large extension of Dissent and its aims. Much of the work was based in the provinces. In so far as it was associated with a political party, it was with the Liberals.

These developments were related to the growth of the Press, especially in the provinces. By 1868 fourteen provincial towns in England possessed daily newspapers, most of them Liberal in tendency. The authority of *The Times* was reduced as other and cheaper London dailies, principally the *Daily Telegraph* and the *Standard*, won wider if less distinguished circulations. The repeal of the 'taxes on knowledge' made this change possible.

Another fundamentally critical movement which had its origins in this period deserves notice here, although as yet it was of very limited scope. In 1848 Queen's College, London, was established, the first specific effort to remedy the deficiencies of educational provision for women. F. D. Maurice was the Principal. In 1853 the example was followed at Cheltenham Ladies' College. Five years later the foundation of *The Englishwoman's Journal* inaugurated the organized feminist movement, concerned with women's rights. In 1865 Elizabeth Garrett Anderson, having become thoroughly qualified medically as far as examinations were concerned, induced the Society of Apothecaries to enable her to practise as a doctor, the first woman to do so in Britain on a professional basis.

Parliamentary Politics and the Second Reform Act
By comparison with the previous and still more with the subsequent period, the years between 1850 and 1868 knew a weak party system. Not only were the main parties ill-disciplined and at times divided, but until 1859 there existed two additional parties, the Peelites and an independent Irish party. This latter group broke away from alliance with the

Liberals after Russell made his Protestant stand in 1850, and worked for land legislation giving more rights to tenants; it sometimes numbered 50 M.P.s. From 1851 to 1859 leadership of the Liberals was disputed between Russell and Palmerston, and from 1866 to 1868 the party was split over Parliamentary reform. Disraeli was at no time during this period secure as deputy to Derby. The Governments of these years were all weak in Parliament. Four of them, Russell's first and Derby's three, had only minority support at best. Further, on only one occasion, in 1868, was a Ministry unequivocally brought down by a General Election. In all other changes of government the House of Commons had a large part. The most resounding crash was that of the apparently powerful coalition of 1852-5, placed in a minority by more than 150. This was in time of war, and no attempt was made to consult the electorate in this case. But it was striking how regularly M.P.s reacted against the verdict of Elections. In 1858 and 1866 Cabinets with a paper majority were turned out shortly after the electorate had increased their nominal strength. In 1852 and 1859 the Conservatives, defeated in the Commons, won seats at an Election, but not enough to give them a majority. It appeared that the independence of M.P.s was restored against both Ministers and voters, and in some cases the activity required of the monarch in the search for a substitute Government recalled the days of George III.

It would not be right, though, to suggest that the party system had broken down completely. The very persistence of the Peelites in keeping themselves separate from the major parties testifies to the value placed on political consistency. In the great division of 1859 which brought Palmerston to power 637 out of 654 M.P.s took part, and there was little cross-voting. Protectionists and Liberals, despite many attempts to detach individuals, always declined to collaborate with one another. Even those who made a point of calling themselves 'Liberal-Conservative', which was a title used by others than Peelites, were seldom inconstant voters. The true 'non-party' man is hard to find. Although there were some who rejoiced at the decline of party, the great majority of those who had to take the decisions acted in accordance with the conventions built up in the previous period. The Queen and the Prince maintained their constitutional resolves: she always first applied, after the resignation of a Government, to a leader of the largest Opposition party.

Loose and confused parties obviously go with weak Governments and little legislation. The historian would like to be able to decide which caused which, or what caused all. The following explanation seems at any rate plausible. At least before the days of strong national party organizations, strong enough to make it politically suicidal for an M.P. to be disloyal, party solidarity and a clear two-party division can only be maintained for long by widespread feeling on what are conceived to be vital issues. The split of 1845–6 took place on such a question, but Protectionism was soon 'dead and damned'. Nothing came to replace it, except matters of foreign policy, which were all ephemeral, unlike the wars of 1793–1815, which had fostered new party divisions of long standing. The number of contests at General Elections fell to a low point in 1859. It is the change of mood of the late 'forties which is decisive. The majority of the influential public, with the Church question and Free Trade both dormant issues, was interested only in small and tentative domestic changes, and concerned instead with the defence and promotion of British interests in the world at large. Some measure of Parliamentary order could be preserved, but no strong discipline, until the appearance of a new alignment of public feeling in 1868.

Palmerston was the beneficiary of this attitude. He did not in all respects embody it. He was a consistent advocate of the unpopular French alliance, which twice, in 1851 and 1858, enabled his Parliamentary enemies to humble him. He was a vigorous reformer in the field of Public Health, as he showed during his tenure of the Home Office from 1852–5. But he was justly identified with the assertion of British interests abroad. After his eclipse in 1851–2, events worked in his favour. Russell had ostentatiously taken up the causes of Free Trade, Protestantism and Parliamentary reform. The first two were popular enough, but Russell soon lost any special property in them; the third attracted little support until 1866. During the Aberdeen Ministry Russell was, officially, the more involved with foreign affairs: he was even for a short time Foreign Secretary. When Palmerston resigned at the end of 1853, it was ostensibly in opposition to Parliamentary reform. But the impression was created that it was Palmerston who was the true advocate in the Cabinet of a strong line against Russia, and the man to win the Crimean War, while Russell, by fussing continually about his status in the Government, by abandoning it at the height of the war and by failing to obtain Austrian assistance on a mission to Vienna after the fall of Aberdeen, discredited himself with both the public and his colleagues. During the negotiations which led to the formation of Palmerston's Ministry in 1855 the Queen gave Russell the opportunity to try to form a Government, in order to show him how low his standing now was. Only Palmerston would serve under him. It was therefore natural that in 1859 Russell should take second place. Palmerston's nine years as Prime Minister, briefly interrupted, resemble Liverpool's liberal phase. He preserved himself, generally, from defeat by the Lords or by the conservatives of all parties in the House of Commons, because he was clearly more conservative on Parliamentary reform than any likely alternative Liberal, perhaps (after 1859) than the official Conservatives. He maintained Radical support, generally, by allowing the passage of minor reforms, by permitting the extension of Free Trade and by liberalism in foreign policy. In spirit Palmerston was a Canningite to the end.

As with the death of Liverpool, the death of Palmerston broke up parties, and in the subsequent confusion proposals for fundamental reform were found attractive by public and politicians alike. As in the 'thirties, a bout of major legislation was introduced by the passage of a Parliamentary Reform Act. Historians have lately expended much effort in trying to explain this event.[1]

The problem, of course, is of a different order from that of the causes of the First Reform Act. No doubt, in the very long run, given the continuing advance of industrialization and the development of mass-communications, Parliamentary

---

[1] The best single account is in F. B. Smith, already cited. M. J. Cowling, *1867: Disraeli, Gladstone and Revolution* (Cambridge, 1967) subtly modifies Smith's picture. R. Blake, *Disraeli* (London, 1966) and P. Smith, *Disraelian Conservatism and Social Reform* (London, 1967) complete a body of testimony which makes it impossible to accept G. Himmelfarb's view, expressed in *Journal of British Studies* 1966, that Tory Democracy was a consistent and developed creed at this time.

Briggs, *Victorian People*, chs, VIII–X, is still useful. On the development of opinion, see J. R. Vincent, *The Formation of the Liberal Party, 1857–68* (Cambridge, 1966) and R. Harrison, *Before the Socialists* (London, 1965). On Gladstone, W. E. Williams, already cited.

reform, culminating in democracy, was certain to come in
Britain. But the first step had been exceedingly difficult to take.
Once one Reform Act had been passed, however, it was bound
to be followed up in the comparatively short run, and with less
travail. It was scarcely possible after 1832 to rebut the argument
that the growth of new towns and the decay of old required
further modifications to be made in the system of representation. The franchise qualifications remained too arbitrary to be
easily defended.

In 1851 Russell became the first Front Bench politician to
take up again the cause of Parliamentary reform, proposing a
very modest enfranchisement. In raising the question he of
course hoped for political advantage for the Liberals. But little
accrued at first. The existing electorate and the existing
Members were on the whole content with the privileges they
had. Only three years after the last grand Chartist demonstration, Reform aroused slight interest among the intended
beneficiaries and the public at large. The issue became a
plaything of Parliamentary politics, something which a
Government could scarcely avoid bringing up, but which,
once the House was confronted with it, produced a line-up
of forces sufficient to defeat the proposal. Of the first five
ministerial Bills of the period, all very moderate, three were
dropped in the face of opposition and apathy (1852, 1854,
1860), and two were defeated in the House (1859, 1866).
After 1851 the next landmark in the story was the conversion
of the Conservatives to further Reform. But at their first
attempt to legislate, in 1859, they failed to win enough Radical
support to counterbalance the opposition of some Conservatives and Whigs.

Russell's very moderate Bill of 1866 alienated the conservative Whigs, the 'Adullamites', led by Robert Lowe, a
virulent and doctrinaire critic of any approach to democracy.
There appeared, as usual, to be a majority in the Commons
against Reform. The Derby Administration, formed after
Russell resigned, was composed of politicians who had helped
to defeat the 1866 Bill, and was in a decided minority. Yet
by August 1867 Disraeli had carried a much more Radical
Bill than Russell's, or than any of those so far proposed by
Governments.

These were the main provisions of the Act and of the

measures for Scotland and Ireland passed in 1868. The important enfranchisement was of all borough householders, whether owners or not, in England, Wales and Scotland, who paid their own rates. This provision largely explains why the Acts added nearly a million to the electorate, mostly in the large towns. There was some lowering of qualifications in the counties, which increased their electorate by about 250,000 votes. As for the redistribution clauses, 52 seats were taken from English and Welsh boroughs, and one seat from the Scottish counties; 28 county seats were created, 22 borough seats, and 3 University seats. A number of changes were made in constituency boundaries, with a view to separating urban from rural areas, as this was supposed to be to the advantage of the Conservatives. A clause which has aroused much interest provided that in three-member constituencies, of which there were 12 (7 counties and 5 boroughs), a voter might vote for only 2 candidates, and in the City of London, which had 4 Members, for only 3. The intention was to give representation to the minority party. The Act for Ireland made almost no difference. A special Act passed in 1850 had somewhat extended the franchise there, but it was still after 1868 narrower than it had been before 1829.

At a high Parliamentary level the story of the 1867 Bill's passage is excessively complex. These seem to be the decisive moments. First it had to be decided that the Conservatives should bring in a Bill at all. Disraeli himself had doubts, but Derby and the Queen and most other politicians were clear that the question must be settled, or Parliament would discredit itself, the Conservatives be ruined and the people roused. Secondly, the nature of the Government's Bill had to be determined. The Cabinet after long debate was prevailed upon to accept 'household suffrage, coupled with plurality of voting.' All the Reform Bills of this period embodied some sort of 'plurality of voting', giving more votes than one to persons with degrees or considerable shareholdings or sizable Savings Bank accounts. This kind of 'safeguard' against the 'rule of numbers' was very popular with the governing classes as well as with Radicals like J. S. Mill.[1] At the last moment the Cabinet reversed its decision, and so a weak Bill was outlined to the

---

[1] J. H. Burns, 'J. S. Mill and Democracy', *Political Studies* 1957.

Commons late in February 1867. It aroused such objections that Derby reverted to the bolder plan, although it cost three resignations from the Cabinet. A 'comprehensive' measure was introduced in mid-March. Thirdly, over the next four months the Bill was drastically altered in the House of Commons, so that the safeguards against household suffrage nearly disappeared. The greatest single change was Hodgkinson's amendment, unexpectedly accepted by Disraeli on 18 May, enfranchising many of the 'compound householders', tenants whose rates had been paid by their landlords, by the bizarre device of abolishing the practice.

Many of the other details were also concessions made on the spur of the moment to varying Parliamentary combinations. The division in the Liberal party produced by Russell's Bill lasted long enough to allow the Radicals to vote as they pleased, and Disraeli's performance was a uniquely brilliant example of Parliamentary skill in an extraordinary situation. But certain generalizations can be made about the aims of the principal actors and the state of politics, which largely account for the passage of the Act of 1867. It was not a mere succession of accidents. Derby and Disraeli, and many of their followers, cared more that their party should pass some great measure, and therefore, in the context, a Parliamentary Reform Bill, than they cared about its precise terms. The Conservative Ministers who resigned, seeing the issues as matters of life and death to the party and the State, were untypical. Experience of the working of the Constitution since the passage of the First Reform Act had shown that extension of the franchise and redistribution of seats need not seriously affect the dominance of the aristocracy and the land. The Conservatives had never had a Parliamentary majority since 1846. They could hardly be worse off under a new electoral dispensation. If they were in charge of carrying a Reform Bill, they might hope to make it more advantageous to their party than a Liberal measure would be. There was much uncertainty about the effects of many of the changes discussed. In this sense the Act was, as Derby called it, 'a leap in the dark'. But in one or two ways the Conservatives had good reason to think it might help them in future Elections. It provided for a larger increase in the number of county seats than the 1866 Bill, and most counties were Conservative strongholds. Again as compared with

Russell's Bill, it probably also preserved or created more borough seats likely to return a Conservative. On the other hand, the further extension of the borough franchise could hardly make the larger towns much more Liberal in tendency. Throughout his career, except, oddly enough, in 1866, Disraeli was a consistent Parliamentary reformer. But he was a party man before he was a Parliamentary reformer. Insofar as his claim is justified that he had educated his followers in this field, it was not because he had instilled into them devotion to Tory Democracy. Rather, he had seized opportunities to identify the party's obvious interest in office and vote-winning with support for Parliamentary reform, as a matter of expediency. The break with Peel had so far brought no good to the Conservatives. Perhaps a new electoral régime would restore their fortunes, and vindicate Disraeli.

Gladstone's and the Liberals' attitudes present a different problem. Even while Palmerston lived, Gladstone had moved into what by Parliamentary standards was an advanced position on Reform. In 1864 he said, though he told his affronted Prime Minister he did not mean, that 'every man not presumably incapacitated . . . is morally entitled to come within the pale of the constitution', that is, be admitted to the franchise. The way in which he arrived at this view is instructive. Gladstone was like no one else, but it was his combination of attitudes, not the attitudes themselves, which was distinctive. In the 'thirties he had opposed the First Reform Act, Liberal foreign policy and concessions to Nonconformists. His experience at the Board of Trade under Peel made him a fanatical Free Trader. The defection of Newman from the Church of England began a process whereby Gladstone, while himself remaining a High Churchman, came to value liberty for all denominations, an outlook utterly opposed to that of his book of 1838. A visit to Naples late in 1850 turned this critic of Palmerston's handling of the Don Pacifico affair into a moralizing enemy of reactionary absolutism, who in 1859–60 supported the cause of Italian liberty more strenuously than any of his Cabinet colleagues except Palmerston and Russell. During this Ministry Gladstone worked with Cobden and Bright, Parliamentary reformers, in the cause of Free Trade. He worked with Russell, Parliamentary reformer, on foreign policy. He found himself progressively more sympathetic with working-class and Nonconformist deputations and audiences. He was impressed, during the American Civil War, both by the refusal of Lancashire cotton-workers, despite the hardships the war brought them, to support the Southern States on which they depended for their raw material, and by the fact that the spokesmen of the working class had been right, whereas he had been wrong, about the outcome of the conflict. This was 'a great lesson to us all, to teach us that in those little tutored but reflective minds . . . opinions and sentiments gradually form themselves . . . which are found to be deep-seated, mature and ineradicable.' He was overwhelmed by the reception he was given when he spoke to large provincial audiences. 'God knows I have not courted them. . . . It is, however, impossible not to love the people from whom such manifestations come, as meet me in every quarter.' While Gladstone condescended, a deputation of the workmen of York deferred:

> We have marked your manifestations of sympathy with the down-trodden and oppressed of every clime. You have advanced the cause of freedom in foreign lands by the power and courage with which you have assailed and exposed the misdeeds and cruelties of continental tyrants. To the provident operative you have by your Post Office Savings Bank Bill given security for his small savings. . . . These acts, together with your speeches . . . on the Borough Franchise Bill, make up a life that commands our lasting gratitude.

Gladstone was becoming a superior demagogue, and already the essence of Gladstonian Liberalism was present in his attitudes: the moralist appeal to a General Will, believed to be, when speaking *ex cathedra*, infallible.[1]

During the course of 1867, however, Gladstone was often to the Right of Disraeli on Parliamentary reform. He took much more seriously than the Conservative leader the details of the measure, especially the restrictions on household suffrage in the original drafts. Further, he was trying to restore the unity of a party which counted Lowe among its members. Yet the Liberals in general, and Gladstone in particular, retained the support of the Reform movement outside Parliament. The Reform Act was taken, and on the whole rightly, to be a concession to the Opposition, albeit to different elements at different moments, rather than a Conservative initiative.

---

[1] Quotations from Williams, *Rise of Gladstone*, pp. 84, 107, 110. See G. M. Young, 'Mr Gladstone' in *Today and Yesterday*.

Historians have been especially interested in seeking an answer to the question: what part was played in the passage of the Act by public pressure? In the middle of the 'sixties Parliamentary reform had suddenly again become a popular cause. Part of the explanation, no doubt, was comparatively high food prices in 1866–7. But the dear corn of 1853–4 had evoked a demand for war with Russia. It was the changed situation at Westminster, and a new shift of mood in the country, away from complacent interest in foreign affairs, which made the essential difference. Lowe's extreme denunciations in 1866 of the poorer voters and non-voters contributed to the revival of the demand for Reform, just as Wellington's diehard stand in 1830 had brought the Grey coalition together. Bright now mounted a successful campaign in the provinces for household suffrage. The Reform League, founded in 1865 to work for manhood suffrage, asserted: 'Let us once be able to maintain by the force of intellect and truth our rights as workmen in that House, and depend upon it we shall rise in the social scale.'[1] There was a more moderate Reform Union, whose aims were more in line with Gladstone's and Bright's.

These organizations were, in part, attempts to transfer to the national scene the spirit of class co-operation already carefully cultivated in some of the great towns, especially in Birmingham, where in the Elections of the 'fifties and in that of 1865 non-voters were taken into consideration by the Liberal leaders. From this point of view also, Gladstonian Liberalism existed before the Second Reform Act and helped to pass it. Even the origins of the National Liberal Federation may be traced back to the Birmingham Liberal organization of these years. Broadly, the cities were Liberal, Nonconformist and individualist. Their articulate inhabitants were interested in winning political rights rather than social reforms. In general, without the growth of the provincial Press, the consolidation of the skilled workers' unions and the Nonconformist revival, it would hardly be possible to explain the movement for Parliamentary reform.

The 1867 Reform Bill was the only one since 1832 to be debated at a time when there was great public interest in the

---

[1] Quoted in Harrison, *Before the Socialists*, p. 81 n.

question, and it was the only one that was passed. This is not a mere coincidence. But it is not a simple matter to say precisely how opinion influenced Parliament. Some historians have laid much stress on the so-called Hyde Park riots of July 1866 and May 1867, monster meetings of the Reform League which got slightly out of hand. It is plainly true that the Derby Government lost face by its failure to enforce its prohibitions of the meetings in question. It is more important, though, that a steady pressure was kept up on Parliament by orderly provincial meetings throughout the autumn and winter of 1866 and the spring and summer of 1867. The Government did not meet the protesters' demands in full, but the agitation, though much less violent than that of 1831–2, had somewhat the same effect. Ministers, and M.P.s in general, felt themselves compelled to pass some measure, which had to be broad enough to be plausibly described as a settlement of the question, with a view to placating respectable reformers and detaching them from the extremists. Without pressure from the public, Disraeli would not have retained control of his party as he allowed the Bill to become radical.

As soon as the Bill had been passed, the Liberals were in a position to reunite. At least as important as the story of the session of 1867, but much less studied, is that of the session of 1867–8, during which Gladstone again took command of his party and fashioned it into a new progressive instrument. He cultivated Nonconformity, carrying the abolition of compulsory church rates against the Government. He took up the question of the disestablishment of the Irish Church, thus attracting Irish support and involving himself in elaborate autobiographical explanations of his change of front. Through the Whips he collaborated with the Unions and the Reform League, the latter supplying electoral information in return for a subvention from party funds. In the General Election he made Irish disestablishment the programme of his party, submitting a clear issue to the voters for the first time since 1831. In the result he was able to form a Government with a majority in the Commons of over a hundred, committed to legislative action on a large scale. This, too, was something unknown since the early 'thirties.

12 The building of Clifton Suspension Bridge, Bristol, in 1863. The bridge was completed in 1863–4 as a memorial to I. K. Brunel (1806–59) and followed a modified version of his design of 1830–1. The foundation stone had been laid in 1836, but shortage of money had delayed the project.

13 Dowlais iron works, near Merthyr Tydfil, Glamorgan, 'from the cinder heaps', 1875.

14 The reredos (centre panel) in St Paul's Church, Brighton, by Edward Burne-Jones, 1861. Joseph is evidently a portrait of William Morris, and the King in the centre is Swinburne.

15 Dinner in the Iguanodon Model at the Crystal Palace (31 December, 1853). The designer of this and other 'gigantic restorations of the Extinct Inhabitants of the Ancient World', 'trustworthy lessons to the world at large in a branch of science which had hitherto been found too vast and abstruse to call in the aid of art to illustrate its wonderful truths', had brought together for this festivity 'great names . . . in the sciences of palaeontology and geology'.

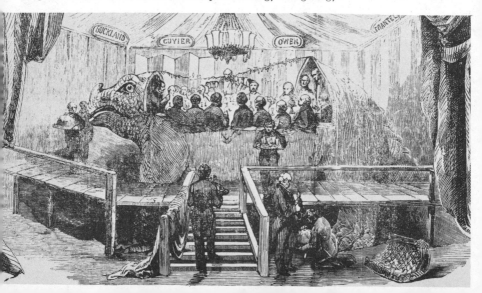

15

Culture and Society
1850-1868

IN 1851 was held 'the Great Exhibition of the Works of Industry of All Nations'. Historians have found it an inexhaustible source of humour, ugliness, illustrations and lessons. It was the first large exhibition ever held anywhere in the world. As such it is a landmark in the history of the 'public'. Jeremiahs did not believe it would succeed: there would be vandalism, or no one would come. In fact the crowds were amazingly orderly, from which the moral was drawn that the failure of the British to revolt in 1848 was no accident and that they were contented, law-abiding and respectable. Further, the crowds were enormous. Latterly, the attendance reached 100,000 a day. The total was over 6,000,000. The provision of non-alcoholic refreshments, catalogues and lavatories was novel, and set the pattern for similar events in Britain. The profit was over £180,000. London had appropriated the Industrial Revolution.

It had its lunatic side. There were exhibited:

> Railway trains constructed to prevent collision. Square carriage wheels, termed *scrapers*, to advance by steps and without jolting.
> Silent alarum bedstead to turn any one out of bed at a given hour.
> Piece of mechanism intended to represent the proportions of the human figure; it admits of being expanded from the standard size of Apollo Belvedere to that of a colossal statue. Composed of more than 7000 pieces of steel.

Many of the exhibits, though more practical, were hideous. It seems hard to escape the conclusion that the triumph of industrialization, bringing mass production and a flood of new materials, together with pride and confidence in material progress, were fatal to taste. The greatest aesthetic success of the affair was the building in which it was housed, the Crystal Palace, which was an expanded version by Paxton of one of his

Chatsworth conservatories. It was prefabricated, 1848 feet long, 408 feet wide and 100 feet high at maximum, and was the classic glass-and-iron functional building of the nineteenth century.

The Exhibition illustrated Britain's superiority in technology. It was appropriate that, among the advertisements in the catalogue—with those of the Religious Tract Society, Novello's for cheap editions of oratorios, Madame Tussaud's, Colman's for mustard, Dinneford's for magnesia and the St Helen's Crown, Sheet and Plate Glass Company – there figured that of John Murray for G. R. Porter's *The Progress of the Nation* and Longmans' for J. R. M'Culloch's *Descriptive and Statistical Account of the British Empire*. These works, published in the late 'thirties, were the first notable statistical glorifications of Britain's industrial progress. 'The progress of the human race, resulting from the common labour of all men,' ran one of the Exhibition's mottoes, 'ought to be the final object of the exertion of each individual. In promoting this end, we are carrying out the will of the great and blessed God.'[1]

Self-satisfaction apart, the promoters of the Exhibition, chief of whom was Prince Albert, saw in it a triumph of peace and internationalism. It was comprehensive, of course, and so there was even a medieval court. There was also a model artisan dwelling. Art, Industry and Social Progress were supposed to go hand in hand. With the profits the museum site in South Kensington was bought, on which was erected 'an accumulation of cultural institutions as compact and varied as exists . . . anywhere'.[2] The only one of the buildings completed in this period, however, was a museum on the site of, and partly preserved within, the Victoria and Albert Museum. The Albert Hall was not finished until 1873.

Paxton's vein of architecture was still being worked in the 'fifties and 'sixties for the railways. In London the arches over the rails at King's Cross (1851–2) and St Pancras (1868) Stations are the best examples. In a different field, the dome of the circular Reading Room of the British Museum (1854–7) is outstanding. However, functionalism was not widely popular, whereas Gothic was. As if to counterbalance the austerity of

<hr>

[1] All quotations so far from the Great Exhibition catalogue.
[2] N. Pevsner, *The Buildings of England: London, except the Cities of London and Westminster* (London, 1952), pp. 252–3.

the Station behind, Sir George Gilbert Scott built the St
Pancras Hotel in a style which 'is a combination of various
medieval features the inspection of which calls to mind the
Lombardic and Venetian brick Gothic . . . while the critical
eye of the student will observe touches of Milan . . . , interlaced
with good reproduction of details from Winchester and
Salisbury Cathedrals, Westminster Abbey, etc.'[1] By the
criterion of output, Scott was easily the most important British
architect of the nineteenth century. Between 1847 and 1878
he built or restored at least 39 cathedrals and minsters, 476
churches, 25 schools, 23 parsonages, 43 mansions, 26 public
buildings, 58 monuments and 25 colleges or college chapels.
Earlier he had built at least 50 workhouses. He did not positively
insist on Gothic. He agreed, 'for the sake of his family', to build
the new Foreign Office of 1868–73 in the 'Italian' style on
which Palmerston had insisted. But almost all his other work
was Gothic of a kind. His restorations are notorious for their
ferocity, but he himself defended them as comparatively mild,
since the Camden Society liked them more drastic still. In
general, sharing Pugin's love of Gothic but lacking his Catholicism and philosophy, he proved the perfect popularizer of the
Revival. His best-known piece is the Albert Memorial, of
1863–72. The most thoroughgoing High Church Gothic
building of the period is All Saints', Margaret Street, by
William Butterfield, completed in 1859. In 1867 G. E. Street
won, with a Gothic design, a competition for the central
Law Courts. These are the architects who are considered to
have been the most distinguished of the Gothic Revival.

Ruskin, although his aesthetic theories so much resembled
Pugin's, was bewitched by what he called *The Stones of Venice*.
The polychromy and some of the forms he advocated in the
book of that title, which appeared in 1851, are to be found in
the Oxford Museum (1854–9) and Keble College, Oxford
(1868–70), the former inspired by Ruskin himself, the latter
built by Butterfield. Under Ruskin's influence, Italian styles
which were not very specifically Gothic became popular at this
time, as exemplified in the Free Trade Hall at Manchester
(1856). 'Classical' styles were still sometimes employed, as in
Leeds Town Hall (1853–9). Amid so much elaboration of

---

[1] Quoted in Pevsner, op. cit., p. 368.

ornament, the Red House at Bexley, built by Philip Webb in 1859, represented a specially simple design for a private house, and inaugurated a long British tradition. Its owner was William Morris, who will figure largely in the next Part.

In literature, as has been stressed, the mixture is somewhat as before. With *Enoch Arden* in 1864 Tennyson captured a still wider public, aligning himself with the ethos of self-help so characteristic of the 'sixties. Less noticed, Matthew Arnold's poems were mostly published in the early 'fifties. Dickens continued to succeed with almost every production, including *Bleak House* (1852–3), *The Tale of Two Cities* (1859) and *Great Expectations* (1860–1). Two new novelists of special importance, however, emerged during this period, Anthony Trollope and George Eliot.

Trollope positively embodies the complacency, the indulgence towards anachronism and anomalies, and the unheroic worldliness of the middle period of Victoria's reign. He seized in *The Warden* (1855) on an excellent milieu for novels, the clerical life of 'Barsetshire', into which the reforms of the Ecclesiastical Commission and the intensities of Low and High Church were but slowly penetrating. *The Warden* is a manifesto directed against several of the stronger literary trends of the day. It dissociates itself from the ruthless revelation of abuses, as defined by the standards of utilitarianism and illustrated in *The Times*; from Carlyle, 'Dr Pessimist Anticant', who compared 'ancient and modern times, very little to the credit of the latter'; and from Dickens, Mr Popular Sentiment, who set the world right 'by shilling numbers'. Five other Barchester novels followed, *The Last Chronicle of Barset* appearing in 1867. Trollope also allowed himself to be amused by the politics of the day, though he described them as even more pointless than they were. He was thankful they led to few reforms, he sympathized with the Protectionist squires and laughed at working-class politicians. He revered, and wrote the life of, Palmerston. In his *Autobiography* of 1883 he described how he had written his novels in measured stints, disclaiming Romantic inspiration. Nothing better shews the oppressiveness of the age than the fact that Trollope, the prophet of normality, as decorous as one can imagine, felt it necessary to censor himself. The 'fifties are clearly the highpoint of nineteenth-century prudery.

George Eliot, the pseudonym of Mary Ann Evans, started her career as a novelist only two years after Trollope's *The Warden* appeared, and on a similar subject. *Scenes of Clerical Life*, indeed, opens with a passage rather in Trollope's spirit, doubting whether reform and restoration have improved the Church. She was, however, in many respects the opposite of Trollope. She was aggressively intellectual, she purveyed German philosophy and theology, she wished to assert the independence of her sex, and she was a subtle psychologist. *Middlemarch*, reckoned to be her greatest book, came out only in 1871–2, but *The Mill on the Floss* appeared in 1860 and *Silas Marner* in 1861.

What exactly Henry Adams meant by his statement, quoted at the head of this Part, that the English mind was utterly *décousu* in the 'sixties, when he was Secretary to the American Legation in London, he made it as difficult as usual to find out. But among the literary manifestations which impressed him, as it well might, was the early poetry of Algernon Swinburne, far from the philosophical sobriety of Tennyson. *Atalanta in Calydon* appeared in 1865. The most important intellectual influence of the 'sixties, however, was the impact of Darwin, which may certainly be regarded as 'disintegrating', breaking up a whole way of thought, in its first effect.

General evolutionary notions and attitudes were, as has been seen, characteristic of much early nineteenth-century thought. Wordsworth's *Prelude*, written by 1805 but published posthumously in the same year, 1850, as *In Memoriam*, illustrates the point, as do the works of Coleridge, Gladstone, J. S. Mill and Tennyson himself. Already, for those who studied these matters, Lyell had pushed far back the origins of Life and indicated a pattern of organic development. What Darwin added to this general evolutionism in *The Origin of Species* (1859) was an explanation of the variety of existing species of plants and animals in terms of an autonomous process which he thought of as operating, at least from the time when Life began, into the future. In Paley's time the study of the variety of species had been a matter for Natural Theology, and it had been widely believed that the glory of the Creation was displayed in their once-for-all differentiation, as proclaimed in *Genesis*. Darwin definitively removed this subject from Theology.

Living things necessarily produce numerous variants, he argued; and those variants prosper which are 'the fittest to survive in the struggle for life'. The principle of Natural Selection explains the whole process and the existing situation. 'Unbroken Evolution under uniform conditions,' says Henry Adams, 'pleased every one – except curates and bishops; it was the very best substitute for religion; a safe, conservative, practical, thoroughly Common Law deity.'[1] Bishops denounced it, but were easily proved ignorant when they did so. In a famous confrontation of 1860 Bishop Samuel Wilberforce of Oxford was worsted by the biologist, T. H. Huxley. In the same year the orthodox had to face another attack, a collection of *Essays and Reviews* by young clergy, some of which were condemned by church courts as heretical, though the Judicial Committee of the Privy Council upheld their appeals. This was the point at which the Church and Science, and, within the Church, dogmatic and undogmatic religion – the High and the Low Church here on the same side *versus* the 'Broad' Church – fought their pitched battles. But of course the war was of long standing.

It would be possible to write many volumes on the implications of Darwin's work. The relationship between Darwinism and religion is not simple. Literal interpreters of the Bible had for centuries found themselves in growing difficulties. Darwin's ideas were scarcely more damaging than Lyell's, though they made more of a stir. Undoubtedly *The Origin of Species* shook the belief of many. Yet some churchmen soon found it possible to adapt evolutionary ideas so that they did not conflict with Christianity.

Spencer claimed Darwin as a supporter, as did many who applied the notion of the survival of the fittest to conflicts between races or to capitalist competition. Marx and Engels thought they were doing for the study of society what Darwin had done for biology. As Burrow says:

The uniformitarian's rejection of catastrophism [i.e. Lyell's attitude in geology], the Darwinian's of Special Creation, are paralleled by the rejection of the Social Contract, the Great Man theory of history, and the mechanical conception of society as an artifact, transformable almost

---

[1] Henry Adams, *The Education of Henry Adams* (Modern Library, New York, 1931), p. 225.

at will; all the newer theories were concerned to present the relation of past and present as a steady growth, a chain of cause and effect related in accordance with discoverable natural laws.[1]

Newman's theology of Development, positively applauding modifications of dogma over time, is another intellectual position which can be added to the catena, even though Darwin and Newman had no other attitude in common. Many of those who sympathized with Darwin, like Spencer, conceived of Natural Selection as a progressive process. The ideas of Progress and Evolution are obviously related. But they are distinct. For Darwin the process he was describing was morally neutral. Some thinkers who were evolutionists in other fields shared his approach. For example, what are usually thought of as primitive societies developing towards civilization were now being conceived as deserving of equal respect and attention with so-called advanced societies, as by Henry Maine in his *Ancient Law* (1861).

Roman Catholic writers had a notable impact in this period. Newman tried to win acceptance for his *Idea of a University* among the Roman Catholics of Ireland in lectures of 1852, but not yet under that title. In 1864 he published *Apologia pro Vita Sua*, an account of his conversion to Rome, in the hope of justifying himself against the attacks of Low Churchmen. His chief poem, *The Dream of Gerontius*, appeared in the following year. The two prose works, superbly argued and magically written, convey some of the attraction which his hearers had found in his Oxford sermons. The lectures did not achieve their immediate object of establishing an Irish University such as Newman wanted; rather they provided a justification for Oxford and Cambridge. The *Apologia* contributed much to make Roman Catholicism respectable among British intellectuals. A very different Roman Catholic, Sir John Acton, made his name in the years around 1860. He had a cosmopolitan aristocratic background, being closely related to members of the nobility of Britain, Naples and the Holy Roman Empire. He made himself a phenomenally learned historian, as he displayed in a succession of short-lived reviews, the *Rambler*, the *Home and Foreign Review* and the *North British Review*. Quite unlike Newman, he passionately supported

---

[1] J. W. Burrow, *Evolution and Society* (Cambridge, 1966), p. 111.

freedom of religion, and believed in Progress. In consequence he had differences with the Papacy.

One more of the literary manifestations of the period must be mentioned. In 1865 appeared, over the pseudonym Lewis Carroll, *Alice's Adventures in Wonderland.* Special writing for children is a feature of the nineteenth century; and, although some upper-class Victorians were notoriously restrictive parents, in no previous period was so much concern shown over the happiness and education of the young.

16

Britain and the Rest of the World 1850-1868

IN imperial affairs the chief interest in this period centres on India, but certain developments elsewhere should be briefly noticed. Responsible government was extended to Australia and New Zealand during the 'fifties. In 1858 Canada was allowed to lay a tariff on British goods. In 1865 the Colonial Laws Validity Act considerably extended the powers of colonial legislatures. In 1867 a federation was established in Canada, including some of the maritime provinces as well as Quebec and Ontario. On the other hand, a rebellion in Jamaica in 1865, repressed with unnecessary severity by Governor Eyre, led to the abolition of the island's representative assembly.

It is principally in relation to this and the next period that a debate has arisen among historians about the nature of the Empire and of imperialism. Traditionally, the 'fifties and 'sixties have been regarded as the years of the nineteenth century when Ministers were most reluctant to annex territory, when they most cheerfully conceded responsible government, when there was least public pride in the colonies and when the Cobdenites' distaste for military adventures was most widely shared. Yet, it has been argued, the Empire expanded vastly, apparently regardless of these views. It is possible to point to two insignificant withdrawals: Britain gave up sovereignty over what became the Orange Free State in 1854, and surrendered the troublesome protectorate of the Ionian Islands in 1864. Otherwise the record of territories occupied or annexed between 1851 and 1871 includes Berar and Oudh in India, Burma, Lagos, Basutoland, Griqualand, Queensland, the territories of the Hudson's

Bay Company and British Columbia. Britain reasserted her control of the Chinese economy by the Second China War of 1856–60. She might keep few soldiers in Britain, but the Indian revenue supported an army of 200,000. She continued to dominate the economy of South America. Emigration proceeded on a tremendous scale. British foreign investment at least trebled. All these extensions of British influence abroad should, it is claimed, be considered 'imperialist'. The difference between formal and informal Empire is trivial. Britain used in each area whatever method was appropriate to impose her power and secure her trade. The grant of responsible government itself was 'simply a change from direct to indirect methods of maintaining British interests'. Free Trade required military and naval backing. The Pax Britannica was an armed peace.[1]

Clearly it is true that to discuss the development of the Empire purely in constitutional and theoretical terms is misleading. It made little difference to the inhabitants whether Oudh was annexed by the Company or the Crown, and whether Sarawak was the private domain of the Brooke family or a province of the formal Empire. Even in cases like these, though, it might make some difference. The Maoris were evidently in a better position after the annexation of New Zealand. And in many instances the difference between formal and informal Empire was enormous. It would be hard to show that, with all Britain's investment in the United States and all the emigration there from the British Isles, Britain had much control over the country's political development. She declined to interfere in Latin American politics. Again, that Canada could lay a tariff on British goods was bound to injure the trade of the mother-country.

No discussion ought to assume that 'British interests' were ever readily identifiable. What they were was a matter of opinion. Further, immediate interests were subordinated to other concerns. Some Christian missionary propaganda was doubtless tinged with hypocrisy, but it is impossible to account for the details of African expansion without allowing for the campaign against the slave trade, which obsessed Palmerston almost as much as the Evangelicals. David Livingstone, who

---

[1] This paragraph is intended as a modified summary of J. Gallagher and R. E. Robinson, 'The Imperialism of Free Trade', *Econ.H.R.* 1953.

explored much of central Africa in a series of journeys between 1841 and 1873, discovering the Victoria Falls in 1855, was chiefly concerned to eradicate slaving. Many Free Trade advocates were genuine internationalists.

The position varied over time: the 'sixties were less notable for imperial expansion, as for interference in Europe, than the 'fifties. But Britain's Governments were always refusing to give aid to her merchants, and left them to meet economic competition themselves. In summary, during these years the attitudes of British Ministers and opinion restricted the scope of imperialist development, although none the less the expansion that occurred was vast.[1]

The Indian 'Mutiny'

From 1847 to 1856 the Earl (later Marquess) of Dalhousie was Governor-General of India. He continued the policies of Bentinck: in particular, he extended the educational system by giving grants-in-aid to private Colleges and by founding the first three Indian Universities. His special impress was his public works programme, cutting irrigation canals, building roads and planning railways, all on a vast scale. He also set out to reduce the power of the independent princes, taking over Oudh on the ground that it was misgoverned, refusing to allow rulers without direct heirs to adopt successors and informing the old Emperor that his title would lapse with his death.

In 1857 the progress of Westernization was brutally interrupted. On May 11 the troops at Meerut 'mutinied', marched to Delhi and proclaimed the Emperor their leader. Oudh, and within it Lucknow, was the other main centre of revolt. The immediate occasion of the rising was the introduction of new cartridges, which the soldiers had to bite before loading, and which contained fat of animals sacred to the Hindu and impure to the Mohammedan. But the grievances of the rebels were much wider. The 'Mutiny' 'was a last passionate protest of the conservative forces in India against the relentless penetration of the West'.[2] For a time the situation looked black for the British, some famous atrocities were

---

[1] Cf. D. C. M. Platt, 'The Imperialism of Free Trade: Some Reservations', *Econ.H.R.* 1968.

[2] Spear, *India*, p. 270.

committed against them, and it was not until 1859, after some savage reprisals, that order was completely restored.

One result of the 'Mutiny' was the assumption by the Crown in 1858 of the powers of the East India Company. A Secretary of State for India replaced the President of the Board of Control, the Governor-General became the Viceroy. The European element in the Indian Army was strengthened. Although public works programmes were maintained, future Viceroys showed themselves less hasty Westernizers. The princes were taken into partnership; there was less determination to create and uphold an Indian intelligentsia; more respect was paid to Indian traditions. The heroic, iconoclastic period had lasted rather longer in India than at home. The reaction was stronger. Men with experience of Indian conditions were to contribute powerfully to the strains in late nineteenth-century British thought which questioned the validity of democracy, of radical reform, and of the whole approach of utilitarianism.

The Crimean War and Foreign Policy

From March 1854 to March 1856 Britain was at war with Russia. It is important to have some idea how she came to involve herself in this, her only European land war between 1815 and 1914, and with what consequences to herself and other countries. Early in 1853 Russia, expecting that the Ottoman Empire would shortly break up and relying on the sympathy of Austria and Britain, made very strong demands at Constantinople. She asserted in particular an unrestricted right to intervene to protect the Orthodox Christian subjects of the Sultan. The Turks rejected these claims, and in June Russia occupied the Principalities of Moldavia and Wallachia, roughly the modern Romania. War between Russia and Turkey broke out in October. For many months the other Powers worked to keep and then restore the peace, but when it came to the point the attitude of Russia was always unconciliatory. The Turks were supported more or less strongly by Britain, France and Austria, because they believed Russia to be intransigently expansionist and the Ottoman Empire a bulwark of the *status quo* against a new bid for hegemony. Britain and France formally declared war on Russia after making an alliance with the Sultan in March 1854.

Britain's policy has been much criticized. Cobden and Bright took the view that what Russia claimed was quite reasonable, and that in any case the issues were not vital enough for Britain to fight about them. Critics more ready to accept the realities and conventions of international politics have concentrated blame on the divided counsels of the Aberdeen Government, in which the Prime Minister was pacific and tentative while Palmerston was bellicose and decisive. It may be that vigorous action early in 1853 would have made Russia reduce her demands before it was too late. Once that stage had passed, it is difficult to see what the British Government could have done to avoid joining in the war unless it was prepared to permit the Turks to be crushed by Russia or protected solely by France. Both the British and French Governments were egged on by the violent reaction of public opinion in their countries to the Russian naval victory at Sinope in November 1853, which was regarded as a 'massacre'. This was an occasion when *The Times* modified its attitude because opinion ran ahead of it. But even without the pressure of the public the Government would probably have felt bound to fight.

Because of the failure to win a quick victory, the hardships suffered by the troops and the inefficiencies revealed in the Government's and the generals' handling of the war, a strong body of opinion demanded administrative reform, denouncing aristocratic incompetence. The Civil Service reforms of 1855 were hastened. Florence Nightingale's success in improving hospital services in the Crimea helped the development of nursing in Britain. But in fact the war was finally too successful, was too short and had too slight an impact on the population as a whole to make possible a general overhaul of administration. As soon as peace was restored, the feeling in favour of economy reasserted itself and the army, as hitherto, was starved of money for comforts and ancillary services. Aristocratic incompetents continued to be able to buy themselves commissions. At the top, the fusion of the Secretaryship *for* War with the Secretaryship *at* War did little to strengthen the chain of command.

By the time peace was made, Russia had long abandoned the Principalities, which soon became a virtually independent state. The Treaty of Paris of March 1856 guaranteed the Turkish Empire and, to weaken and humiliate Russia, neutralized the

Black Sea. The War had certainly secured the position of the Ottoman Empire, though it did not lead to the reforms there for which Palmerston and his supporters hoped. It also, as some of its advocates in Britain had believed it would, improved chances for liberal movements on the Continent, in Germany and Italy if not in Poland, by turning Russia into a revisionist power. The Anglo-French alliance remained of importance for several years, giving British Ministers some influence over the policies of the most creative and powerful European ruler of the late 'fifties and early 'sixties.

The Crimean War was in a sense the apogee of the bellicose feeling associated with Palmerston. For the rest of this period Britain's policy was declining in effectiveness, and Palmerston's own part in it was becoming smaller. In his second Cabinet he was controlled much more strictly by his more cautious colleagues than in any other Administration in which he served after 1830. Though he made known his clear-cut opinions to the Press, to envoys of Britain and to those of other Powers, it was another policy than his which was officially endorsed by the Government as a whole and which alone might be enforced by arms. In 1864 Bismarck, the Prussian Chancellor, called Palmerston's bluff, ignoring his pro-Danish speeches. In 1866 the Austro-Prussian War proceeded without even arousing much interest in Britain. It has been suggested that Cobden's views had triumphed. That is to exaggerate. But a more genuine non-intervention than Canning's and Palmerston's, almost isolationism, was in the ascendant.

PART FOUR

I contend that we are the first race in the world, and that the more of the world we inhabit, the better it is for the human race.

C. J. RHODES, 1877

Queen	Every Bill and every measure
	That may gratify his pleasure,
	Though your fury it arouses,
	Shall be passed by both your Houses!
Peers	Oh!
Queen	You shall sit, if he sees reason,
	Through the grouse and salmon season;
Peers	No!
Queen	He shall end the cherished rights
	You enjoy on Friday nights:
Peers	No! No!
Queen	He shall prick that annual blister,
	Marriage with a deceased wife's sister:
Peers	Mercy!
Queen	Titles shall ennoble, then,
	All the Common Councilmen:
Peers	Spare us!
Queen	Peers shall teem in Christendom,
	And a Duke's exalted station
	Be attainable by Com-
	Petitive Examination!

W. S. GILBERT, *Iolanthe*, 1882.

17

Narrative of Events
1868-1885

IN Gladstone's Administration Clarendon was Foreign Secretary until 1870, Granville thereafter; Lowe was Chancellor of the Exchequer until 1873; and Bright was President of the Board of Trade until 1870, the first Nonconformist to sit in a Cabinet. The Government has a well-deserved reputation for the scope of its reforming legislation. The Prime Minister himself was mainly interested in Irish questions, and displayed his phenomenal skill both in drafting measures intended to solve them and in carrying the Bills through Parliament. In 1869 the Irish Church was disestablished and to some extent disendowed. Derby just lived to condemn the change which he had left the Whig party in order to oppose in 1834; but the Lords acquiesced, since the electorate seemed to have given approval. In the following year Gladstone put through his first Irish Land Act.

1870 also saw the passage of the Education Act, under the direction of W. E. Forster, which provided for almost universal elementary education. In the same year the majority of appointments to the Civil Service were made subject to competitive examination. The Universities Tests Act of 1871 opened most of the posts at Oxford and Cambridge to Nonconformists.

This Government tackled army reform more boldly than any other Administration of the nineteenth century. Edward Cardwell as Secretary for War in 1868 abolished flogging in peace-time; then secured the subordination of the Commander-in-Chief to the political head, and that of all land forces, including the militia, to the Commander-in-Chief; the introduction of short-service engagements; the abolition of purchase of commissions; and the regrouping of infantry regiments on a county basis. All these changes were bitterly opposed by most officers, including a group of M.P.s. The House of Lords was overridden only by inducing the Queen to use her prerogative and revoke the royal warrant which authorized purchase of commissions. These reforms were a delayed attempt to remedy some of the defects revealed in the Crimean War.

In 1872 the Ballot Act was passed; and a Licensing Act, restricting drinking hours in public houses. In 1873 Gladstone attempted to endow an Irish national University, was defeated in the Commons, and resigned. But Disraeli refused to take office without a regular majority. The Liberal Government in the remaining months of the session carried the most comprehensive measure of Law Reform of the century, the Judicature Act. This statute provided that the rift between common law and equity should be bridged, all judges in all courts administering both. Further, seven out of the eight central courts were brought together, and a court of appeal established above them.

The main concerns of foreign policy between 1868 and 1874 were these. In 1870-1 the European balance was disturbed, more dramatically than by any other event between 1815 and 1917, by the Franco-Prussian War, from which a unified Germany resulted. The British Government confined its intervention to attempting, successfully, to preserve Belgium from invasion and, unsuccessfully, to persuade Count Bismarck, the German Chancellor, not to annex Alsace-Lorraine from France. Russia took the opportunity of the War to denounce the 'Black Sea clauses' of the Treaty of 1856. Granville saved face to the extent of obtaining the ratification of this step by all the Powers. In 1871-2 the Government accepted responsibility and paid compensation for the damage done to the United States by the *Alabama* during the Civil War.

Gladstone dissolved Parliament early in 1874. He had been trying to persuade the Cabinet to accept a Budget involving the repeal of the income tax, but the defence departments were too strong for him. He put the issue to the electorate, and was defeated.

Disraeli became Prime Minister with an overall majority of about 50. He went to the Lords as Earl of Beaconsfield in 1876. The 15th Earl of Derby, son of the Derby who had been Prime Minister, was Foreign Secretary until 1878, when the

Marquess of Salisbury succeeded him. Sir Stafford Northcote was Chancellor of the Exchequer, R. A. Cross Home Secretary. In domestic affairs the Government is chiefly remembered for its social legislation, in 1875 on Trade Unions, Public Health and housing, and in 1878 on Factories.

The Balkans after 1878

———— Proposed boundary of big Bulgaria (Treaty of San Stefano)
– – – – Frontiers settled by Congress of Berlin

Foreign and imperial questions, however, overshadowed domestic. In 1875 revolts of a nationalist character occurred in the Turkish provinces of Bosnia and Herzegovina, and later in Bulgaria. In June 1876 Serbia and Montenegro attacked Turkey in support of the revolts, but were soon defeated. So far Britain maintained her old policy of upholding the integrity of the Ottoman Empire. In attempting to restore order in the rebellious areas, however, the Turks massacred many thousands of civilians in what became known as 'the Bulgarian atrocities', which evoked an outcry in Britain. At a Conference of the Powers at the end of 1876 Britain agreed that, despite the Turks' victory, an independent Bulgaria should be carved out of their Empire. But the Turks refused to accept any such proposal. In

April 1877, therefore, having secured the support of Austria-Hungary by promising her Bosnia and Herzegovina, Russia declared war on Turkey. Russia's main object was to recover from Romania southern Bessarabia, ceded in 1856. She also intended to promote the establishment of an independent Bulgaria, though not always the 'big' Bulgaria she had originally proposed to the Conference. The Turks resisted quite effectively, and, though Russian troops reached the outskirts of Constantinople in the New Year, the Tsar had then to conclude an armistice. But the Treaty of San Stefano of March 1878 satisfied all Russia's demands, establishing a 'big' Bulgaria and shelving Austrian claims. The other Powers now worked to set aside the results of the war. Beaconsfield carried the Cabinet in favour of calling up the reserves.

A European Congress, the grandest since 1815, met at Berlin in June–July 1878. Largely because they had taken care to make previous agreements with the states concerned, Beaconsfield and Salisbury (now Foreign Secretary) achieved what they wanted at the Congress. 'Big' Bulgaria, which had by this time become a symbol of Russian imperialism, was divided into three: one part, the northern, independent; the second, named 'Eastern Rumelia', under Turkish protection; and Macedonia, within the Ottoman Empire. Austria-Hungary occupied, without annexing, Bosnia and Herzegovina. Russia took southern Bessarabia and also some hitherto Turkish territory on the eastern shores of the Black Sea. Britain guaranteed Turkey-in-Asia, asserted a new right to send her navy into the Black Sea, and annexed Cyprus from Turkey. This was a large step towards the partition of the whole Ottoman Empire. From the British point of view, what seemed to be achieved was that it was a partition rather than a Russian conquest. It was regarded as a great triumph for Beaconsfield, and the peak of his career.

Outside Europe, Disraeli had in 1875 arranged for the British Government to buy nearly half the shares in the Suez Canal Company. In 1876 Queen Victoria was made Empress of India. In the following year the Transvaal was annexed.

As soon as the Congress of Berlin was over, the Government began to lose ground. Depression in agriculture now became severe. During 1879 Britain was humiliated in the course of imperial adventures on two occasions, in January against the

Zulus, in September in Afghanistan. Gladstone, in his 'Midlothian campaign', attacked the whole foreign and imperial policy of the Government. When Beaconsfield dissolved Parliament, early in 1880, the Liberals won an overall majority of about 70. Gladstone again became Prime Minister, and Granville Foreign Secretary. Bright was joined in the Cabinet by another Nonconformist, Joseph Chamberlain, a Birmingham manufacturer of Radical views, ruthless in his methods, who had already proved a notable Mayor and a great party organizer. Gladstone appeared to have committed himself to reversing the annexation of the Transvaal, but at first decided against it. The white inhabitants revolted, and defeated a British force at Majuba Hill in 1881. The Government now conceded the Transvaal independence under British suzerainty. In the case of Afghanistan, Gladstone and his advisers tried withdrawal first, but then found it necessary to assert control again. In 1882 they took the most far-reaching decision in the imperial history of the whole period, to invade Egypt. Britain thus became involved in the Sudan, where a force under General Gordon was besieged by a native army in Khartoum in the winter of 1884–5. The city fell, and Gordon was killed, in January 1885. Relief arrived two days later.

The principal achievement of the Ministry in internal affairs was the passing of the Third Reform Act in 1884 and the Redistribution of Seats Act in 1885. Much of its time, however, was devoted to Ireland.

At the General Election of 1874 a Home Rule party under Isaac Butt had won 60 seats. The early efforts of the group to convert the House of Commons to their programme by constitutional means failed. Soon the more radical of the Home Rulers adopted the weapon of obstructing Parliamentary proceedings, which was easily done under the lax rules of the day. The leader of this faction was Charles Stewart Parnell, a young Protestant landlord from a Roman Catholic area, embittered against British domination. As the condition of Irish agriculture worsened in the late 'seventies, violent attacks on landlords became frequent. In 1879 Parnell helped to form the Irish National Land League, which linked the activities of the Home Rulers at Westminster with the agrarian revolt in Ireland.

After the Election of 1880 Parnell was elected leader of the
Home Rulers in the Commons, but did not at first command
their united support. The Government tried to meet the
agrarian situation by a Compensation for Disturbance Bill,
which the Lords rejected. Parnell then summoned Irishmen to
a campaign of 'boycotting' landlords. Forster, Chief Secretary
for Ireland, imposed a Coercion Act, against massive obstruction, early in 1881, but it was coupled with a new Land Act,
Gladstone's personal draft again, which the Lords were
frightened enough to pass and which went so far towards
solving the problem that Parnell felt his leadership threatened
by moderates. He retaliated by calling for renewed violence
in Ireland, and was imprisoned in October 1881 in Kilmainham
jail. In April 1882 he negotiated with the Government a
'treaty' in which he abandoned the Land League, accepted the
Land Act and promised the Liberal party cooperation. Coercion was dropped in return for an Arrears Act. Forster resigned.
His successor, Lord Frederick Cavendish, was assassinated
immediately, when he visited Ireland. In the upshot, coercion
was reimposed, but the whole party and the whole national
movement in Ireland were united behind Parnell in a renewal
of the moderation of Butt. Even the Irish Roman Catholic
Church, in defiance of the Pope, came to support him.

Until the passage of the Redistribution of Seats Act, Parnell's
party generally backed the Liberals. Then it took advantage of
Liberal disunity and Conservative overtures of friendship,
and helped defeat the Government in June 1885. Lord
Salisbury agreed to become Prime Minister. His willingness
sprang partly from the uncertainty of his position of leadership.
On Beaconsfield's death in 1881 Salisbury had become leader
in the Lords, Northcote had remained leader in the Commons.
But a group of dissidents in the Commons, 'the fourth party',
led by Lord Randolph Churchill, had escaped Northcote's
control and threatened Salisbury's. The latter's position was
strengthened when he became Prime Minister.

After the General Election held later in the year, Parnell's
supporters numbered 86. This was enough to give the Liberals a good working majority if they allied with the Home
Rulers; otherwise neither English party would command a
Commons majority. During the election campaign, the most
prominent Liberal speaker had been Chamberlain, pressing
what was called his 'unauthorized' programme.

At the end of the year it was suspected, but still not confirmed, that Gladstone had become a supporter of Home Rule, and the Conservatives hastened to dissociate themselves from it. Politics were poised for the greatest upheaval since 1832.

18

The Economy
1868-1885

1873 is a great economic divide. It was the peak of the trading boom of the mid-nineteenth century. There followed, until 1896, what is often known as 'The Great Depression'. This is a thoroughly misleading term, but that the economic climate changed in the 'seventies cannot be doubted.

It is still revealing, however, to look at the economic development of the period 1868 to 1885, or of a period as close to that as the statistics allow, in somewhat the same way as for previous periods. Despite all the novelties of these years, the continuity with earlier development is impressive. To take, as usual, population change first, the crude British birth-rate reached its highest recorded level, around 36 per 1000, in the 'seventies, and the 26,000,000 in the Britain of 1871 became 33,000,000 in 1891. Ten more towns passed the figure of 100,000 inhabitants between these dates, making a total of 28 towns of that size outside London. Four of these new recruits were in Lancashire, Blackburn, Bolton, Oldham and Preston; and the population of the county as a whole increased over the two decades by more than 1,000,000, to almost 4,000,000. This growth reflects the remarkable resilience of the cotton industry after its setback of the early 'sixties. Three old towns of the Midlands and East Anglia entered the category: Leicester, Nottingham and Norwich. Their emergence marks the rise of the factory in two hitherto domestic industries, making hosiery and boots and shoes. Aberdeen, Birkenhead and Cardiff all qualified as ports, Cardiff as the world's greatest coal-exporter, the others also as shipbuilding towns. The tenth in the group, Brighton, was the first seaside resort to enter this league.

The Growth of Towns (from the census figures of 1811 and 1891)

1811

Glasgow
Edinburgh
Liverpool
LONDON (11)

1891

Aberdeen
Dundee (2)
Edinburgh (3)
Glasgow (7)
Newcastle-upon-Tyne (2)
Sunderland
Blackburn
Bradford (2)
Bolton
Preston
Salford (2)
Leeds (4)
Oldham
Hull (2)
Birkenhead
Liverpool (5)
Manchester (5)
Sheffield (3)
Nottingham (2)
Norwich
Stoke-on-Trent
Leicester (2)
Birmingham (5)
LONDON (43)
Cardiff
Bristol (2)
Brighton
Plymouth
Portsmouth (2)

Where there is no number in brackets the
population was between 100,000 and 150,000

• Towns of more than 100,000 people
  Numbers in brackets give population to nearest 100,000

Glasgow, Liverpool and Manchester now had over half a million inhabitants each. London continued to grow as fast as any, from nearly 4 to over 5½ millions, but otherwise, at least until about 1880, the North and its towns were still gaining from the South. The agricultural labour force continued to decline, and some southern rural counties were depopulated. Heavy emigration occurred in the years around 1870 and in the 'eighties.

Of the staple industries cotton exported an ever larger proportion of its output, four-fifths in these years, and contributed a good third of the value of all exports. The industry's production from 1866–70, by volume, was about 50 per cent higher than from 1861–5 and slightly higher than from 1856–60; the figures for 1871–5 were about 25 per cent better than those for 1866–70, and those for 1876–80 almost as good; in 1880–4 there was an improvement over the previous decade of about 12 per cent. Woollen textile production grew at roughly the same rate – more slowly than before.

The iron industry, however, advanced very rapidly, largely through the exploitation of new processes for the making of steel. Wrought iron production grew, though more slowly than before, until 1882; as for steel, Britain manufactured perhaps 100,000 tons in 1860, over 200,000 in 1870 and almost 2,000,000 in 1885. Iron and steel output now amounted to 10 per cent of the whole national product. Exports of iron and steel combined passed 2,000,000 tons in the late 'sixties, 4,000,000 in the early 'seventies, then, after dropping below 3,000,000 in the latter part of that decade, reached 5,000,000 in the early 'eighties. Railway-building remained of importance. At home more than 4,000 miles of railway were opened between 1868 and 1885. Abroad 60,000 miles were built in the 'seventies and 100,000 in the 'eighties. Shipbuilding, the most successful British industry of the second half of the nineteenth century, also using great quantities of iron and steel, constructed four-fifths of the world's rapidly increasing output. As far as this sector was concerned, Britain followed the course expected of an industrializing country: she became from the 'sixties a great importer of iron ore, which she manufactured for export. Coal exports, on the contrary, more than doubled in this period and accounted for a growing proportion of total output.

These continuities with the experience of the early Industrial Revolution must be remembered. In a book whose terminal date is 1885 it is necessary to be especially careful not to allow the picture to be dominated by what appear to be harbingers of the economic transformation of twentieth-century Britain. But unquestionably there were great changes during this final period, of which some took immediate effect and others revealed their significance only later.

One of the changes was touched on in the Introduction. Britain, although still pre-eminent, was losing ground relatively. There remained respects in which she was drawing away from her competitors, as in the size of her merchant marine and her output of ships, but in general the gap was being closed. The most spectacular advances were made by Germany, which outdistanced France as Britain's main European rival in the 1860s. It has been estimated that in 1860 Britain possessed steam engines with a capacity of 2,450,000 h.p., France 1,120,000 and Germany 850,000. In 1880 Britain had 9,200,000, France 4,520,000 and Germany 6,200,000. As for iron and steel, in 1873 Germany produced over 2 million tons of pig iron, against France's 1·4 million and Britain's 6·6. In the late 'seventies British steel was cheap and plentiful enough to put many German firms out of business. But in the 'eighties the tables were turned: while British output of pig iron was nearly stable, Germany's nearly doubled. Still, in 1890 Britain made 5·3 million tons of steel, Germany only 3·2. The estimate was quoted in the Introduction that the United States' manufacturing production passed Britain's in the early 'eighties; but the definition of manufacturing used includes baking, and more sophisticated American manufactures made little impact in export markets until the 'nineties. From Britain's point of view in the 'eighties, the United States was her granary. Again, though the later superiority of the German chemical industry is notorious, it was not fully apparent until the 'nineties. The most complete industrial failure in Britain had little to do with foreign competition: the tin and copper mines which, disfiguring the Cornish landscape, had participated in the growth of the early Industrial Revolution virtually ceased to be worked in the 1860s. The end of mining did not, however, stop the growth of manufacturing. Britain, now using ore from overseas, had a world monopoly of tinplate production.

Other countries were bound eventually to catch up. There were even disadvantages in having led the way, for example the possession of much out-of-date plant. But in 1885 Britain's pre-eminence and the continuity of her industrial success still stand out most strikingly, despite growing competition.

As for her trade, though it too was declining relatively to other nations', it remained astonishingly large. In 1885 it amounted to 20 per cent of world trade, while the trade of Germany, France and the United States, taken together, totalled only 27 per cent. In the boom years before 1873 trade between Britain and the industrializing countries grew especially fast. Thereafter the trend set in which persisted until the end of the century. The markets of Germany, France and the United States, now protected by high tariffs, became relatively less accessible to British goods than those of less de-veloped countries, especially in the Empire. India, for example, took more of Britain's output of cotton textiles, which were no longer so easily sold in the more advanced countries. It was especially serious that the markets of Germany and the United States were becoming harder to penetrate, since they were show-ing the greatest increase in demand.[1]

Two tendencies already observable in previous periods developed so rapidly after 1873 that the change amounts to a change of kind rather than a change of degree. First, Britain's imports of food expanded vastly. The average annual import of wheat in the 'sixties was under 30,000,000 cwt., in the 'seventies over 45,000,000, in the 'eighties over 56,000,000. More generally, 'In 1868 the United Kingdom still produced four-fifths in value of what the inhabitants consumed of grain, meat, dairy produce and wool. ... In 1878 the United Kingdom supplied her inhabitants with scarcely one-half.'[2] In 1877, for the first time, the value of foodstuffs imported was greater than that of raw materials. These facts have many implications. Such large amounts of food existed to be imported only because of the development of the prairies and transport in the United States and similar changes elsewhere. The bulk of the grain came from the United States, the wool from Australia, meat

---

[1] P. Temin, 'The Relative Decline of the British Steel Industry, 1880–1913', in *Industrialization in Two Systems* (ed. H. Rosovsky) (London, 1966). I owe this reference to Professor D. M. Joslin.

[2] L. H. Jenks, *The Migration of British Capital* (London, 1938), p. 329.

from both. These areas were opened up only with the aid of British capital and emigrants. The new supplies were cheap. Even in years of good harvests in Britain, imported wheat now undercut the home producer. In bad years, which in the 'seventies were commoner than good, his position was hopeless. In the early 'eighties wheat prices fell below 40 shillings a quarter, lower than at any time since the mid-eighteenth century, and they continued to fall henceforward, until around 1900. Wool prices broke also. The benefit to the consumer is as obvious as the damage to the farmer. 1873 certainly marks the beginning of the agricultural depression. Until then, the high cost and difficulty of transporting bulk produce across Continents and oceans, the limited scope of settlement in the United States and Australia, the disruption caused by the American Civil War and the exceptional efficiency of British farming, nurtured by lavish capital expenditure, had delayed the onset of severe competition. When it came, it was made much worse by the appallingly bad weather of the 'seventies in Britain. In areas where wheat cultivation predominated, farmers suffered real hardship, land reverted to grass or pasture and eventually landlords had to reduce rents. The position was worst in the East Midlands and East Anglia. Where other grains were the main crops, and anywhere near enough to big towns to profit by a shift to dairy-farming and market-gardening, the story was more cheerful. Cattle-farmers suffered little, because low grain prices reduced their costs and meat imports were insufficient to diminish the demand for home produce. In Wales rents held up, in the Fylde Lord Derby's estates were prosperous as never before. The agricultural depression was not general. But even between 1879 and 1887 a million-and-a-half acres, a tenth of the arable area of Britain, ceased to be so cultivated. As has been seen, the agricultural labour force declined. On the other hand, the total area of farming land was still growing. The effects of the depression in Ireland and on the aristocracy will be considered later.

Secondly, there was a marked shift in favour of the consumer during these years. The fall in food prices was greater than average, but the inflation of the period before 1873 was sharply reversed and almost everything became cheaper. Indices are agreed that 1885 was the cheapest year covered by this book, with 1848-52 the only near competitors. The fall continued until about 1900. Money wages fell slightly from a peak in the mid-'seventies, but real wages, even corrected as far as possible for unemployment (which was particularly high in 1879 and in the mid-'eighties), rose decisively. It is estimated that they were 30 per cent higher in the early 'eighties than in the 'fifties and early 'sixties. This trend too continued until about 1900. Between 1868 and 1885 consumption per head of both tea and sugar in the United Kingdom rose by more than 50 per cent. In 1884–6, for whatever combination of reasons, the proportion of the population relieved under the Poor Law was lower than ever before in the nineteenth century, 2·8 per cent. Related to this improvement in the general standard of living was a notable development of the service industries and a diversification of manufacturing. 'Persons engaged in transport, commerce, art and amusement, literary, scientific and educational functions had risen between 1871 and 1881 from 947,000 to 1,387,000, or from 8·8 per cent to 11·7 per cent of the self-supporting population.'[1] The early 'eighties were the period of fastest development of multiple shops. In 1875 29 firms had 978 branches, in 1885 88 had 2787. Their chief fields of operation, apart from newspapers and sewing-machines, were groceries, meat and footwear. The International and Home & Colonial Stores became well-established. Boot's original chemist's shop was opened in 1877, and had branches by 1885. Bicycles and perambulators both date from the 'seventies, and their popularity from the 'eighties. From this period come marketed sauces and meat extracts, and, at least on any large scale, marketed jams and tinned foods. At length the mass of the population was deriving undoubted benefit from the Industrial Revolution.

Such calculations as can be made of the growth of national income give this period the best record of any in the nineteenth century. From 1861 to 1891 real national product per head is believed to have doubled. For what it is worth, the 'eighties are thought to have had a higher growth-rate than any other decade of the century. What, then, is 'depressed' about this period? Undoubtedly, after 1873, agriculture, at least as to wheat and wool. The staple industries, too, had a bad time in

---

[1] C. H. Wilson, 'Economy and Society in Late Victorian Britain', *Econ.H.R.* 1965, p. 185.

the later 'seventies. Overall, the rates of growth of cotton, wool and coal production were lower, and similarly with iron after the great boom ended in 1873. The most marked drop in a series showing percentage increase of industrial production per decade of the nineteenth century is that between the 'seventies and 'eighties. The 'seventies show an increase of 33 per cent over the 'sixties. This is substantially lower than the figures for the 'twenties and 'thirties, but not very different from those for the 'fifties and 'sixties. The rise from the average of 1865–1874 to the average of 1875–1884 is only 23 per cent. The relative decline continues until the mid-'nineties. The series, however, gives undue weight to long-standing industries. The rate of growth of exports and of trade as a whole also fell. In the late 'seventies foreign investment was comparatively low, and the days were now past when more capital was sent abroad than interest was earned there. There was a depression of prices, and a depression of industrial profits, at least in the established industries.

In particular sectors, then, and especially by value, there was relative decline. In the case of some branches of agriculture, there was absolute decline. The years immediately after 1873 constituted a grave setback in almost every field. But, per head and overall, in real terms the rate of growth of national product was more impressive than ever before.

It is the later continuance and intensification of the new trends of the 'seventies and 'eighties which have made historians criticize severely Britain's performance in these years. In the long term it was clearly desirable that she should invest more capital in industry, old and new. High general growth rates can only be sustained by high industrial growth rates. In some sectors at least there were weaknesses which more capital and better management might have remedied, for example in chemicals. There was certainly an ominous deficiency of technical and scientific education. There must have been a diversion of resources of manpower, especially of potential managers, away from industry both into commerce and finance and into administering and extending the Empire. But, up to 1885 and for some years thereafter, it was reasonable to be satisfied with the profits of British investment, trade, industry, shipping and financial services, especially in view of the unparalleled growth of per capita income. Entrepreneurs could hardly be expected to make contingency plans against the outbreak of a Great War in 1914.[1]

It must be noticed finally that certain new demographic trends began in this period, although nobody could know then that they would endure. Before 1880 the crude death-rate in Britain was always above 20 per 1000 per year and at its highest just over 25. Beginning in 1881 the rate fell below 20 per 1000 per year, and, with the single exception of 1891, never rose above that figure again. At length improvements in medical care, public health and food supplies had a distinguishable effect. The age-groups affected most were those below 35. The birth-rate was falling too, from the peaks of the 'seventies at least, but in the period covered by this book it did not go below the figures recorded for the early years of compulsory registration from 1838. It is likely that there is a direct connexion between the fall in infant mortality and the fall in the birth-rate. However, it is clearly not fortuitous that, following the prosecution of Charles Bradlaugh in 1877 for publishing a book on birth control, its sales rose from about 100 a year to 130,000 a year. Some historians have plausibly suggested that the desire to restrict the size of families was strengthened by the rise in middle-class standards of living in the 'fifties and 'sixties. Now that a larger domestic staff and a costlier education for children were considered necessities for the well-to-do, the economic pressure is plain. As yet it was only among the middle classes that the decline in the birth-rate was evident.[2]

There was almost no surplus rural and agricultural population left, at any rate in England. The country now had a smaller proportion of its inhabitants engaged in agriculture than any other. It was truly urbanized. This point reached, it is not surprising that patterns of migration changed. In the 'eighties, for the first time for probably two centuries, the towns of the North, though they grew by natural increase,

---

[1] A full list of references on 'the Great Depression' would fill pages. The controversy is as voluminous as that on population rise in the early Industrial Revolution. For a summary and bibliography see S. B. Saul, *The Myth of the Great Depression, 1873–1896* (London, 1969). P. Mathias, *Retailing Revolution* (London, 1967) is useful on shop development. For agriculture there is a magisterial article by T. W. Fletcher, 'The Great Depression of English Agriculture, 1873–1896', *Econ.H.R.* 1961.

[2] J. A. Banks, *Prosperity and Parenthood* (London, 1954).

did not attract so many migrants as they lost, whether to the South of England or to other Continents.[1] Movement away from the cities created by the Industrial Revolution has continued ever since.

---

[1] A. K. Cairncross, *Home and Foreign Investment, 1870–1913* (Cambridge, 1953), pp. 69–71.

19

Society and Politics
1868-1885

The Approach to Democracy

This was the classical age of the two-party system. It set a pattern which writers on the subject have quite incorrectly treated as normal: the Liberals and the Conservatives, each solidly united behind a great leader with a wide popular appeal, alternated in power, on the results of General Elections held every five or six years, using the substantial majorities accorded them to put through large programmes of reform, on their differing principles. In fact, this model does not apply perfectly even to the age of Gladstone and Disraeli. First, the former's popular appeal was much more conspicuous than the latter's. Secondly, in the case of both the Liberal Governments of the period, their initial majorities soon dwindled, and Gladstone resigned both in 1873 and 1885 as a result of Commons defeats. Thirdly, in the late 'seventies and early 'eighties there existed, as well as the two major parties, a highly independent party of Irish M.P.s. The question of reforms will be considered later. However, there is undoubtedly a sharp contrast between this period and the previous one. Parties were now more clearly differentiated and better disciplined; popular participation was greater; and legislation was more important. There is something of a contrast also with the period after 1886, when the presence of the Liberal Unionists further complicated the situation, when the Conservatives and their allies held power for 17 out of 20 years, and when domestic reform again receded into the background.

Between 1868 and 1885, however, behind the classical pattern, the system was developing very rapidly. The essential steps were being taken towards the democratization of politics and the parties. This can be illustrated in various ways. To begin with, it had hitherto been exceptional for the electorate to make the choice of a Government. Only in the special case of Melbourne's second Ministry had it turned out a Government by converting a Parliamentary majority into a minority. In 1868 an already minority Government lost seats, and Disraeli acknowledged the power of the electorate and created a constitutional precedent by resigning office before the new Parliament met. In 1874 the position was close to that of 1841, the General Election reinforcing the verdict of by-elections. But in 1880, for the first time, a Government with a considerable and perfectly firm Parliamentary majority was displaced by the electorate at one blow, the other party winning a still larger majority. The House of Commons, clearly, no longer chose the Government.

It is striking that at each of these General Elections the proportion of constituencies contested rose. In 1868 two-thirds were fought, as many as in 1832 and more than in any other previous Election. But, whereas decline set in after 1832, in 1874 the proportion of contests rose to nearly three-quarters, in 1880 to over four-fifths, and in 1885, after another Reform Act, to nineteen-twentieths, the highest ever before 1924. Further, the pattern of results over the country as a whole became more uniform.

Legislation also advanced democracy. In 1869 the electorate was further extended. Hodgkinson's amendment had proved unworkable: many ratepayers would not or could not pay their rates personally, and so could not vote in 1868. The new measure restored the possibility of compounding for rates while allowing the compounder in some circumstances to vote. By the Municipal Franchise Act of the same year, single women who were ratepayers received the vote in borough elections. The Ballot Act of 1872 made voting secret, reducing improper influence at elections and satisfying a Radical demand a century old. Then in 1883–5 the whole electoral system was remodelled, more fundamentally than by any of the other bouts of Parliamentary Reform.

The Corrupt Practices Act of 1883 made it at last possible to reduce drastically corruption at elections. The Act provided that it should no longer be necessary, in order to procure a conviction, to prove that a man giving a bribe to a voter or otherwise improperly influencing him was the agent of the candidate concerned. It further set very low limits on what a candidate might spend. The expenditure at the election of 1885, per head of the electorate, was less than a quarter of that of 1880.[1]

In 1884, by the Third Reform Act, the franchise in county constituencies was put on much the same basis as had been established for the boroughs in 1867, and the qualifications to vote were made the same for Ireland as for the rest of the United Kingdom. In consequence, an electorate of about three millions rose to about five millions, 60 per cent of adult males. Women were still unenfranchised for Parliamentary elections.

By the Redistribution Act of 1885 the old constituency structure was simply swept away. Just over 100 boroughs ceased to be constituencies at all, because their population was below 15,000. Others with fewer than 50,000 inhabitants lost one Member. These seats, and a handful more, were transferred to counties and large towns. The only constituencies unaffected were a few of those which already had only one Member, and a group of 24 boroughs with a population of between 50,000 and 130,000, which retained their two Members. All other counties and all larger towns were divided up into new single-member constituencies. The boundary commissioners were instructed to have some regard to existing local boundaries, and also to 'the pursuits of the population', but of necessity they created in most cases artificial electoral districts. Thus 'community' representation was abandoned, and the great traditional discrepancies vanished. Wales, Scotland and the North of England were now as adequately represented, on a population basis, as the South of England. Rural and urban areas were equally treated. Allowing for some flexibility, the day of equal electoral districts had arrived. Now the most glaring anomaly was a new one: it was decided not to reduce the representation of Ireland to take account of the decline in its population. Next came the survival of nine University seats.

Between 1867 and 1885, again, party organization developed enormously. The Birmingham Liberal Association led the way. Although founded before the Second Reform Act was passed and already then concerned to associate non-electors with electors, it faced new problems after the Act had doubled the

---

[1] C. C. O'Leary, *The Elimination of Corrupt Practices at British Elections, 1868-1911* (Oxford, 1962).

town's electorate. The matter was further complicated by two other legislative provisions, the 'minority clause' of the Second Reform Act and the system of election for school boards prescribed in the Education Act of 1870. Under this system each elector had as many votes as there were seats on the board; he need not use them all, and could give as many of them as he liked to one candidate. These arrangements made electoral organization especially worthwhile. For the Election of 1868 the Birmingham Association created for itself an elaborate ward organization which gave at least the appearance of democracy. All members, whether or not they had paid a subscription, had the right to vote for members of ward committees, which elected a central representative committee of 400 members, which in turn delegated its power to an executive committee of over 100 members, some of them co-opted, which finally appointed a small effective management committee. Technically, the central representative committee chose Liberal candidates for municipal and Parliamentary elections. This structure was the type for the later national party organization. It was known as the 'Caucus', was the first to give ordinary voters a say in the choice of their candidates, and was much more effective than previous organizations in getting out the party vote.

There was no difficulty in procuring the election of three Liberal M.P.s for Birmingham, despite the 'minority clause'. The town's Liberal majority was very large. At the first school board election, though, the Association, or more precisely its close relative, the Education League, was defeated by the Church party. The League was not identical with the Liberal party, but a ginger group within it; and its opponents exploited the more effectively the oddities of the election system. In 1873, however, with Francis Schnadhorst as its organizer, the League won control of the school board, and Chamberlain became Chairman. In the same year he was also elected Mayor.

Four years later, with a view to pressing the aims of Birmingham Liberals on the party as a whole, the same group of men founded the National Liberal Federation, which sought to bring together the numerous Liberal associations all over the country and to standardize their organization. These objects were not fully achieved until 1888. But already by the end of the period covered by this book the Birmingham

Federation was the most important organization in the party and had greatly influenced the others. It had become less dissident when Chamberlain had entered the Cabinet, and backed the Government generally, most obviously in carrying and enforcing new rules of Parliamentary procedure. These rules had been proposed in 1881–2 to thwart obstruction by the Irish party, but were generally destructive of private M.P.s' independence. The 'Caucus' also tried, not very successfully, to make election candidates toe its line.

On the Conservative side Disraeli blessed the foundation in 1867 of the National Union of Conservative and Constitutional Working-Men's Associations. This body (which soon dropped 'Working-Men's' from its title) held an annual conference and helped to mobilize voters in the constituencies. In 1870 Disraeli established the Conservative Central Office under John Gorst, who was also prominent in the National Union. After the election victory of 1874, however, the party leaders lost interest in both organizations. The National Union again attracted attention in the 'eighties because, during Lord Randolph Churchill's challenge to the regular leadership, he tried to use the annual conference to strengthen his position. But in 1884 he made a deal with Lord Salisbury under which the organization was restored to docility. In the same year Churchill founded the Primrose League, designed to bring women into the work of the party and to increase the supply of voluntary workers in general, as the new electoral system required. There was as yet little sign on the Conservative side of mass participation in the choice of candidates or the determination of policy, but at least there were the beginnings of a national party organization, which was to be much extended immediately after the end of the period. Salisbury said his epitaph would have to be: 'Died of writing inane answers to empty-headed "Conservative Associations".'[1]

Superficially, then – constitutionally, electorally and organizationally – democracy was advancing. The various factors in the process interacted. The legislation helps to explain the development of organization. No doubt both together help to explain the increase of electoral activity. The Act of 1867 and subsequent measures created much uncertainty in the minds of

---

[1] 9 March 1884 (Lady G. Cecil, *Life of Robert Marquis of Salisbury*, vol. III (London, 1931), p. 108).

election managers. Their forecasts proved wrong both in 1874 and 1880. Hence, partly, the number of constituencies contested, without which there could hardly have been such large transfers of seats in the House and such large majorities. These, better disciplined with the improved organizations, could be mobilized to pass reforms previously considered hopeless.

Less tangible influences were working in the same direction. In discussing the background to Gladstone's success in 1868, it has already been argued that there is more to take into account than the Reform Act of 1867 and the manner of its passage. During the months following the settlement of the Reform question, a Parliamentary coalition of Whigs, Liberals, Radicals and Irish, the old combination of 1835, was reconstructed, but backed this time by an alliance in the country between reformers variously interested in education, church matters, Trade Unions and temperance. Though the Conservatives carried Reform, it was Gladstone and his supporters who exploited it. As Derby had foreseen, his party could not hope to win an Election until after the Liberals had exhausted a reforming mandate. It was certainly not party organization which gave Gladstone his majority in 1868. He had the help of the Nonconformists and their societies, of the Trade Unions and of the small number of up-to-date organizations in the big towns. Otherwise his appeal had to be to opinion. He made speeches in the constituency he was fighting, S. W. Lancashire, on a scale hitherto unknown. He lost the seat, but the speeches were reported nationally in the Press and had wide effect. Gladstone adopted the role of Bright in the office of Palmerston.

Gladstone's personal part in the politics of these years can hardly be exaggerated. It is impossible to imagine anyone else making so much capital out of the new electoral system. If he had not lived to play the demagogue, the Liberal party must have wasted some of its opportunities.

> I am by no means sure, [he said] upon a calm review, that Providence has endowed me with anything that can be called a striking gift. But if there be such a thing entrusted to me it has been shown at certain political junctures, in what may be termed appreciations of the general situation and its result. To make good the idea, this must not be considered as the simple acceptance of public opinion, founded upon the discernment that it has risen to a certain height needful for a given work, like a tide. It is an insight into the facts of particular eras, and

their relation one to another, which generates in the mind a conviction that the materials exist for forming a public opinion and directing to a particular end.[1]

This was how he saw his demand in the Election of 1868 for a mandate to disestablish the Irish Church. It was not how he saw the crusade of 1876–80 against the Turks' Bulgarian policy and 'Beaconsfieldism'. He felt then that he was carried along by the public. But this was truer at first than later. He had resigned the leadership of the party after the election defeat of 1874, which he took as a personal rejection. He at first devoted himself to tree-felling, to ordering his vast collection of papers, and to theology, especially the question of Papal Infallibility. Very soon, however, the agitation arose against the Government's policy towards the Ottoman Empire. It was a movement of moralists and of churchmen of all denominations. What persuaded Gladstone to come out of his retirement was a meeting of working-men in Hyde Park in August 1876 which supported the agitation.[2] He closed the file on which he was working, docketing it: ' "Future Retribution": From this I was called away to write on Bulgaria.' He completed in a week a pamphlet on *Bulgarian Horrors and the Question of the East*. It was published almost at once and sold 200,000 copies in a month. While the party in Parliament, under Granville in the Lords and the Marquess of Hartington in the Commons, was divided, outside Westminster Gladstone refashioned the coalition of 1868. He seemed to have failed in 1878, when Disraeli was triumphing. But Gladstone agreed to stand for Midlothian at the next General Election, and during 1879–80, in his campaigns there, he set new precedents in speech-making, appealing to the people to sit in judgment on the whole record of the Conservative Government. When the country responded, Gladstone became Prime Minister, although not the official party leader in either House. Hartington and Granville told the Queen there was no alternative.

Organization mattered more in this Election than before. Though Chamberlain much exaggerated the success of the National Liberal Federation, it had some impact. But there was still nothing resembling a countrywide party organization.

---

[1] J. Morley, *The Life of W. E. Gladstone* (London, 1903), vol. II, pp. 240–1.
[2] R. T. Shannon, *Gladstone and the Bulgarian Agitation* (London, 1963), for this point and the whole agitation.

The victory, like that of 1868, was achieved by an alliance in the country behind a coalition in Parliament, both welded together by Gladstone. It is very significant that, whereas in 1875 Chamberlain had written Gladstone off – 'an ex-Minister of the first rank who devotes his leisure to a critical examination of the querulousness of an aged priest is hardly in sympathy with the robust commonsense of English Liberalism'[1] – in 1877 he was pressing him to sanctify the inaugural meeting of the National Liberal Federation with his presence. Hartington had refused to attend. Gladstone, by agreeing to do so, probably contributed more to the success of the Federation than the Federation did to the victory of 1880. It was Gladstone who made the new voters Liberal, and Gladstone who made the Elections national rather than local contests.[2]

Gladstone's success as a party leader, however, does not rest solely on the fact that he was so effective a demagogue. He was also a marvellous administrator and, more significantly still, a traditionalist, even aristocratic statesman. He genuinely regretted his demagogy, his support of denominationalism, his disputes with the House of Lords. They were all undertaken *faute de mieux*. His ideal remained the old Tory ideal of a beneficent paternalism in Church and State. In a letter to his grandson and heir, written in 1897, he expressed the hope that the family property based on Hawarden Castle might be enlarged.

> The influence attaching to [estates] grows in a larger proportion than mere extent, and establishes a natural leadership, based upon free assent, which is of especial value at a period when the majority are, in theory, invested with a supremacy of political power which, nevertheless, through the necessities of our human nature, is always in danger of slipping through their fingers.[3]

Unfortunately, landlords as a body had abused their trust. They had been personally extravagant and politically irresponsible. This was Gladstone's justification for attacking the House of Lords. They ought to have led the people in the right paths. Since they had not done so, others must do it for them.

---

[1] Quoted in J. L. Garvin, *Life of Joseph Chamberlain*, vol. I (London, 1932), p. 222.

[2] T. Lloyd, *The General Election of 1880* (Oxford, 1968), should be compared with B. McGill, 'Francis Schnadhorst and Liberal Party Organization', *Journal of Modern History* 1962.

[3] P. Magnus, *Gladstone* (London, 1954), p. 433.

The same sort of argument applied to the Church. In Ireland she had proved unequal to the duties of an Establishment. In England she had shown herself unfitted for the full role Gladstone had attributed to her in his book of 1838. The next best thing was to encourage all reputable denominations. The Midlothian campaign he defended on the ground that Parliament was not doing its duty. Yet part of him remained a committed landowner, Anglican and House-of-Commons man.

With these attributes he was a nearly perfect leader for the Liberal party in these years. Kitson Clark, in his *The Making of Victorian England*, calls successive chapters 'The Nobility and Gentry – Old Style' and 'The New Politics and the New Gentry'. Historically, the one did not simply succeed the other. Between 1867 and 1885 they co-existed, and Gladstone contrived to live in both worlds. The Second Reform Act established mass electorates in the large towns. Until after the Liberal party split over Home Rule in 1886 they always produced a large majority of Liberal M.P.s. The *Radical Programme* of 1885 could reasonably say:

> The great towns as they now are, constitute the source and centre of English political opinion. It is from them that Liberal legislation receives its initiative; it is the steady pressure exercised by them that guarantees the political progress of the country.[1]

In the English counties, on the other hand, the Conservatives had a large majority, and increased their representation as a result of the redistribution of 1868. In the smaller boroughs, which still included after the Second Reform Act over 50 constituencies with an electorate of less than a thousand, the Liberals tended to do rather better than the Conservatives. This would not have remained true, and so the Liberals would never have won an election, if the leaders had ignored the interests of these towns, most of them closely involved with agriculture.

Among both the counties and the smaller boroughs there survived seats which were virtually in the gift of landed patrons, to the number of about 80. Of these, though the majority were normally Conservative, about 30 were generally

---

[1] Quoted in H. J. Hanham, *Elections and Party Management: Politics in the Time of Disraeli and Gladstone* (London, 1959), p. 91. This book is the main authority for this discussion of politics between the Second and Third Reform Act.

Liberal. Earl Fitzwilliam could write to Granville in 1880 as follows:

> I believe it is mainly thro my instrumentality that six liberal members have found seats in this parliament. My own political opinions are well known, and I have every reason to believe, that it was confidence in the moderation of my views, which brought about this success – you will therefore understand that I must take a deep interest in the formation of a cabinet which I and mine will have largely contributed to place in power.[1]

There were good reasons, therefore, apart from personal predilection, why Gladstone put so many peers in his Cabinets. They could allege the same claim as Chamberlain put forward, that they had powerfully contributed to the victory of 1880, as by their inactivity or opposition they had abetted the defeat of 1874. In the absence of arrangements for collecting small subscriptions from the party's poor supporters, the great Whigs' donations constituted the chief source of election funds. It is often forgotten, too, that the House of Lords remained comparable with the House of Commons in power and prestige. A Government needed as much Front Bench talent in the Upper House as in the Lower. The Liberals, in a minority in the Lords, had a special problem here. In addition, politicians as a whole, and probably the public, still 'deferred'. Further, they accepted the notions that to deserve appointment to the Cabinet a man needed to have had junior ministerial experience, and that anyone who had once held major office had a presumptive claim to hold it again. Derby had had to make exceptions to the first principle on a large scale in 1852. Gladstone made special cases for Bright in 1868 and Chamberlain in 1880. But there was remarkable continuity of personnel from one Whig-Liberal Cabinet to another, and evidently this was considered right. Despite the fact that there were nearly 100 Nonconformists amongst them, and from 1874 even a few working-men, the majority of Liberal M.P.s were still Anglican country gentlemen. Hence, partly, the presence of Earl Granville in every Liberal Cabinet from 1851 to 1886, of the Duke of Argyll from 1852 to 1881, of the Earl of Kimberley from 1868 to 1895, and of the Marquess of Ripon from 1863 right down to 1908. Gladstone himself, of

---

[1] Hanham, op. cit., p. 28.

course, had a longer Cabinet life still, from 1843 to 1894. But, apart from him, it was the peers, who could easily start a political career early and had secure seats in the Lords, who provided the continuity. That it was necessary to humour them is evident from the importance attached to the defection from the Liberals in the 'eighties of Hartington and Goschen, who had both entered the Cabinet for the first time in 1866 and were still serving with the Conservatives at the turn of the century. The electoral reforms of 1883–5, followed by the Home Rule split, much reduced the weight of the Whig peers in the party. But at least until then it was necessary for the leader, if he was to win elections, to preserve the balance between the old and the new politics. The Radicals recognized Gladstone as far the most sympathetic leader they could hope for, while the Whigs, fearing that without him the Radicals might break away and form a new and more advanced party, confided in his conservative predilections.

For the Conservatives there was the same problem of balancing old and new, with the balance naturally tilted towards the old. In general, of course, they could not be the initiators and innovators in this field. Most of their followers even in the 'new' constituencies must be presumed to have been deferential, content to be ruled by squires. The preservation in 1867 of the old franchise in the counties ensured the continuance of Conservative control there, using traditional methods. Conservative leaders scarcely competed with the Liberals in electioneering speeches. But there was reality to Disraeli's intermittent visions of Tory Democracy and the Tory working-man, especially in areas where the Liberals were the oppressive 'Establishment' or, as around Liverpool, tied to Roman Catholicism. To win a majority, the Conservatives certainly needed to take some urban seats. They began in this period to benefit from the growth of suburbs, the physical separation of employers from workmen, middle-class from working-class, made more general by the development of public city transport. Districts like Edgbaston and Headingley joined Clifton as superior residential areas distinct from industrial and commercial slums in the same cities. Business, especially commerce and banking, was ceasing to be purely Liberal. The Conservative party was no longer overwhelmingly agrarian. There was a time-lag, as on the Liberal side, before Cabinet composition reflected this change adequately; but Cross was a Lancashire banker, and W. H. Smith, of the railway book-stalls, became First Lord of the Admiralty in 1877. Cross had won S. W. Lancashire against Gladstone in 1868 and Smith sat for Westminster. After the reforms of 1883-5 the Conservatives lost ground in rural areas, but, as well as strengthening their hold on Lancashire, gained heavily in the metropolitan boroughs and in the middle-class constituencies carved out of the large towns. It now seemed essential for them to take more seriously, not only Churchill's talk of Tory Democracy, but also the organizations and the genuine constituency opinion which he had exploited for his personal advantage. However, the Home Rule split and the uncovenanted accession to the Conservative side of both Hartington and Chamberlain postponed the reckoning.[1]

Little attention has been given to the question why the Third Reform Act and the related measures were passed. The two Front Benches worked together, with the aid of the Queen, against old-guard opposition from back-benchers of both parties. The Liberals had not intended to propose such a drastic redistribution. That the Conservatives pressed for something like equal electoral districts astonished Gladstone and must surprise anyone familiar with the debates of 1867. One factor influencing their attitude was the belief that the division of towns for electoral purposes would be to their advantage. They thought of themselves as undermining the 'Caucus'. But, especially given the lack of interest shown by Parliament and the public in the Corrupt Practices Act, it seems right to conclude that between 1867 and 1883 the supporters of the old politics had simply been discredited. In particular, it was scarcely possible for the party of the counties and of agriculture to defend the narrowness of the county franchise against the Liberal demand for extension. In general, while it was still thought necessary to tie the right of voting to the possession of a minimum of property or income, evidently, in the climate of opinion created by Gladstone and the Liberals since 1867, the old system as a whole was felt to be indefensible. In this case, the prior change of opinion was very much more significant than the Acts it furthered. The years 1886 to 1906

---

[1] J. Cornford, 'The Transformation of Conservatism in the Late Nineteenth Century', *Victorian Studies* 1963.

were hardly years of reform. But Parliament could not foresee this outcome. As with other legislation, it showed itself remarkably ready to act against the personal interests of its membership.

The Spirit of the Laws

Walter Bagehot, writing a preface in 1872 to a new edition of his *English Constitution* of 1867, made necessary by the passage of the Second Reform Act, expressed the fear 'that both our political parties will bid for the support of the working-man,' perhaps suggesting the public discussion of:

> topics which will bind the poor as a class together; topics which will excite them against the rich; . . . make them think that some new law can make them comfortable – that it is the present law which makes them uncomfortable – that Government has at its disposal an inexhaustible fund out of which it can give to those who now want without also creating elsewhere other and greater wants.[1]

A. V. Dicey, whose *Lectures on the Relation between Law and Opinion in England during the Nineteenth Century* (1905) established the view that Benthamism was the chief inspiration of the legislation of 1825–70, believed that 'collectivism' displaced it in the late 'sixties. 'The Reform Acts, 1867–1884, were carried in deference to the wishes and by the support of the working classes, who desired, though in a vague and indefinite manner, laws which might promote the attainment of the ideals of socialism or collectivism.' Collectivism he identified with a kind of socialism, 'which favours the intervention of the State, even at some sacrifice of individual freedom, for the purpose of conferring benefit upon the mass of the people'. Its characteristics include a willingness to breach freedom of contract, a desire to 'equalize advantages' and a tendency to treat men 'not so much as isolated individuals, but as beings who by their very nature are citizens and parts of the great organism – the State – whereof they are members.'[2]

Whereas Dicey's claims for Benthamism have been much disputed, those he made for collectivism have scarcely been challenged. Yet they are the more misleading. *A fortiori*, Bagehot's fears proved irrelevant to the period under discussion.

---

[1] W. Bagehot, *The English Constitution* (Oxford, 1928), p. 269.
[2] Quotations from 2nd ed., pp. 254, 64, 301.

THE EDUCATION ACT OF 1870

The best evidence for Dicey's view is the Education Act of 1870. This measure led to a large extension of State intervention, the greatest of the whole nineteenth century in practice if not in theory. It limited individual freedom, as understood by Dicey. It conferred benefit upon the mass of the people. It equalized advantages. It may be added that it cost a lot of money. The education vote was about £1,000,000 a year in the 'sixties; by 1885 the figure was about £4,000,000, by far the largest amount for any public service apart from 'Law and Justice' and defence. Local authorities were also spending £4,000,000 a year on education in the 'eighties, as much as on the police and more than on any other public provision except the Poor Law and roads.

By comparison with previous educational measures, the Act of 1870 was sweeping. Its essential aim was to create enough school places for all children between the ages of 5 and, generally, 13. To begin with, a last special opportunity was given to the voluntary societies. There was to be a 'period of grace' in which they could still obtain government building grants on the old basis. From the last day of 1870, however, these grants were to cease. Thereafter, the voluntary schools could hope only for maintenance grants, from the central government, equivalent to the amounts privately subscribed. In areas where voluntary effort had failed to make adequate provision by the end of 1870, there were to be elected school boards, which were to levy rates for the building of new schools, 'to fill the gaps'. This procedure was compulsory. On the other hand, it was a matter for individual boards to decide whether parents should be compelled to send their children to the schools provided. As for the religious difficulty, the boards were not permitted to allow the teaching in their schools of 'formularies distinctive of any creed'. That apart, they could prescribe what religious instruction should be given, excluding it altogether if they wished. Such instruction, though, had to be arranged at times when children could easily be excused from it if their parents so desired. Finally, by clause 25, the boards were empowered to assist poor scholars in denominational schools by grants in aid of fees. No other payments could be made out of the rates to help voluntary schools.

During the 'period of grace' 1600 successful applications for building grants were made. In many areas the 'Establishment' preferred to provide a sufficiency of school places by private effort, rather than risk the intrusion of a school board. Gladstone displayed his duality again. Nothing could be worse, he thought, than a school board for Hawarden. By 1880 the number of denominational schools had risen from 8,000 to 14,000 in ten years, and the number of children attending them from 1,200,000 to 2,000,000. Between 1820 and 1883 Anglicans raised £12¼ millions for the building and maintenance of Church schools, which compares with £15 millions during the whole previous history of the National Society. Roman Catholics also subscribed largely. The Dissenters made lesser efforts because they were more satisfied with the new State system.[1]

All the great towns, and many other places, had to elect school boards. By 1880 they ran over 3,000 schools, some of them in buildings originally erected for voluntary and private schools, and educated 750,000 children in them. On the whole, they were better equipped than the denominational schools. There was great variety of religious teaching. The London Board gave a lead which was widely followed, in prescribing Bible-reading 'with explanation'. After long struggles, the Radical Birmingham Board in 1879 allowed Bible-reading 'without note or comment'. Manchester's Board satisfied most Anglicans. Some boards in fact allowed the catechism into their schools. In Liverpool even the susceptibilities of Roman Catholics were considered, to the point that the Douai version of the Bible might be used. Clause 25 caused violent disputes, and had to be modified in 1876. By 1885 the church schools as a whole were educationally and financially on the defensive, though they contained the majority of the children, and though in most areas the 'Establishment' and snobbery were on their side.

As usual in educational history, it was political and religious disputes rather than the quality or breadth of teaching which engaged public attention. In this context the Act certainly marked a great extension of secularism. Already for forty years the State had had to be neutral as between the denomina-

---

[1] I have found especially useful M. Cruickshank, *Church and State in English Education* (London, 1963).

16 Formal Empire: Detachments of the Indian Army among the Afghan snows, and in fact surrounded, 23 December, 1879. (Sherpur, Laager and Abattis, with the Paghman range in the background.)

17 (*below*) Informal Empire: A cricket match on the parade ground at Kohat, N.W. Frontier of India, 1863 or 1864.

18 (*overleaf*) The centre of Birmingham, 1886; The Grecian Town Hall is on the right, the Council House (1874–9) in the centre, the Library in the right foreground and Mason College (founded 1874) which was to become the core of the University of Birmingham, in the left foreground.

tions. Now it effectively set itself up in competition with them. Immediately the 1870 Act intensified denominational disputes. In the long run it nullified them. The teachers constituted, in Disraeli's words, a 'new sacerdotal class.'[1]

Educationally, of course, the Act was of enormous importance, especially as strengthened in 1880, when school attendance was made compulsory over the whole country. By the end of the period, in England and Wales, only about 10 per cent of those marrying were illiterate. The number of children being educated, and the number of certificated teachers, trebled between 1870 and 1885. The quality of the education provided, measured by its cost per head, rose by about 70 per cent over the same period. New types of periodical were founded with the new educated class in mind, such as *Tit-bits* in 1880; and it is hard to imagine the 'new unionism' of the 'eighties, catering for unskilled workers, without the Education Act.

The Act, though, had very grave limitations. That the Act did not apply to Scotland, where educational provision was already more generous, is unimportant. The Scottish measure of 1872 was less radical. But it is significant in reference to Dicey's arguments that the voluntary principle was so elaborately respected. It is also highly important that nothing whatever was done by the State to make secondary or University education available to the poor. A Royal Commission report of 1867, which recommended that the State set up a national system of secondary education, was shelved. Many of those who supported and worked the Act intended to give only such schooling to the working class as would fit them better for their traditional employments. It should be added, however, that some progressive school boards were already by 1885 assisting a few secondary students, that private efforts much improved and extended secondary education in this period, and that several new University Colleges, including some which admitted women, were founded.

Some account of the passage of the 1870 Act must be given. It will be remembered that the Newcastle Commission had reported complacently on the state of popular education in 1861. The satisfaction this Report gave did not survive the publication of some private surveys of school provision in the

---

[1] G. E. Buckle, *Life of Benjamin Disraeli*, vol. V (London, 1920), p. 122.

great towns. In any case the mood of the educational debate
changed very quickly at the end of the 'sixties. The development
has not been fully studied, but it seems that these are the main
factors. The passage of the Second Reform Act led conservatives of both parties to take more seriously the education of
what Lowe called 'their masters', the new electorate. Then the
Liberal-Nonconformist resurgence of 1867–8 led to a much
wider demand than had existed previously for unsectarian
State education, preferably free and compulsory as well. The
most militant Dissenting elements were now found in favour
of a State system, on condition that it was not dominated by
the Church; and presumably their successes in other fields in
these years led them to think that that condition could now be
secured. There was opposition to this line within Nonconformity, especially among Congregationalists, who were
mostly voluntaryists. There was, additionally, dispute about
the meaning of 'unsectarian'. But the new movement put the
question on to the legislative programme. It also, like the
Nonconformist assault of the early 'thirties, called forth the
power of the 'Establishment'. A National Education Union,
based in Manchester, rivalled the League, based in Birmingham, and even defeated it, as has been seen, in its own strong-
hold. The Union reflected a shift in Anglican attitudes in
favour of State intervention. Other influences were the difficulties of the Education Department of the Privy Council,
administering what was virtually a State system without
adequate statutory sanction; the generally greater drive of
Gladstonian government as compared with Palmerstonian;
and the result of the Austro-Prussian War, which was thought
to demonstrate the advantages of the Prussian educational
system.

In Parliament the original Bill was considerably modified,
mainly to suit the Methodists. But it was finally passed by a
combination of Conservatives and moderate Liberals, most
of the Radicals and Nonconformists voting against. The Ayes
believed that they had achieved the best possible terms for
the Church, the 'Establishment', voluntary effort and religion. The Noes would not be content with less than their
ideal.

At no stage is there much sign of concern for the views of
the working men themselves. The Reform League had de-

manded the same as the National Education League, but its main stress was elsewhere, and its educational opinions attracted little attention. As with the great mass of nineteenth-century legislation for the poor, especially the urban poor, the Education Act of 1870 did what their 'betters' thought to be good for them rather than what they themselves requested.

TRADE UNION LEGISLATION

The Liberals were clear that they must take some action about the legal status of Trade Unions, to repay the working-class organizations for their support in 1868. Within the party, however, there were many manufacturers and some doctrinaire upholders of freedom of contract. The Trades Union Congress first met in 1868, and appointed a Parliamentary committee from 1871, with the principal object of rewriting the law of Master and Servant, and the law on combinations. In 1871 it extracted a measure giving the Trade Unions legal status. At least the verdict in *Hornby v. Close* was over-ridden. But another Act passed at the same time, the Criminal Law Amendment Act, reiterated the existing law on strikes, which, though variably enforced, could be interpreted to make almost any action involved in a strike illegal. Under this Act seven Welsh women were imprisoned for saying 'Bah' to a blackleg. In 1873 the Chipping Norton justices imprisoned strikers' wives!

Union membership increased very rapidly during these boom years, and the movement had now reached the agricultural labourers. So dissatisfied were the more radical Trade Union leaders with this legislation that they put up independent candidates at elections in 1873–4. Several Conservative M.P.s pledged themselves to help repeal the Liberals' measures. Largely because of support from Cross, the Unions got almost all they wanted in three Acts of 1875. The first, the Employers and Workmen Act, replaced the Master and Servant Acts, making a contract of employment purely a matter for the civil law. The Conspiracy and Protection of Property Act checked the judges' application to strikes of the law of conspiracy. The third measure repealed the Criminal Law Amendment Act. Peaceful picketing was now expressly permitted. 'Collective bargaining, in short,' wrote the Webbs, 'with all

its necessary accompaniments, was, after fifty years of legislative struggle, finally recognized by the law of the land.'[1]
Dicey himself says of these Acts:

> The compromise of 1875 represents in the main the combined influence of democracy and collectivism – an influence, however, which was still balanced or counteracted by ideas belonging to individualistic liberalism.[2]

Certainly, it dealt with men in groups, and in a trade dispute waived the ordinary law of contract.

LAND LEGISLATION

It was for Ireland that the largest measures of land reform in this period were enacted. Gladstone had convinced himself by the time of the Election of 1868 that it was his 'mission to pacify Ireland'. To do this he conceived it necessary, not only to disestablish the Irish Church, but also to change the Irish land law, to meet the grievances of the tenants. His first Irish Land Act, of 1870, extended the 'custom of Ulster' over the whole country, giving the tenant compensation for improvements he made to his holding. It further aimed to compensate him for disturbance if unjustly evicted. There was also a clause, as in the case of the Irish Church Disestablishment Act, under which tenants might be assisted by government grants to buy the land they leased. This Land Act had one serious flaw. For the sake of individualist theory and landlord interest, tenants were allowed to contract out of the provisions of the Act.

By the beginning of Gladstone's second Ministry the problem of Irish land had changed. In so predominantly agricultural a country as Ireland the bad harvests of the late 'seventies and the competition of cheap grain from abroad added up to ruin. The land could be profitable neither to tenant nor landlord. The Land League had the whole island in rebellion. The second Irish Land Act, of 1881, claimed to guarantee to the tenant a fair rent, fixity of tenure and free sale of his holding. It enforced its provisions by setting up a Land Commission of judges to determine rents. This was to abandon completely any notion of freedom of contract between landlord and tenant. Not until the First World War was any form of rent control introduced in

---

[1] S. and B. Webb, *The History of Trade Unionism* (London, 1920), p. 291.
[2] Dicey, *Law and Opinion*, p. 272.

Britain, but by this Act it was imposed universally in Ireland. The Arrears Act of 1882 attempted to deal with the case of tenants who had simply not been able to pay rent during the years of depression.

Even the 'revolutionary and socialistic' second Land Act did not solve the problem. Endless court cases followed, since a 'fair' rent was not defined. The Act was attempting to make 'dual ownership' work, but, as usual, the Irish appeared to have altered their Question as soon as Parliament had answered it. Only peasant proprietorship could meet the case now, and this could be achieved only if the State would provide the full cost of land purchase. The first measure to go so far was passed by the Conservatives in 1885, but the sum of money it made available was very small.

For Britain also, important reforms were made in the land law, but not of so startling a character. By the Agricultural Holdings Acts of 1875 and 1883 tenants in England and Wales gained much greater rights to compensation for improvements they made to their holdings. In 1876 a general Commons Act reversed the legislative trend of many centuries, and established a presumption in favour of the public's rights to commons as against prospective individual purchases and enclosers. By the Settled Land Act of 1882 'entails', arrangements controlling the descent of land over several generations, were much restricted, in the interest of the life tenants and a freer market in land. These statutes obviously have a mixed bearing on Dicey's thesis.

THE SOCIAL REFORMS OF DISRAELI'S MINISTRY

Disraeli's Ministry of 1874–80 has long enjoyed a reputation for promoting social legislation, and the Prime Minister has had much of the credit. Compared with the Liberals', the Conservatives' record in some fields is certainly impressive. Some of the measures concerned have already been discussed. Of these the most important, the Trade Union legislation, owed most to the sympathy of Cross. Disraeli was totally lacking in the capacity to devise detailed schemes of legislation. The most that can be said for him in this connexion, which still gives him great importance, is that, particularly in speeches of 1872, he had committed his party in general terms to social legislation, and that he backed Cross in the Cabinet.

It has been usual to list two other Conservative measures as specially notable in this field, the Public Health Act of 1875 and the Factory Act of 1878. These, however, were scarcely more than consolidating statutes. The most interesting of the other Acts passed by Disraeli's Ministry was the Artizans' Dwellings Act of 1875. It offered government loans to local authorities to enable them to buy up, perhaps compulsorily, property declared to be insanitary, so that it could be replaced by new houses. This embodies a glorious mixture of theories. The interference with property rights was justified solely by health considerations. The building of the new houses was firmly left to private enterprise.[1]

GLADSTONIAN LEGISLATION

Apart from Irish legislation, which was always treated as exceptional, and the Education Act, the record of Gladstone's Ministries gives little support to Dicey. The main work of 1868–74, it would seem, was to rationalize administration and to bring nearer equality of opportunity for the middle classes, particularly the Nonconformists. This latter was obviously among the motives of the Universities Tests Act, and of the Civil Service and army reforms. The Licensing Act also was most popular with Nonconformists. In 1870 and 1882 the first Acts were passed in the interests of a more distinctively middle-class minority, namely, to protect the property of married women.

Liberals in general, and Gladstone most intensely, were conscious of the party's debt to 'the Celtic fringe' and of the growth of nationalism in Wales, Scotland and Ireland. The Second Reform Act made Scotland even more of a Liberal preserve than before, and effectively emancipated Wales, enabling the Nonconformist majority to overwhelm the Anglican landlords. The Third Reform Act made Southern Ireland solidly Parnellite, which for many purposes meant Liberal. Before 1885 the Liberals did not become committed to Welsh or Scottish Disestablishment or Irish Home Rule, but worked, in subtler ways, to please their non-English supporters. Gladstone appointed in 1870 the first Welsh-speaking Bishop of St Asaph for centuries. In 1881 his Government passed the first statute which treated Wales as distinct from England, charac-

---

[1] P. Smith, *Disraelian Conservatism and Social Reform* (London, 1967).

teristically the Welsh Sunday Closing Act. Throughout the second Ministry the Cabinet was occupied with proposals for giving limited self-government both to Scotland and Ireland. In 1885 the Liberals secured the establishment of a separate Scottish Office.

CENTRAL AND LOCAL GOVERNMENT FINANCE

In general, it became ever more remarkable how little the central government cost. In 1885 its gross income reached £88 million, the highest figure to date. The gross expenditure of the central government, however, was smaller in absolute terms than it had been during the last years of the Napoleonic and Crimean Wars. The revenue constituted only about 8 per cent of the estimated national income, as against about 20 per cent in 1821 and about 13 per cent both in 1841 and 1861. The standard rate of income tax was even lower than in Palmerston's day: it actually fell to 2d in the pound. Gladstone's proposal to repeal it was not so fantastic, nor so out of tune with the times, as has been supposed, and it was defence estimates that thwarted him in Cabinet, rather than the costs of 'collectivism'.

Receipts of local authorities, on the other hand, nearly doubled between 1868 and 1885, to over £50,000,000, that is, they rose faster than national income. Birmingham under Chamberlain is the model municipality of the period, buying up its gas and water works, building a town hall, clearing slums. In none of these endeavours was it actually a pioneer. But it led the way for many other towns to a generalized 'civic gospel' which might even rejoice in worthwhile expenditure. One aspect of this development was the growth of 'municipal trading'. Not only did more authorities buy gas and water works, but under an Act of 1870 all corporations had the power to build tramways, though not to run them. To some extent the central government felt it should leave 'collectivism' to the localities. 'We are a Senate,' said Lord Salisbury of Parliament, 'not a vestry.'[1] As yet, though, the organization of local government was absurdly muddled; outside the towns the J.P.s still ran it in an old-fashioned manner; and the new Local Government Board, created in 1871, did little save replace the Poor Law Board.

---

[1] Quoted in P. Smith, op. cit., p. 267.

CONCLUSION

Dicey was clearly right in attributing some of the legislation of this period to the spirit of 'collectivism' or 'socialism', if by these terms is meant 'a willingness to breach freedom of contract', 'equalization of advantages', 'treating individuals as members of groups', 'sacrificing individual freedom for the purpose of conferring benefit upon the mass of the people by State intervention'. The last of these definitions involves no new principles, but its extension to education was momentous. Equalization of advantages, also not new, was carried much further. The Trade Union Acts of 1875 were genuinely novel in treating individuals as members of groups and in breaching freedom of contract. The Irish Land Acts breached it further.

Dicey's definitions, however, were very limited. They had to be if they were to apply to this period. This is neatly illustrated by Cross' disarming remark in introducing his housing measure: 'I take it as a starting-point that it is not the duty of the Government to provide any class of citizens with any of the necessaries of life.'[1] The Poor Law of course did just this, but was the product of an earlier age, which some in this period still wished to abolish, in the interests of individualism. But in high politics there was no idea before 1885, or for some years thereafter, of the Government's setting up pension or insurance schemes or building houses for the poor. Yet in Germany health insurance was introduced in 1883 and accident insurance in 1884.

From 1868 to 1885 virtually no additional controls were imposed on hours and conditions of work. The State took over the management of no commercial enterprises. Even free elementary education did not come until 1891. By Dicey's own definitions, there were serious gaps in the legislation. The equalization of advantages did not extend to making it noticeably easier for workmen to rise in the social scale. The doctrines inspiring the Irish Land Acts were not allowed to affect law in Britain.

Other evidence can easily be adduced to the same effect. Chamberlain's 'unauthorized programme' of 1885 was the culmination and extremity of Birmingham radicalism. He called it 'socialism', 'the death-knell of the *laissez-faire* system'.

---

[1] P. Smith, op. cit., p. 221.

The proposals varied from speech to speech, but at most they amounted to

> an extension of popular government to the counties, free education, land for the labourers, artizans' dwellings, the rights of the poor in commons and charitable endowments, a revision of taxation, including the consideration of the taxation of ground rents and the contribution of personal property to local rating; revision of the income tax with regard to precarious incomes: reform of the death duties, and graduated taxation.[1]

What was meant by 'land to the labourers' was the end of primogeniture and entail, recovery of commons, easier enfranchisement of leaseholds, higher rating of large estates and the provision of allotments or smallholdings by compulsory purchase. With regard to artizans' dwellings, Chamberlain did not intend more than that local authorities should have greater power to take up loans to finance slum clearance. There was no question of government, central or local, building the new houses.

Again, T. H. Green is usually taken to be the leading light of the Idealist school of Oxford philosophy at this time, exalting the State and defining freedom so that it embraced 'positive' opportunities, of education for example, as well as 'negative' liberties. He and his associates helped to inspire the sweeping social reforms of the Liberal Government of 1905–14. Yet Green's specific legislative proposals corresponded almost exactly with what Gladstone's first two Governments managed to achieve, most prominently the promotion of temperance and Irish land reform.[2]

Henry George, an American thinker, author of *Progress and Poverty* (1879), is generally regarded as a notable contributor to working-class socialism, indeed as the man who virtually brought it to life when he made a speaking tour of Britain in 1881–2. His programme, however, was confined to a modified form of land nationalization, namely, the levying of a tax on landowners which would take away all they drew in rents. It was claimed that the proceeds of this 'single' tax would suffice for all the needs of government.

This period, then, was a period of 'collectivism' or 'socialism'

---

[1] See P. Fraser, *Joseph Chamberlain* (London, 1966). The quotation comes from J. Chamberlain, *A Political Memoir* (ed. C. H. D. Howard) (London, 1953), p. 110.
[2] M. Richter, *The Politics of Conscience* (Cambridge, Mass., 1964).

only in a very limited sense. Even in that sense, these attitudes were not dominant. The politics of the period, and its legislation, are best understood in other terms, those of the main contemporary debate. The principal battle was between Nonconformity and the Church, which was still identified with the landed aristocracy and its privileges. Outside England nationalism heightened the feeling. The Liberals were the party of movement, and the Nonconformists were the only important policy-makers in the party, apart from Gladstone himself. Many of them were narrow, negative, destructive, as portrayed in Matthew Arnold's *Culture and Anarchy,* largely written and published in their year of triumph, 1868. They were determined, he said, to disestablish and disendow the Irish Church, but it did not matter to them that thereby a significant endowment was lost for ever to religious purposes. They were obsessed by the fear that 'the management of education should be taken out of their hands', rather than concerned 'to model education on sound ideas'. They chipped away at the land law which operated to maintain the power and wealth of the aristocracy, with no idea how a new élite might be found to replace them. They worried away at the trivial question of the legal prohibition on a man's marrying his deceased wife's sister. They opposed increasing government expenditure on social services. The members of the National Education League, it is true, showed themselves more positive than many Nonconformists, in advocating a State system of education. But they too proved captious at the details of the religious settlement of the 1870 Act and petty over clause 25. They helped to deny Gladstone the opportunity to improve Irish Universities, because it involved spending public money on a Church they hated. The relationship of Nonconformity with the party was complex. They made or unmade much of its policy; they had much to do with both its victories and defeats at elections; and their support was essential to its success. But the party was also essential to theirs. The history of the Birmingham organizations is instructive. They could not prevail when they provoked a coalition between Gladstone, moderate Liberals and the Conservatives. They were forced to the conclusion that they had more power within the party than outside it. Ideas of establishing an independent Radical party were never pressed. Rather, the Nonconformists sought to capture the Liberal party, and Gladstone, for themselves. Chamberlain's purpose in 1885 seems to have been to drive the Whigs out of the party while retaining Gladstone and the moderate Liberals. Probably this policy would have defeated its own objects, as Chamberlain's other 'unauthorized' crusades did, over Education in the early 'seventies and over Tariff Reform after 1903. He always overestimated his own, Birmingham's and Nonconformity's independent power. But, so long as he did not threaten the unity of the party, it was unlikely to be defeated in an Election, and there would be little it could do which he and Nonconformity disliked.

It might appear, and Chamberlain often suggested, that the towns were fighting the countryside. It would be more accurate to say they were fighting *over* the countryside. An astonishingly high proportion of politicians' time was spent on the problems of the continuously declining agricultural areas. As well as destitute Irish peasants, they worried about starving Scottish crofters and English labourers wanting allotments. There was also the question of extending the county franchise and its corollary, the introduction of representative county government. The Farmers' Alliance was an important ally of the Liberals in the Election of 1880, and Gladstone considered he had brought off a great political *coup* when he repealed the Malt Tax in the budget of the same year. Parliament, of course, always found rural questions more congenial than urban. And, just as in the United States the urban poor voted for free homesteads in the West, so in Britain they voted for 'three acres and a cow'. It should be remembered that most of them had rural fathers or grandfathers, and were familiar with rural problems.

Historians have often been tempted, with reference to this period as to others, to explain the limitations of government action by the nature of Parliamentary membership and of the electoral system. But it is difficult to do so for the age of Gladstone and Disraeli.

Gladstone found it politic and agreeable to surround himself with peers, but it almost seems that he did so in order to bewitch them into supporting proposals which they and sometimes he thoroughly disliked. The House of Lords gained only about 100 members in the whole period covered by this book, which means that it became relatively more exclusive. With a few exceptions such as literary men, soldiers, sailors and one or two politicians, all newly-created peers were substantial owners of landed property. None of them were mere industrial-ists and businessmen. Yet as a body they acquiesced in such measures as the second Irish Land Act and the Redistribution Act of 1885. As well as Whig tradition, rebellion in Ireland, agricultural depression and the persuasions of Gladstone, royal influence and the efforts of Conservative leaders help to account for this moderation. The electoral reforms of 1884–5 were the last measures to be agreed between the parties and the Houses through royal mediation. In this period the attitude of mind instilled into the peerage in the 'thirties prevailed, and ideas of constitutional balance survived. It was the Lords' habit to con-cede. Only after 1886 did the Upper Chamber become the creature of the Conservatives, and the Queen so partisan that she abandoned attempts to reconcile the Houses.

It is not clear that the mass town electorates enfranchised in 1867 exerted more influence than the unenfranchised rural labourers. But in any case they did not demand what simpliste sociology would expect them to demand. As the Webbs lament, 'the draft "Address to the Workmen of the United Kingdom" which the Parliamentary Committee [of the T.U.C.] submitted to the Congress of 1885, fell far short of Chamberlain's "un-authorized programme".' In 1885 'all observers were agreed that the Trade Unions of Great Britain would furnish an im-penetrable barrier against Socialistic projects.'[1] This hypothesis of Vincent's helps to explain some of the workers' attitudes:

> that while the Industrial Revolution produced proletarians in some factory districts . . ., over the country in general the economic growth with which it was associated worked for quite a long time in favour of a wider distribution of small property and a diminution of the relative power of large property.[2]

Certainly voting was not on what are usually regarded as class lines. 'The voting of Anglican clergy, sextons, organists, and gravediggers was more unevenly split between the parties, by a long way, than was voting of the most reactionary or the most revolutionary secular occupation.'[3] The 'classes' that mattered were still the 'Establishment' and the rest. The working class, as far as can be discerned, did not generally demand collectivist

---

[1] S. and B. Webb, *History of Trade Unionism*, pp. 373, 374.
[2] J. R. Vincent, *Pollbooks, How Victorians Voted* (Cambridge, 1967), p. 7.
[3] ibid., p. 18.

measures, however defined. What it wanted was to change the social structure in favour of Nonconformists and of the overlapping group of small independent men, who, incidentally, were felt to need special assistance in rural areas.

In the light of past history, mere participation in government was deemed a high privilege; Gladstone's appeals to the wisdom of the people were found enormously flattering. Maitland in 1888 was to condemn, in his *Constitutional History of England*, the kind of historical writing which spends pages on party struggles, but forgets institutions as soon as they are established and laws as soon as they are passed.[1] But the fault was particularly easy to condone in the period just before he wrote, for it was then that parties first became institutions and that their struggles mattered most, as democracy permeated politics.

Anticipations
As in strictly economic affairs, so in social and political matters, there are evident in this period anticipations of twentieth-century developments. First, as was perceived by Maitland long before most commentators, the output of legislation had become so great that Parliament had of necessity to delegate much legislative power to Ministers. New regulations and orders made by or on the advice of Ministers, under the authority of Acts of Parliament, already filled as large a volume each year as new Statutes of the Realm.

Secondly, the ways in which people outside the government service and outside Parliament sought to influence ministerial policy were changing. The characteristic method of the early nineteenth century, a society using meetings, petitions, pamphlets and so on, was much less important later. The extension of the franchise had brought politicians and the public into closer contact with each other. The Press afforded means for continuous dialogue between them. But the greater rigidity of Parliamentary alignments had reduced the extent to which agitation outside could act on individual Members, regardless of party. A political campaign was now much more likely to be attached to a party, as, for instance, Chamberlain's causes became embodied in the National Liberal Federation. Home Rule created

---

[1] F. W. Maitland, *Constitutional History of England* (London, 1908), p. 537.

its own party. The close discipline of the Parnellites, and their success in bringing their case before Parliament, encouraged the Labour movement to form a party in 1900. For special interests, like the railways, the shippers and the brewers, which at one time had been able to achieve much through a few M.P.s, it became necessary to organize lobbying more effectively and perhaps to identify themselves with either Liberals or Conservatives.[1]

Thirdly, the relationship between the components of 'High Society', the Court, the aristocracy and the plutocracy, was changing, as was the nature of their connexion with the political and intellectual élites. From the Regency down to the death of Prince Albert, they were all closely interconnected. Thereafter disruption was quite rapid. The Court went into endless mourning. The Queen became somewhat more active again in the 'seventies, but spent as much time as possible away from London, at Balmoral in Scotland, at Osborne in the Isle of Wight, in Germany, or, if Ministers pressed her, at Windsor. Intellectual Republicanism seems to have reached its highest point about 1870 and to have declined later in the century. The Queen did not cease to command, as a figurehead, the devotion of the mass of the people, which was to be revealed in the Jubilees of 1887 and 1897. But her Court did not recover its significance for 'High Society'. To some extent the void was filled from the 'seventies by the Court of the Prince of Wales, where the aristocracies of birth and wealth were welcome, and where some effort was made to cater for political and intellectual society. But the Prince's Court lacked the prestige of the monarch's, it was not entirely respectable, and in any case the difficulty of relating the various élites was growing. The hold of the landed aristocracy on politics was diminishing, and many lesser politicians could hardly attune themselves to Court life. The class of intellectuals was emerging as to a greater degree distinct from the governing class.

At length the power of the aristocracy was seen to be seriously threatened. The contraction of the agricultural population and the effects of the agricultural depression, which rendered it very difficult to profit much from rents, made it increasingly absurd that the peerage was still restricted to large landed proprietors.

---

[1] P. Mathias, 'The Brewing Industry, Temperance and Politics', *Historical Journal* 1958.

Indeed, few of the latter were able to maintain their position without converting themselves into businessmen as well. In 1880 there was still a sufficient supply of Liberal peers for the aristocracy to be credibly regarded as a governing class of broad enough sympathies to command continued deference. But no sooner was Gladstone's Government in office than the defections began: the Marquess of Lansdowne among others in 1880, over the Compensation for Disturbance Bill; the Duke of Argyll among others over the Second Irish Land Act. The Whigs and the Radicals campaigned in virtual opposition to each other in the Election of 1885. This time no Bulgarian agitation arose, to enable Gladstone to reunite the coalition. Instead, in 1886 Home Rule made the split in the party still more serious, and apparently irreversible. The aristocracy was already approaching the position of a mere interest attached to one party. However, though the militia had been wrested from the direct control of Lords Lieutenant, they continued to play a great part in choosing J.P.s. Representation was introduced into the government of the counties only in 1888, and the powers of the House of Lords were not curbed until 1911.

I have been at pains to deny that socialism, on any definition which would be considered appropriate in the mid-twentieth century, had much influence in the 1870s and 1880s, and to shew that, even on definitions acceptable to publicists of the period, it was less important than has been supposed as an inspiration for reforms. But the beginnings of serious socialist thought and action in Britain are to be found at this time. The general situation was favourable. The 'Great Depression' discredited for some the orthodoxy of Free Trade economics. In 1881 the Fair Trade League was founded, to work for a measure of protection for British producers against foreign competition. It was a period of growing concern with discovering the truth about the conditions in which the poor lived, and with considering how they might be improved. The Salvation Army was founded in 1878 by William Booth, who had been for thirteen years a 'missionary' in the East End of London. The organization belongs to the Evangelical tradition in that it was primarily devoted to spreading the Gospel. It belongs to the new tradition of 'social work' in that it was especially directed at the population of the slums. In 1883 was published *The Bitter Cry of Outcast London*, the most effective of several accounts of conditions in the East End produced in these years. In 1884 was established the first significant 'University settlement' in the East End, Toynbee Hall. By then Charles Booth had begun work on his vast survey of London, which began to appear in 1889.

When Karl Marx died in 1883, his principal work, *Das Kapital*, was still not translated into English. However, his thought was at last beginning to exert influence in Britain. Three years before Marx's death, H. M. Hyndman, a wealthy Trinity man, read *Das Kapital* in French, and was converted to its brand of 'scientific' socialism. In 1881 he founded the Democratic Federation, to propagate his views. The tours and writings of Henry George, though he was far from Marx's position, led many people nearer to it. The most significant convert made by the Democratic Federation was William Morris. He was already famous and prosperous as a result of his promotion of new styles and standards in design of all kinds of furnishings. In 1876 and the following years, he had taken an enthusiastic part in the agitation over Bulgaria. He served as Treasurer of the Eastern Question Association and was especially active in mobilizing working-class support. But the behaviour of Gladstone's second Ministry quickly disillusioned him. As soon as he joined the Democratic Federation in 1883, he read and absorbed Marx's writings. He had abandoned the mid-Victorian programme of class co-operation and adopted revolutionary aims:

> The basis of all change must be . . . the antagonism of classes: I mean that though here and there a few men of the upper and middle classes, moved by their conscience and insight, may and doubtless will throw in their lot with the working classes, the upper and middle classes as a body will by the very nature of their existence, and like a plant grows, resist the abolition of classes: neither do I think that any amelioration of the poor on the only lines which the rich *can* go upon will advance us on the road; save that it will put more power into the hands of the lower class and so strengthen both their discontent and their means of showing it: for I do not believe that starvelings can bring about a revolution. I do not say that there is not a terrible side to this: but how can it be otherwise? Commercialism, competition, has sown the wind recklessly, and must reap the whirlwind: it has created the proletariat for its own interest, and its creation will and must destroy it: there is no other force which can do so.[1]

[1] Morris to T. C. Horsfall, 25 October 1883 (ed. A. Briggs, *William Morris: Selected Writings and Designs* (London, 1962), p. 150).

19 Oxford undergraduates working on the South Hinksey Road improvement scheme originated by Ruskin, c. 1875. The scheme was a practical application of the 'gospel of work' and involved, among others, Arnold Toynbee. The road was ill-constructed, but the message was successfully conveyed.

20 Gladstone electioneering, c. 1885.

21 The Crystal Palace after its removal to Sydenham, c. 1887. The landscaping makes an interesting and characteristic contrast with that of Petworth (Plate 1). Socially, too, the function of the Palace, as a pleasure ground for workers and their families, paying for admission, illustrates society's rejection of the values which Lord Egremont's fête embodied.

In 1884 he broke away from Hyndman's organization (now called the *Social* Democratic Federation) and founded a Socialist League, intended to be the nucleus of a new political party. Another body of middle-class sympathizers with socialism dates from 1884, the Fabian Society, which soon contained among its members George Bernard Shaw, an Irishman later to become through his plays the best propagandist of the creed in Britain, and Sidney Webb, who was to be one of its most important theorists. The Society was explicitly opposed to revolution. As yet, there was very little sign of working-class socialism of a Marxian character, but the movement for the eight-hour day and the first extension of Trade Unionism to the unskilled have been traced to the early 'eighties.[1] In 1885, it so happens, James Ramsay MacDonald, illegitimate son of a Scottish ploughman, brought up in poverty in the fishing village of Lossiemouth, first took the train for England, where, in Bristol, later in the year, he joined the Social Democratic Federation. Within forty years he was Prime Minister.

---

[1] A. E. P. Duffy, 'New Unionism in Britain, 1889–1890: A Reappraisal', *Econ.H.R.* 1961.

20

Culture and Society
1868-1885

IT seems natural to characterize the last period covered by this book, as far as the history of the arts is concerned, as one of progressive disintegration. In retrospect, the 'fifties appear a moment of unity, when almost all new buildings were Gothic, when almost everyone was a believer, when writers wrote in a direct style, with a high moral tone, distinguishing unsubtly between good and evil. Comparatively, the 'seventies and early 'eighties were years of diversity and doubt.

The period is notable in secular architecture for the spreading popularity of what was called the 'Queen Anne' style, and of related rejections of Gothic, as practised especially by Philip Webb and Norman Shaw. The influence of the architecture of Anne's reign on their buildings was seldom specific, but they liked to use bare red brick and they avoided Gothic forms. Churches were nearly always made Gothic, but a more correct and austere style, derived from English medieval architecture rather than from French or Italian, become fashionable. J. L. Pearson is the best-known of the architects concerned, and St Augustine's, Kilburn (1870–80) probably his best-known building. Perhaps more important than this trend was a reaction against the drastic restoration of old churches. Scott had been quite capable of 'restoring' a whole building on the evidence of one bricked-up window. William Morris founded in 1877 the Society for the Protection of Ancient Buildings, devoted to safeguarding them in their mixture of styles and in their oddities from those who wished to unify them ruthlessly. The test-case, which provoked Morris to establish the Society, was Tewkesbury Abbey. The preservation movement nicely typifies a loss of confidence in late Victorian taste. In one sense the adoption of Gothic itself had betrayed a lack of artistic assurance. Now it was admitted that the nineteenth century could not make as good Gothic as the Middle Ages.

More important even than this aspect of Morris' work was his improvements in the decorative arts. He followed in the theoretical tradition of Pugin and Ruskin. Art was a reflection of a good society. The Industrial Revolution had made society bad, in that it divorced the workman from direct creation. Mass-produced structures like the Crystal Palace did not deserve to rank as architecture; machine-made patterns were not art. In furniture Morris' firm, started in 1861, made relatively simple but fairly conventional Gothic pieces, but used all the conveniences of mechanization. In tiles, wallpaper, textile patterns, stained glass and (after 1885) printing the work was more original, and the method of production more in accordance with his theories. Even so the reproduction of patterns was often mechanical. In all these fields Morris' designs, usually based on medieval examples, exerted great influence, and, more important still, his concern for the quality of such work inspired later developments in quite different styles.[1]

Britain was the home of the Gothic Revival. Nowhere in the world was it so pervasive, and nowhere else were its theories so significant. But the British took Gothic with them on their travels: hence the Anglican churches scattered over the Continent. They carried it with them when they emigrated. It captured other nations to some extent. The tradition of building associated with Shaw and Webb was also a British product, but was scarcely exported at all outside the English-speaking countries. Morris' 'arts and crafts' movement has no parallel abroad at all.

At last it is worthwhile to say something of British musical composition. The early Gilbert and Sullivan operas fall into this period: *Trial By Jury* (1875), *H.M.S. Pinafore* (1878), *The Pirates of Penzance* (1879), *Patience* (1881), and *Iolanthe* (1882). The musical Renaissance is usually dated from the performance of Hubert Parry's *Prometheus Unbound* in 1880. It clearly owed much to a broader cultivation of music in the country, for instance to the Crystal Palace concerts after 1855 and to the Hallé Orchestra's concerts in the North after 1857. The Royal

---

[1] P. R. Thompson, *The Work of William Morris* (London, 1967).

College of Music was founded in 1882 in competition with the Academy.

Tennyson continued to write freely, and so did Swinburne, and in 1868–9, with *The Ring and the Book*, Robert Browning made his name, rather late in life, as a poet. Oscar Wilde's first book of verse was published in 1881. Quite unknown to the world at large, Gerard Manley Hopkins, a convert to Roman Catholicism and a Jesuit, was writing the revolutionary poetry which, when published in the twentieth century, had immense influence.

Prose-writing was more notable. Thomas Hardy's first successful novel was *Far from the Madding Crowd* (1874), George Meredith's *Beauchamp's Career* (1876). The work of both authors illustrates the disintegration of the mid-Victorian unity. Meredith's involved writing is characteristic of the later nineteenth century, Hardy's belief in Fate rather than God one of the many aspects of the period's 'doubt'. Both, implicitly if not explicitly, criticized the conventional view of marriage. Samuel Butler's *Erewhon* (1872) was more forthright, an attack on law, morality and religion as found in Victorian society. The Churches figure as 'Musical Banks' purveying Handelian harmony, the Universities as 'colleges of unreason'; even the family is not spared. *Erewhon* represents the extreme of revolt in this period, and was too much for the vast majority. There was great social risk in admitting unbelief. The House of Commons spent weeks over a period of five years refusing Charles Bradlaugh, elected M.P. for the first time in 1880, the right to take his seat, initially because he would not swear the oath of allegiance and later because, while he now agreed to swear it, he had stated that it was not binding on his conscience, since he was an atheist. But Bradlaugh had made his name anathema to the respectable by supporting republicanism and birth control.

In educated circles disbelief was tolerated, if not flaunted and if not associated with too open a disregard for conventional morality. In the special case of George Eliot, living with another woman's husband, many people recognized her as a moralist, not just as a novelist, and public homage was paid to her even by some of the younger members of the royal family. Her philosophic position was widely shared by intellectuals.

I remember [wrote F. W. H. Myers, a young don in 1873, at the time of the incident] how at Cambridge I walked with her once in the

Fellows' Garden of Trinity, on an evening of rainy May; and she, stirred somewhat beyond her wont, and taking as her text the three words which had been used so often as the inspiring trumpet-call of men – the words God, Immortality, Duty – pronounced with terrible earnestness how inconceivable was the first, how unbelievable was the second, and yet how peremptory and absolute the third. Never, perhaps, have sterner accents confirmed the sovereignty of impersonal and unrecompensing Law. I listened, and night fell; her grave, majestic countenance turned towards me like a sibyl's in the gloom; it was as though she withdrew from my grasp, one by one, the two scrolls of promise and left me the third scroll only, awful with inevitable fates. And when we stood at length and parted, amid that columnar circuit of forest trees, beneath the last twilight of starless skies, I seemed to be gazing, like Titus at Jerusalem, on vacant seats and empty halls – on a sanctuary with no Presence to hallow it, and heaven left empty of God.[1]

At length, in the upper classes anyway, religion was on the decline, and, despite the continuing advance of Roman Catholicism and the persistence of Anglo-Catholicism as a minority movement within the Church of England, dogmatism was decaying among those, the great mass of the respectable, who were still believers. It is symbolic that, whereas in 1870 the largest group of new works published was on religious subjects, in 1886 there were fewer of these, and novels had taken first place.[2]

Other prose work in this period was especially important. Matthew Arnold, principally in *Culture and Anarchy*, was the prophet of a literary culture as virtually a substitute for religion. Two pieces of art criticism, Walter Pater's *Studies of the Renaissance* (1873) and J. A. Symonds' *History of the Italian Renaissance* (1875–86), both restored interest in their period and helped to found another movement of a kind unknown in the preceding decades, the 'Aesthetic' movement, valuing Art and the pleasure derived from it for their own sake. R. L. Stevenson's *Treasure Island* (1883) and H. Rider Haggard's *King Solomon's Mines* (1885) represented a new vogue for 'adventure-stories', the latter obviously related to rising imperialism. The period is particularly notable in historiography. William Stubbs followed his *Select Charters* (1870), documents of English medieval history, with his *Constitutional History of England* (1874–8). William Lecky's *History of England in the Eighteenth Century* began to

---

[1] Quoted in W. Allen, *George Eliot* (London, 1965), pp. 13–14.
[2] R. C. K. Ensor, *England, 1870–1914*, (Oxford, 1936), pp. 159–60.

appear in 1878. *The Dictionary of National Biography* was started in 1885.

Certainly there were some signs of disintegration. But they must not be exaggerated. By comparison with the modern situation, late Victorian culture was highly unified. Intellectuals were to some degree becoming distinct from the 'Establishment', but there was still a very close network connecting the more intelligent of the aristocracy with churchmen, the Universities, the professions, artists and writers. If the public now provided sufficient financial rewards to successful authors for them to be independent of aristocratic patronage, and if they were treated with a respect unusual in earlier history, they were a small and select band. It is not difficult to shew that, just as statesmen were related to each other, so were men of science and letters. There was a small group of upper middle-class families which contributed a high proportion of the intelligentsia of the late nineteenth century: interrelated Darwins, Wedgwoods, Huxleys, Macaulays, Arnolds, Butlers, Trevelyans and Stephens.[1] It was possible to enter the circle from outside, but many were born into it. Hence English intellectuals were not alienated from their society, as those of other countries often were. These families formed a link between the 'Establishment' proper and those whose talents demanded admission to it.

---

[1] N. Annan, 'The Intellectual Aristocracy', in *Studies in Social History* (ed. J. H. Plumb) (London, 1955).

21

Britain and the Rest
of the World
1868-1885

BETWEEN 1869 and 1871 two events transformed the world situation. First, in 1869 the Suez Canal was completed. Economically, it proved very beneficial to Britain: her ships made up over three-quarters of the tonnage that used it. It facilitated and cheapened her trade with India and the Far East. But it created problems for her Ministers, by making the Eastern Mediterranean even more important than hitherto to her interests. Secondly, the unification of Germany profoundly modified European power-politics. With the defeat of Napoleon III in the Franco-Prussian War it was scarcely possible any longer to regard France as the major European land power. Germany under Bismarck took the leadership of the Continent. At least for his lifetime, this change improved the prospects of peace. The only Power both able and willing to pursue an expansionist policy within Europe for the rest of this period was Russia.

Partly because of the opening of the Suez Canal and the consequent concern of the Powers over the state of the Eastern Mediterranean, European and extra-European affairs became more closely entangled together in this period. The Ottoman Empire was now more genuinely the route to India. Cyprus was taken by Britain as a kind of compensation for the weakening of the Turks in 1876–8, and also to balance a proposed French foray into Tunis, which took place in 1881. The return of competition for colonies among the Great Powers inevitably linked European and extra-European questions.

In the early years of the period the near-isolationism of the 'sixties was maintained, even strengthened. As long as Belgium was left alone, the British Government showed little inclination to interfere in the Franco-Prussian War. Clarendon and Granville, both undemonstrative Foreign Secretaries, were succeeded by Derby, 'the most isolationist Foreign Secretary that Great Britain has known'.[1] Disraeli, of course, believed in assertions of British power, and Salisbury was more positive than Derby. But when Gladstone returned to office he included in his Cabinet both Granville and (after 1882) Derby. 'Splendid isolation' was as characteristic of this period as of the last decade of the century, to which the phrase was originally applied.

Among interventionists, Disraeli was at least as ready to use force in defence of the Ottoman Empire as any Minister of the century, and he was less concerned than the other notorious friends of Turkey with the quality of the Sultan's government. He wished to give aid to the Turks whatever they did to the Bulgarians. Salisbury was prepared to work against Russian domination of the Balkans, and backed the mobilization of the reserves in 1878, which led to Derby's resignation. But he had no confidence in the Ottoman Empire, would guarantee only Turkey-in-Asia, and thought the establishment of independent nation-states like Bulgaria the best arrangement that could be hoped for. At the Congress of Berlin Beaconsfield and Salisbury worked skilfully together to secure British interests as they now conceived them, helping to procure a peace which lasted 34 years.

Balkan nationalism was a novelty in 1875. It could hardly have been expected to enter into Palmerston's calculations, because it had barely displayed itself during his lifetime. It necessarily affected Salisbury's, and came to play an essential part in Gladstone's. His sympathy with nationalism spread from Italy to Norway, to Ireland, even to the Sudan, where he saw 'a people rightly struggling to be free', and to the Balkans. He believed it right to sustain true national feeling wherever it was to be found. This was one aspect of a thoroughly moralist approach to foreign policy. He is quite often represented as a non-interventionist, and he certainly sometimes showed exceptional moderation, as over the *Alabama*. In reality, how-

---

[1] A. J. P. Taylor, *The Struggle for Mastery in Europe, 1848–1918* (Oxford, 1954), p. 233.

ever, he was a new and special sort of interventionist. He argued against action when he conceived it to be unilateral and selfish. But he believed it was Britain's duty to act 'to preserve the public law of Europe' and in the causes of justice and civilization. He preferred it to be visible that such intervention was collective, but, if he was convinced that Britain in a particular instance could embody the will or the 'moral force' of Europe or the civilized world, he would support her acting on her own. He would have gone to the aid of the Bulgarians in the name of the Concert of Europe. He justified the occupation of Egypt as an action collective in spirit if not in practice. He leapt to the defence of the Afghans after a border incident with Russia in 1885. 'We must,' he said, 'do our best to have right done in this matter.'[1]

Add to this variety of approach among the principal statesmen concerned the near-pacifism of Bright, and it must seem that Britain was taking advantage of her pre-eminence to indulge disputes within and between parties, and in the result a degree of confusion and vacillation in her policies, which a less powerful country could scarcely have survived. There can have been few periods of such uncertainty in her history.

About her Empire the same extended gamut of opinions displayed itself. Derby, whose office under Gladstone was the Colonial Secretaryship, had the traditional distaste for territorial gains. When an Australian delegation came to him urging annexations in the Pacific, he 'asked them whether they did not want another planet all to themselves.'[2] Gladstone took much the same line as in foreign affairs. Britain had a mission in relation to her existing colonies, a mission to make them free agents whose co-operation with the mother-country, if it were to continue, was to be unforced, and whose subordination, if maintained, was to be willing. The white colonies should be self-governing and look to their own defence. It was not to be hoped that they might assist in defending Britain. That would be to involve them in policies over which they had insufficient control and in affairs which barely concerned them. New annexations should be avoided, as beyond Britain's strength. British dominion in India was to be regarded rather differently. It had

[1] Morley, *Gladstone*, vol. III, pp. 144, 184.
[2] Quoted in W. L. Langer, *European Alliances and Alignments, 1871–1890* (New York, 1931), p. 295, from *Letters of Queen Victoria*.

arisen dubiously, but, now that it existed, it must be maintained. However, its spirit must be to educate the people of India to ultimate self-reliance. These were attitudes of long standing. It was a novelty of this period that some statesmen began to glory in the Empire. Disraeli was their prophet. It was he who had been responsible in 1852 for the famous dismissal of colonies as 'a millstone round our neck'. As late as 1866, he agreed with the future Derby that the separation of Canada was positively desirable. But in 1872, when he set up the Conservatives as social reformers, he also seized for them the imperialist position. He asserted that the Liberals had spent the last forty years trying 'to effect the disintegration of the Empire of England'. They had succeeded in this aim more completely than in any of their other policies, so far as they could succeed by action from Whitehall. But they had failed ultimately 'through the sympathy of the Colonies for the Mother Country. They have decided that the Empire shall not be destroyed.'

> The issue is not a mean one. It is whether you will be content to be a comfortable England, modelled and moulded upon Continental principles and meeting in due course an inevitable fate, or whether you will be a great country, an Imperial country, a country where your sons, when they rise, rise to paramount positions, and obtain not merely the esteem of their countrymen, but command the respect of the world.[1]

Disraeli's stand was extraordinary in comparison both with his own past views and with those of the bulk of his followers. In numerous ways, however, it is characteristic of him, and of his relationship to his party and his time. The history he deployed to support it was at best plausible, like his attempt to identify the interests of Conservatism and those of the working-man. But plausibility is the true coin of politics. Bland disregard of his previous attitudes was one of his attributes and strengths. His later actions shew, as in the case of social policy, that he had little capacity to put his principles into detailed execution. The purchase of the Suez canal shares, it is true, was a *coup* for which he was responsible and which had considerable effects on the history of imperialism. The invention of the Empire of India was his. But in detail he was pushed into annexation and imperial adventure by subordinates 'on the spot', whose actions

---

[1] See *The Concept of Empire* (ed. G. Bennett) (London, 1953), esp. pp. 257–9.

he blessed only after the event. This was true, as will be seen, both of the annexation of the Transvaal and the Afghan expedition. It is somewhat doubtful whether he meant what he said, or understood what he was saying, either in his anti-imperialist or his imperialist utterances. He was in all these respects the opposite of Gladstone, whose history was careful to the point of pedantry, who wrote books to justify his changes of attitude, who was superb at making specific applications of general ideas, and who used words like a casuist. In this particular context, though, Disraeli was outbidding Gladstone in his own trump suit, making morality serve rather than frustrate imperialism, accusing Liberals of

> viewing everything in a financial aspect, and totally passing by those moral and political considerations which make nations great, and by the influence of which alone men are distinguished from animals.[1]

Of course Disraeli was 'educating his party'. The phrase has often been applied to the 'fifties and 'sixties, and it is true that he then had much to do with weaning the Protectionists from Protection and, at some points, with interesting them in Parliamentary reform. But he spent most of his energies during those decades preserving his position as Derby's deputy and heir, and was more active in trying to fashion unlikely Parliamentary combinations than in making policy statements. As leader he proved much more of a creative force, and especially in the great speeches of 1872. It is typical too that the chief influence of these assertions of Conservative principles was delayed. It was not until the 'nineties that his party became unitedly the party of Empire, and later still that Tory Democracy and Tory Social Reform came into their own. Disraeli's greatest contribution was as a myth-maker. It is even more remarkable that he should have become Prime Minister when that was his great talent, and a talent as yet largely unappreciated, than that he should have overcome the disadvantages of his Jewish race and modest social origins. In his lifetime his success rested almost purely on Parliamentary skill. He could have risen so far only in a party denuded of its natural leaders. Having reached 'the top of the greasy pole', he put a stamp on British history which even Gladstone barely equalled.

During the 'seventies and early 'eighties imperialist attitudes

---

[1] ibid. p. 258.

spread. It became common form to say that there was a choice before Britain: of becoming great, or, as Tennyson put it, again in 1872, 'Some third-rate isle half-lost among her seas.'[1] All kinds of movements, relevant in earlier periods only to the domestic history of Britain, became associated with imperialism. Here is Ruskin, giving his inaugural lecture as first Slade Professor of Fine Art at Oxford in 1870:

> There is a destiny now possible to us, the highest ever set before a nation to be accepted or refused. We are still undegenerate in race; a race mingled of the best northern blood. We are not yet dissolute in temper, but still have the firmness to govern and the grace to obey . . . . Will you youths of England make your country again a royal throne of kings, a sceptred isle, for all the world a source of light, a centre of peace; mistress of learning and of the Arts . . .? This is what England must either do or perish: she must found colonies as fast and far as she is able, formed of her most energetic and worthiest men; seizing every piece of fruitful waste ground she can set her foot on, and there teaching these her colonists that their chief virtue is to be fidelity to their country, and their first aim is to be to advance the power of England by land and sea: and that . . . they are no more to consider themselves therefore disfranchised from their native land than the sailors of her fleets do, because they float on distant seas.[2]

Cecil Rhodes, having made a small fortune in the diamond fields discovered in South Africa in the late 'sixties, satisfied his ambition to go up to Oxford in 1873. He there came under Ruskin's influence. He venerated Oxford as Newman, Gladstone and Matthew Arnold did, but was soon planning to tie it to the Empire and to the advance of the Anglo-Saxon race through his Scholarships. Darwinism, and in particular the idea of the survival of the fittest, came to subserve imperialism. Alfred Milner, later to be the archetypal 'Pro-consul', was a product of the Balliol of the 'seventies and of T. H. Green, and deeply involved in the early social work of Toynbee Hall. It is notorious that the public schools, founded to furnish Anglican education for the middle-classes, became seminaries for empire-builders.

The chronology of imperialism is a difficult subject. With all these developments, Gladstone could win the Election of 1880, which he thought meant 'the downfall of "Beaconsfieldism"'.

---

[1] ibid. p. 256.
[2] Quoted in J. G. Lockhart and Hon. C. M. Woodhouse, *Rhodes* (London, 1963), pp. 62-3.

During the 'eighties, however, the imperialist pressures grew rapidly. The Imperial Federation League, which sought to bring the white colonies into effective association, was founded only in 1884, but had behind it fifteen years of schemes and discussions. In 1881–2 J. R. Seeley, Regius Professor of Modern History at Cambridge, delivered some famous lectures on *The Expansion of England*, which held out the possibility that 'Greater Britain', brought together by steam and electricity, would rival the emerging world-powers, the United States and Russia. It could be said that 'the shock caused by the news of the fall of Khartoum has no parallel in the experience of the present generation.'[1] This incident, followed by the Home Rule crisis, which clarified the issue of imperial unity and brought together on one side of the House of Commons and of public debate the great majority of those who placed their hopes for Britain's future on her colonial connexions, made imperialism the prevailing attitude.

For domestic politics and history the development of the imperialist mood is of immense significance. It is a question, though, what difference it made to policy, especially before 1885. There were very few imperialists among the Ministers of 1868–85. Some even of those who were prominent in colonial adventures later were at this time indifferent. Chamberlain himself had advanced only a short way by 1885 from his earlier separatist views.

At a minimum, though, the colonies were perforce taken more seriously by Ministers from about 1870. Gladstone himself spoke more of Britain's imperial mission thereafter than before. He proved right, though not exactly as he expected, that the removal of British troops from some dependencies in the early 'seventies would lead to greater imperial co-operation. The self-governing colonies offered military aid to Britain several times during this period. But, insofar as policy differed in the 'seventies and 'eighties from that of earlier decades, the main cause was events and attitudes outside Britain. Whatever statesmen might feel at Westminster, British subjects overseas commanded skills and weapons which made them capable of imposing order and promoting material progress in large areas of the world where the native inhabitants could do neither. More and more

---

[1] Quoted in Lord Elton, *General Gordon* (London, 1954), p. 430.

colonies existed, some officially 'responsible' for their government, some only loosely controlled, and, further, more and more 'informal' colonies existed. All of them were likely to feel the need for aid from the British Government in maintaining their position, and all of them were in a position virtually to commit Ministers to support actions taken without prior consultation. Moreover, the appearance of rival claims from other States proved a strong incentive to Cabinets to annex territory. If a Government was in any case going to have to answer for the acts of British subjects overseas, and especially if it was going to have to deal with international situations they had precipitated, then it would be better placed the more control it had.

South Africa in 1885

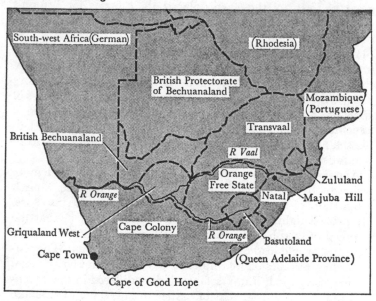

Griqualand West was annexed in 1871 because diamonds were found there and the Orange Free State had a rival claim. The annexation of the Transvaal was arranged by a minor official who was supposed to be trying to secure a South African Federation with a view to obtaining a united front among the white colonists against all natives. He did not exactly exceed

his instructions, and the unsatisfactory terms he made had to
be accepted by Beaconsfield's Cabinet. The Ministry refused to
send additional troops to fight the Zulus, but again a subordinate
in South Africa committed it to war against them, and so to
defeat. In Afghanistan the same Cabinet allowed itself to be
overridden at each stage by its Viceroy. In promoting the
greatest imperial adventure of all, one which led on to many
more, the occupation of Egypt, Gladstone and his colleagues
were not precisely overruled. Disorder in Egypt was threatening the security of traffic through the Suez Canal. The French
would not co-operate. Nor would the Turks. In the end the
Cabinet decided to take over the country 'temporarily'. They
and their successors were to promise to leave 66 times in the
next forty years, and on most occasions they meant it. In the
case of Gordon, Gladstone and his colleagues grossly misman-
aged the situation: they were divided on the Sudan question,
they gave it inadequate consideration and they procrastinated.
On the other hand, they had sent Gordon to the Sudan to
evacuate it, and they could hardly be expected to co-operate
cordially with him when he disobeyed them.

Territorial expansion in this period was, economically, less
successful than hitherto. While emigration reached its highest
level in 1883, most of it was still to the United States. Within
the Empire the older territories were more popular than the new.
A similar pattern is observable in trade and investment figures.
Though trade with the Empire was growing rather faster than
trade with the rest of the world, the great bulk of imperial trade
was with India and Australasia. In general, of course, trade and
investment were growing less rapidly than before, while the
formal Empire was expanding faster. Arguably, though, with
most of the world's surface already bespoken, and now that
other Powers were competing, it was necessary more often than
before to impose political control if any economic advantage at
all was to be forthcoming.

Pressures from the periphery were too strong for Governments. They still adhered to the policy of according responsible
government. In 1872 it was extended to Cape Colony, in
return for an undertaking that Britain would not have to meet
the cost of defending the country. But no Ministry succeeded in
permanently diminishing imperial burdens except in this way.
Among annexations of this period not so far mentioned were Fiji

(1874), British Somaliland (1884), Nigeria (1884), Bechuanaland (1885) and upper Burma (1885). Some of these territories were called 'protectorates', as was the part of New Guinea which the Australians seized without authority from London in 1883. Lord Derby's sarcasm was wasted on them: they thought they *would* like a planet all to themselves. Another mode of postponing annexation was tried in 1881, when the Liberal Cabinet agreed to charter a North Borneo Company. It will be apparent from the dates given that the 'scramble' for Africa, and for the Pacific Islands, began in the last years of this period. Gladstone's Government, the victors of Midlothian, could not escape being involved. They sent representatives to the Berlin Conference of 1884 which partitioned West Africa. Neither at home nor abroad could they or any other Ministers afford the loss of prestige which followed on defeat, or withdrawal, or failure to assist British enterprise.

It was not until after the end of the First World War that Britain's Empire reached its largest extent. Only after the Second World War did it become the Commonwealth. But two remote anticipations of the future, right at the end of the period covered by this book, are intriguing. 'There is no need,' said Lord Rosebery, Gladstone's sponsor in Midlothian, in 1884, 'for any nation, however great, leaving the Empire, because the Empire is a commonwealth of nations.'[1] In the next year was held the first meeting of the Indian National Congress, inspired by the liberalism and nationalism of the West, forming the party which was to win Indian independence.

---

[1] Quoted in P. N. S. Mansergh, 'The Name and Nature of the British Commonwealth' (Inaugural Lecture, Cambridge, 1954), p. 1.

22

Conclusion

A BOOK which attempts to cover seventy years of history in
many aspects cannot be provided with a satisfactory Conclusion.
It is possible to come to conclusions about specific historical
problems, not about whole periods. This Section will include
remarks on some matters which, because of the tendency of
the argument in previous Sections, have been inadequately
treated, and an approach to a conclusion on the problem
which has been most fully discussed in this book, that of the
relationship between the 'Establishment' and 'Other Forces of
Society'.

Two related subjects which deserve further consideration are
foreign investment and emigration. By 1885 the total British
investment abroad was about £1,500,000,000, as compared
with £100,000,000 in 1826, £200,000,000 in 1850, £500,000,000
in 1865 and £1,000,000,000 in 1874. The most rapid growth
had taken place during the great trading boom of the third
quarter of the century. It is likely that throughout the period
covered by this book British investment abroad was at least as
great as that of all other countries combined. Very roughly, a
third or more of all British capital investment was made overseas. The £270,000,000 which it is estimated that the British
Government and British subjects had invested in India by
1885 constituted nearly the whole of Indian investment. Over
half of the total investment in Australia and Canada was
British. Even in the United States at the same time, about a
third of railway securities were held by British investors. In
Latin America also Britain was easily the largest investor,
chiefly in transport and to encourage grain and meat production.

The United Kingdom was equally dominant in the story of

European emigration across the oceans, supplying over half the total. More than 10,000,000 people left the country for America and Australasia between 1815 and 1885. The majority came from Ireland, although from 1869 onwards the British exodus exceeded the Irish. Most went to the United States, though by 1885 increasing numbers were going to Canada and Australia. These immense movements of men and capital had enormous effects. Taken together with other British activities overseas, especially administrative, commercial and religious, they account for many features of the contemporary world. In particular, modern trade relationships between European and non-European countries derive in many cases from connexions first established in the age of Empire.[1] In this period also the foundations were laid of the Commonwealth, the Anglo-American alliance, the worldwide Anglican Communion, democracy in India and many other countries, and the primacy of the English language.

In domestic history certain trends which were mentioned in earlier Parts of the book should be traced further. In the Church of England the number of clergy and the number of ordinands were still growing until the 'eighties, though not fast enough to keep pace with the rise of population. The rate of church-building remained high. While there were fewer new foundations of public schools in the 'seventies and 'eighties than in the previous decades, the number of boys and girls being educated in such schools was increasing rapidly. The University population at Oxford and Cambridge grew fast in the 'sixties and 'seventies, having remained nearly stationary since about 1820. In 1882 Fellows of Colleges at Oxford and Cambridge were allowed to marry and retain their Fellowships.

Organized games were spreading. The first Rugby football international was played in 1871, the first Association international in the next year. The latter game was already becoming a popular spectacle by the end of the period. The Australians first sent a cricket team to England in 1878, when Dr W. G. Grace was at the peak of his career as a batsman. Lawn tennis, invented in 1874, very quickly established itself, superseding

[1] As well as the books by Cairncross, Imlah and Jenks, already cited, see R. Robinson and J. Gallagher, *Africa and the Victorians* (London, 1961), esp. p. 6 n. and W. Woodruff, *Impact of Western Man* (London, 1966).

croquet as a game which the upper middle class of both sexes could play as a social diversion. The Wimbledon tournament dates from 1877.

By the end of the period 4,000,000 newspapers were distributed daily in the United Kingdom.[1] In other words, it took little more than a week to sell as many as were 'stamped' in a year in the 'thirties. In the late 'forties, after the penny post had been operating for a decade, 12 letters were delivered each year in the United Kingdom for each member of the population. In 1884–5 the figure was 38, and after 1872 postcards could be sent as well as letters. Ten times as many passengers (exclusive of season ticket holders) were carried by the railways in the mid-'eighties as in 1850.

Communications, then, were vastly improved, and the public in consequence wider and better-informed. There is much evidence, too, that the middle classes, however defined, were growing in numbers and wealth. Between the Censuses of 1851 and 1871 the group of domestic servants increased by more than 50 per cent, twice as fast as the population. After 1871 the rate of growth slackened, as wages rose. The number of private carriages subject to tax mounted from 60,000 at the beginning of the period to over 400,000 by the end – this despite the development of railways and the widening of exemption from tax. According to the figures of the Inland Revenue, the total of incomes of over £150 per annum grew as follows:

Period	Actual per cent increase	Real increase
1851–61	23·4	12·2
1861–71	44·9	37·2
1871–81	33·2	48·0
1881–91	16·4	33·8[2]

The range of employments recognized as professions, and the numbers practising them, both increased. In 1841 the Census counted as 'professional persons' only clergy, lawyers and 'medical men', and made the total 63,000 for Britain. In 1861 the following groups were first described as professions: actors, authors, artists, musicians, engineers and schoolmasters. In 1881 they were joined by architects and land agents. Here are

---

[1] H. M. Lynd, *England in the Eighteen-Eighties* (London, 1945), pp. 367–8.
[2] Banks, *Prosperity and Parenthood*, the table from p. 132, other figures from pp. 83, 134–5, 91.

some figures for certain occupations of a professional or semi-professional character:

Occupation	Census of 1841	Census of 1881
Accountants	4,416	11,606
Actors	1,357	4,565
Architects	1,486	6,898
Barristers	2,088	4,019
Clergy	14,527	21,663
Engineers (Civil)	853	7,124
Ministers	5,923	9,734
Musicians	3,600	25,546
Physicians & Surgeons	17,500	15,116
Solicitors	11,684	13,376
Teachers	51,851	168,920
'Commercial clerks'	48,689	181,457[1]

Clearly there are statistical oddities here. If the decline in the number of physicians and surgeons is correctly represented, it was presumably due to a stiffening of standards following upon the reorganization of the profession. It is very hard to understand why the group of musicians should have grown so fast. But the general picture of a large increase in the numbers engaged in this category of employments can hardly be false. The information available about shareholding is scanty. It was certainly more widespread than in the early nineteenth century, but the predominant impression is that there were few small investors in this field, partly because there were still in the 'eighties comparatively few industrial and commercial companies whose securities were public.[2] The number of 'businessmen' is unknown, but must have been growing rapidly.

At the beginning of the period covered by this book the 'Establishment' appeared to be entrenched and embattled against 'Other Forces of Society'. In some respects it was still entrenched at the end, and the state of Britain in 1885 can be so described as to suggest that opposing forces had made little headway in seventy years. Despite the remarkable efforts of working-class organizations and movements, full democracy had not yet arrived, and socialism had made very little impact. With all the growth of industry, trade and towns, of the middle classes and Nonconformity, the landed aristocracy, still ex-

---

[1] W. J. Reader, *Professional Men* (London, 1966), table from p. 11, other figures from pp. 147–8.
[2] Cairncross, *Home and Foreign Investment*, pp. 84–9.

tremely rich, as yet undiluted by traders and manufacturers, retained its constitutional equality with the representatives of all other men, and the Church of England preserved its endowments and its position as the Established Church. It has been calculated that between 1835 and 1889 about 500 country houses in the grand sense, each with at least several hundred acres attached, were built or remodelled. The peak of this activity came as late as the early seventies, although by then rather more of it represented 'new' families adopting a traditional style of life than 'old' families refurbishing theirs.[1] By comparison with the rest of the world, Britain's economic development seemed exceptionally advanced, her political and social development unusually conservative. Unlike almost every other country, she had experienced no invasion, revolution or civil war in this period.

If the changes that had occurred are more carefully examined, however, they are seen to be more notable than appears superficially. A violent revolution may result in singularly little change. On the other hand, appearances may remain the same, and the substance be transmuted. *Plus c'est la même chose, plus ça change.* Though by the late nineteenth century the aristocracy had lost none of its land, wealth and constitutional status, it was much less wealthy in relation to the rest of the population, its actual political power had sharply declined as rotten boroughs had been abolished and General Elections had become more meaningful, and the peers retained power and respect only because they had changed their outlook, developing a greater sense of responsibility and a more pliant attitude to proposals for reform. Though the Church had kept its property intact, not only had it been reformed by Parliament, but its place in the constitution and in society had altered. It was less of an aristocratic preserve and refuge, less privileged, more like a denomination, stricter and narrower than it had been, its clergy more professional, its beliefs more specific – and more varied – and yet less widely acceptable. It still played an exceptionally large part in education, but the education was different from what it had been. Criteria of 'Scholarship' and 'Utility', as well as those of 'Godliness' and 'Gentlemanliness', had increased in importance.

---

[1] M. Girouard, *The Victorian Country House* (Oxford, 1971), pp. 5–6.

There remained something like a rift between town and country, and between Church and Dissent. London and traditional Society still held the new towns at arms' length. But the forces which had in 1815 seemed excluded from political participation now had their powerful representatives in the Parliamentary Liberal party. History does not bring problems to a solution, it modifies them. The aristocracy had submitted to some reform of old institutions and of its own attitudes, allied itself with the professional middle class and promoted commercial interests. But most industrialists remained distinct, not having attended old Universities. This new rift has had a continuing effect far into the twentieth century. Similarly, the development of nationalist feeling in Ireland, Scotland and Wales displaced in political importance the differences between regions within England. Soon after the end of this period the battles between aristocracy and middle class, Church and Dissent, were to give way to the war of Capital and Labour.

Three final impressions stand out. First, British achievements during the period were extraordinary, at home and abroad, and the more so because they were accompanied by a minimum of violence. Secondly, the story is in many ways unexpected, even paradoxical: it is not usual for aristocracies to preside over the making of commercial empires or over Industrial Revolutions. Last, it is misleading to think of Britain, the Power or the State, winning such success. Sometimes Governments made large plans which had something like the results they hoped for: the Reform Act of 1832, Peel's Budgets and the whole policy of Free Trade, and the Education Act of 1870 are cases in point. But in most fields Governments declined to plan, and the achievements were those of individuals and groups, commonly involving others than inhabitants of Britain. For this was an age of liberalism and internationalism.

NOTE ON APPENDICES

Except where otherwise stated, all statistics relate to the United Kingdom.

APPENDIX A

The national product of Great Britain in the nineteenth century (in £m.)

	National product at current prices	National product at constant prices	
		Total	Per head
1801	232	138	12·9
1811	301	168	13·2
1821	291	218	15·3
1831	340	312	19·1
1841	452	394	21·3
1851	523	494	23·7
1861	668	565	24·4
1871	917	782	29·9
1881	1,051	1,079	36·2
1891	1,288	1,608	48·5
1901	1,643	1,948	52·5

From P. M. Deane and W. A. Cole, *British Economic Growth 1688–1959* (London, 1962), p. 282.

APPENDIX B

Dates of Dissolutions of Parliament

Sept. 1812	April 1831	July 1847	Nov. 1868
June 1818	Dec. 1832	July 1852	Jan. 1874
Feb. 1820	Dec. 1834	Mar. 1857	Mar. 1880
June 1826	July 1837	April 1859	Nov. 1885
July 1830	June 1841	July 1865	June 1886

NOTE ON APPENDICES

Except where otherwise stated, all statistics relate to the United Kingdom.

Ministries, 1815-1885

Ministry formed	Prime Minister	Chancellor of the Exchequer	Home Secretary	Foreign Secretary
June 1812	Earl of Liverpool	*N. Vansittart *F. J. Robinson, 1823	Viscount Sidmouth *Robert Peel, 1822	*Viscount Castlereagh (from 1821 *Marquis of Londonderry) *George Canning, 1822
April 1827	*George Canning	*George Canning	*W. Sturges Bourne Marquis of Lansdowne (July)	Viscount Dudley
Sept. 1827	Viscount Goderich	*J. C. Herries	Marquis of Lansdowne	Earl of Dudley
Jan. 1828	Duke of Wellington	*H. Goulburn	*Robert Peel	Earl of Dudley Earl of Aberdeen (June)
Nov. 1830	Earl Grey	*Viscount Althorp	Viscount Melbourne	*Viscount Palmerston
July 1834	Viscount Melbourne	*Viscount Althorp	Viscount Duncannon	*Viscount Palmerston
Dec. 1834	*Sir Robert Peel	*Sir Robert Peel	*H. Goulburn	Duke of Wellington
April 1835	Viscount Melbourne	*T. Spring Rice *Sir F. T. Baring, 1839	*Lord John Russell Marquis of Normanby, 1839	*Viscount Palmerston
Sept. 1841	*Sir Robert Peel	*H. Goulburn	*Sir James Graham	Earl of Aberdeen
July 1846	*Lord John Russell	*Sir C. Wood	*Sir G. Grey	*Viscount Palmerston Earl Granville, 1851
Feb. 1852	14th Earl of Derby	*B. Disraeli	*S. H. Walpole	Earl of Malmesbury
Dec. 1852	Earl of Aberdeen	*W. E. Gladstone	*Viscount Palmerston	*Lord John Russell Earl of Clarendon, 1853

APPENDIX C [CONT]

Ministry formed	Prime Minister	Chancellor of the Exchequer	Home Secretary	Foreign Secretary
Feb. 1855	*Viscount Palmerston	*W. E. Gladstone *Sir G. C. Lewis (Feb.)	*Sir G. Grey	Earl of Clarendon
Feb. 1858	14th Earl of Derby	*B. Disraeli	*S. H. Walpole *T. H. Sotheron-Estcourt, 1859	Earl of Malmesbury
June 1859	*Viscount Palmerston	*W. E. Gladstone	*Sir G. C. Lewis *Sir G. Grey, 1861	*Lord John Russell (Earl Russell after 1861)
Oct. 1865	Earl Russell	*W. E. Gladstone	*Sir G. Grey	Earl of Clarendon
June 1866	14th Earl of Derby	*B. Disraeli	*S. H. Walpole *Gathorne Hardy, 1867	*Lord Stanley
Feb. 1868	*B. Disraeli	*G. Ward Hunt	*Gathorne Hardy	*Lord Stanley
Dec. 1868	*W. E. Gladstone	*Robert Lowe *W. E. Gladstone, 1873	*H. A. Bruce *Robert Lowe, 1873	Earl of Clarendon Earl Granville, 1870
Feb. 1874	*B. Disraeli	*Sir Stafford Northcote	*R. A. Cross	15th Earl of Derby Marquis of Salisbury, 1878
April 1880	*W. E. Gladstone	*W. E. Gladstone *H. C. E. Childers, 1882	*Sir William Harcourt	Earl Granville
June 1885	Marquis of Salisbury	*Sir Michael Hicks Beach	*Sir R. A. Cross	Marquis of Salisbury

* Members of the House of Commons.
All those described as Prime Ministers held the office of First Lord of the Treasury, except for Salisbury who appointed to it the Earl of Iddesleigh, formerly Sir Stafford Northcote.

APPENDIX D   Trend in Wheat imports 1810–1890

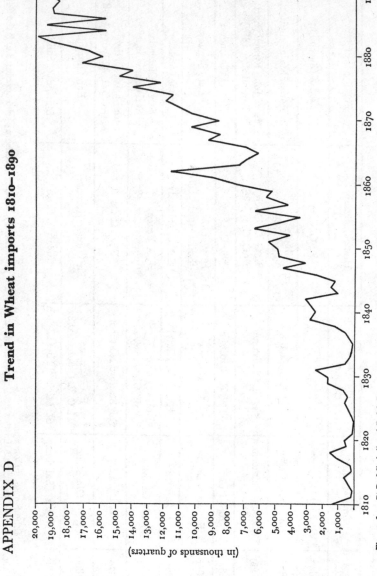

(in thousands of quarters)

Figures from B. R. Mitchell and P. M. Deane, *Abstract of British Historical Statistics* (London, 1962), pp. 97–8.

APPENDIX E

Trend in Sugar Consumption per capita 1810–1890

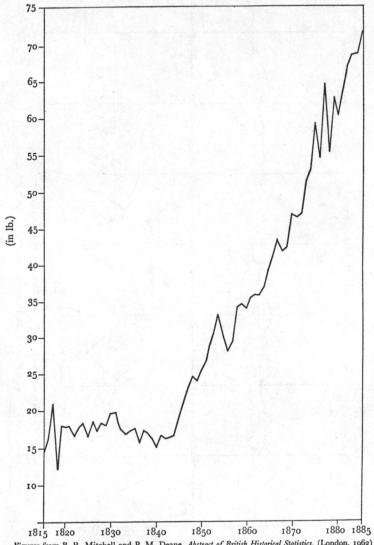

(in lb.)

Figures from B. R. Mitchell and P. M. Deane, *Abstract of British Historical Statistics*, (London, 1962) pp. 355-7.

APPENDIX F   British Prices 1810–1890

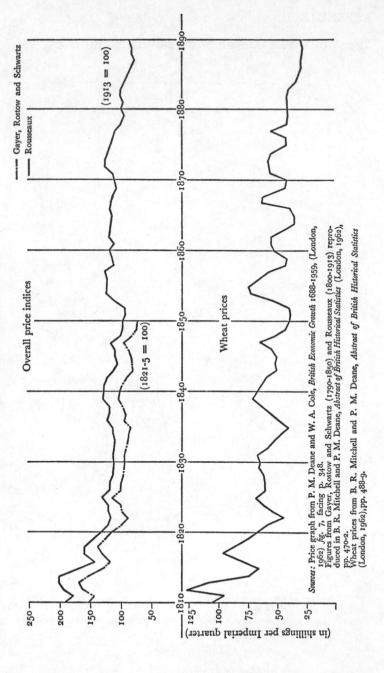

Overall price indices

Wheat prices

----- Gayer, Rostow and Schwartz
—— Rousseaux

(1913 = 100)

(1821–5 = 100)

250
200
150
100
50

125
100
75
50
25

(in shillings per Imperial quarter)

1810   1820   1830   1840   1850   1860   1870   1880   1890

Sources: Price graph from P. M. Deane and W. A. Cole, *British Economic Growth 1688–1959*, (London, 1962) *fig. 7*, facing p. 348.
Figures from Gayer, Rostow and Schwartz (1790–1850) and Rousseaux (1800–1850) repro-
duced in B. R. Mitchell and P. M. Deane, *Abstract of British Historical Statistics* (London, 1962),
pp. 470–2.
Wheat prices from B. R. Mitchell and P. M. Deane, *Abstract of British Historical Statistics*
(London, 1962), pp. 488–9.

APPENDIX G

Population of Great Britain according to the censuses (millions)

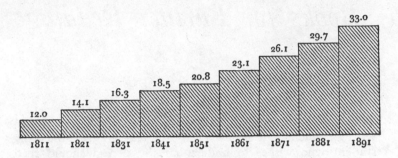

| 12.0 | 14.1 | 16.3 | 18.5 | 20.8 | 23.1 | 26.1 | 29.7 | 33.0 |
| 1811 | 1821 | 1831 | 1841 | 1851 | 1861 | 1871 | 1881 | 1891 |

APPENDIX H

Level of Central Government Expenditure 1810–1890

Figures from B. R. Mitchell and P. M. Deane, *Abstract of British Historical Statistics* (London, 1962), pp. 396-7. Graph represents total gross expenditure in £000,000 sterling

Books for Further Reading

The nineteenth century left behind a prodigious quantity of writing, much of it printed and still readily available. Any student who wishes to understand the period should read something of Jane Austen, Dickens, George Eliot, Trollope and other novelists; of Byron, Shelley, Tennyson, Wordsworth and other poets; and of critics, historians and prophets such as Matthew Arnold, Bagehot, Carlyle, Macaulay, J. S. Mill, William Morris, Newman and Ruskin. He ought also to sample *Parliamentary Debates*, *Parliamentary Papers*, newspapers, and the mass of biographies, diaries and collections of letters published in honour of the great personages of the age. A few contemporary writings are included in the list which follows, but for the most part the reader must be guided by the more elaborate bibliographies he will find in many of the modern works cited, and by his inclination.

1 GENERAL
(a) *Surveys*

Aspinall, A., and Smith, E. A., *English Historical Documents*, vol. XI (1783–1832) (1959).

Briggs, A., *The Age of Improvement* [1784–1867] (1959).

Burn, W. L., *The Age of Equipoise* [the 'fifties and 'sixties] (1964).

Davis, H. W. C., *The Age of Grey and Peel* [1765–1852] (1929).

Dodds, J. W., *The Age of Paradox* [the 'forties] (1952).

Ensor, R. C. K., *England, 1870–1914* (1936).

Escott, T. H. S., *England, Its People, Policy and Pursuits* (1885).

Halévy, E., *A History of the English People in the Nineteenth Century.* Vol. I, *England in 1815* (1924). Vol. II, 1815–30 (1926). Vol. III, 1830–41 (1927). Vol. IV, 1841–52 [incomplete] (1947).

Kitson Clark, G., *The Making of Victorian England* (1962).

Lynd, H. M., *England in the Eighteen-Eighties* (1945).

Woodward, E. L., *The Age of Reform, 1815–70* (2nd ed., 1962).
Young, G. M., *Victorian England: Portrait of an Age* (1936).
Young, G. M. (ed.), *Early Victorian England, 1830–65*, 2 vols. (1934).
Young, G. M., and Handcock, W. D., *English Historical Documents*, vol. XII (i) (1833–74) (1956).

(b) *The European context*
Hobsbawm, E. J., *The Age of Revolution* [1789–1848] (1962).
Taylor, A. J. P., *The Struggle for Mastery in Europe, 1848-1918* (1954).
Thomson, D., *Europe since Napoleon* (1957).

(c) *Reference*
Dictionary of National Biography.
Engel, J., *Grosser Historischer Weltatlas*, vol. III (Neuzeit) (1957).
Mitchell, B. R., and Deane, P. M., *Abstract of British Historical Statistics* (1962).
Victorian Studies, 1957–.

(d) *Other books not fitting well into the following classification*
Bentley, N., *The Victorian Scene* [illustrations] (1968).
Briggs, A., *Victorian People* (1954).
Pelling, H. M., *Popular Politics and Society in Late Victorian Britain* (1968).
Robson, R. (ed.), *Ideas and Institutions of Victorian Britain* (1967).
Young, G. M., *Victorian Essays* (ed. W. D. Handcock) (1962).

2 ECONOMIC AND SOCIAL
(a) *Surveys*
Ashworth, W., *An Economic History of England, 1870-1939* (1960).
Briggs, A., *Victorian Cities* (1963).
Checkland, S. G., *The Rise of Industrial Society in England, 1815–1885* (1964).
Clapham, J. H., *An Economic History of Modern Britain*. Vol. I, 1820–50 (2nd ed., 1930). Vol. II, 1850–86 (1932).
Chambers, J. D., and Mingay, G. E., *The Agricultural Revolution, 1750–1880* (1966).
Deane, P. M., and Cole, W. A., *British Economic Growth, 1688–1959* (2nd ed., 1967).
Glass, D. V., and Eversley, D. E. C. (ed.), *Population in History* (1965).

Habakkuk, H. J., *American and British Technology in the Nineteenth Century* (1962).

Hobsbawm, E. J., *Industry and Empire* (1968).

Imlah, A. H., *Economic Elements in the Pax Britannica* (1958).

Landes, D. S., 'Technological Change and Development in Western Europe, 1750–1914', ch. V of *Cambridge Economic History of Europe*, vol. VI (i) (1965).

Mathias, P., *The First Industrial Nation* (1969).

Perkin, H., *The Origins of Modern English Society, 1780–1880* (1969).

Porter, G. R., *The Progress of the Nation* (2nd ed., 1847, and (ed. F. W. Hirst) 1912).

Rostow, W. W., *The British Economy of the Nineteenth Century* (1948).

Thompson, F. M. L., *English Landed Society in the Nineteenth Century* (1963).

Woodruff, W., *Impact of Western Man* (1966).

(b) *Special studies*

Altick, R. D., *The English Common Reader* (1963).

Ashby, M. K., *Joseph Ashby of Tysoe* (1961).

Banks, J. A., *Prosperity and Parenthood* (1954).

Briggs, A. (ed.), *Chartist Studies* (1959).

Cairncross, A. K., *Home and Foreign Investment, 1870–1913* (1953).

Carrothers, W. A., *Emigration from the British Isles* (1965).

Edwards, R. D., and Williams, T. D. (ed.), *The Great Famine* (1956).

Engels, F., *The Condition of the Working-Class in England in 1844* (1892).

Finer, S. E., *The Life and Times of Sir Edwin Chadwick* (1952).

Flinn, M. W. (ed.), *Chadwick's Sanitary Report of 1842* (1965).

Hobsbawm, E. J., and Rudé, G., *Captain Swing* (1969).

Hobsbawm, E. J., *Labouring Men* (1964).

Jenks, L. H., *The Migration of British Capital to 1875* (1927).

Jones, E. L., *The Development of English Agriculture, 1815–1873* (1968).

Lambert, R. J., *Sir John Simon* (1963).

Nurkse, R., *Patterns of Trade and Development* (1962).

Reader, W. J., *Professional Men* (1966).

Robbins, M., *The Railway Age* (1965).

Roberts, D., *Victorian Origins of the British Welfare State* (1960).

Rolt, L. T. C., *Isambard Kingdom Brunel* (1957).

Saul, S. B., *The Myth of the Great Depression, 1873–1896* (1969).

Simon, B., *Studies in English Education, 1780–1870* (1960).

Thompson, E. P., *The Making of the English Working Class* (revised ed., 1968).

The History of 'The Times'. Vol. I, 1785–1841 (1935). Vol. II, 1841–84 (1939).

Webb, S. & B., *The History of Trade Unionism* (1894).

Woodham-Smith, C., *The Great Hunger* (1962).

(c) *Articles of special importance*

Chaloner, W. H., 'The Hungry Forties' (Historical Association Aids for Teachers, No. 1) (1957).

Fletcher, T. W., 'The Great Depression of English Agriculture', *Econ.H.R.* 1961.

Fairlie, S., 'The Nineteenth-Century Corn Law Reconsidered', *Econ.H.R.* 1965.

Mather, F. C., 'Chartism' (Historical Association pamphlet, 1965).

Mitchell, B. R., 'The Coming of the Railways and United Kingdom Growth', *Journal of Economic History*, 1964.

Robinson, E. A. G., 'The Changing Structure of the British Economy', *Economic Journal* 1954.

Thompson, F. M. L., 'The Second Agricultural Revolution, 1815–1880', *Econ.H.R.* 1968.

Williams, J. E., 'The British Standard of Living, 1750–1850', *Econ.H.R.* 1966.

Wilson, C. H., 'Economy and Society in Late Victorian Britain', *Econ.H.R.* 1965.

3 POLITICAL AND CONSTITUTIONAL

(a) *Books other than biographies*

Bagehot, W., *The English Constitution* (2nd ed., 1872).

Brock, W. R., *Lord Liverpool and Liberal Toryism, 1820–7* (1941).

Cowling, M. J., *1867: Disraeli, Gladstone and Revolution* (1967).

Dicey, A. V., *Lectures on the relation between Law and Public Opinion in England during the Nineteenth Century* (2nd ed., 1914).

Feuchtwanger, E. J., *Disraeli, Democracy, and the Tory Party* (1968).

Foord, A. S., *His Majesty's Opposition, 1714–1830* (1964).

Gash, N., *Politics in the Age of Peel* (1953).

Gash, N., *Reaction and Reconstruction in English Politics, 1832–52* (1965).

Hanham, H. J., *Elections and Party Management: Politics in the Time of Disraeli and Gladstone* (1959).

Hanham, H. J., *The Nineteenth-Century Constitution* [documents] (1969).

Harrison, R., *Before the Socialists* (1965).

Kemp, B., *King and Commons, 1660–1832* (1957).

Mackintosh, J. P., *The British Cabinet* (2nd ed., 1968).

Maitland, F. W., *The Constitutional History of England* (1908).

McCord, N., *The Anti-Corn Law League* (1958).

O'Brien, C. C., *Parnell and his Party, 1880–90* (1957).

Shannon, R. T., *Gladstone and the Bulgarian Agitation 1876* (1963).

Smith, F. B., *The Making of the Second Reform Bill* (1966).

Smith, P., *Disraelian Conservatism and Social Reform* (1967).

Southgate, D., *The Passing of the Whigs, 1832–86* (1962).

Vincent, J. R., *The Formation of the Liberal Party, 1857–68* (1966).

(b) *Biographies*

Blake, R., *Disraeli* (1966).

Garvin, J., *Life of Joseph Chamberlain*, vol. I (1932).

Cecil, Lord David, *Lord Melbourne* (2 vols., 1939 and 1954).

Longford, E., *Victoria R.I* (1964).

Magnus, P., *Gladstone* (1954).

Morley, J., *The Life of W. E. Gladstone* (3 vols., 1903).

(c) *Articles of special importance*

Brebner, J. B., 'Laissez-Faire and State Intervention in Nineteenth-Century Britain', *Journal of Economic History* 1948.

Hanham, H. J., 'The Reformed Electoral System in Great Britain, 1832–1914' (Historical Association Pamphlet, 1968).

Hart, J., 'Nineteenth-Century Social History: a Tory Interpretation of History', *Past and Present* 1965.

Herrick, F. H., 'The Origins of the National Liberal Federation', *Journal of Modern History* 1945.

Kitson Clark, G., ' "Statesmen in Disguise": Reflexions on the History of the Neutrality of the Civil Service', *Historical Journal* 1959.

MacDonagh, O., 'The Nineteenth-Century Revolution in Government', *Historical Journal* 1958.

Moore, D. C., 'The Other Face of Reform', *Victorian Studies* 1961.

Tholfsen, T. R., 'The Origins of the Birmingham Caucus', *Historical Journal* 1959.

4 FOREIGN AND IMPERIAL

Anderson, M. S., *The Eastern Question* (1966).

Bell, H. C. F., *Lord Palmerston* (2 vols., 1936).

Bodelsen, C. A., *Studies in mid-Victorian Imperialism* (1924).

Cambridge History of the British Empire (several vols., 1929–).

Gallagher, J., and Robinson, R. E., 'The Imperialism of Free Trade', *Econ.H.R.* 1953.

Langer, W. L., *European Alliances and Alignments, 1871–90* (2nd ed., 1960).

Mosse, W. E., *The European Powers and the German Question, 1848–71* (1958).

Platt, D. C. M., *Finance, Trade and Politics in British Foreign Policy, 1815–1914* (1968).

Robinson, R. E., and Gallagher, J., with Denny, A., *Africa and the Victorians* (1961).

Seton-Watson, R. W., *Britain in Europe, 1789–1914* (1938).

Spear, T. G. P., *India* (1961).

Temperley, H. W. V., and Penson, L. M., *Foundations of British Foreign Policy* (1938).

Thornton, A. P., *The Imperial Idea and its Enemies* (1959).

Williamson, J. A., *A Short History of British Expansion* (1953).

Woodham-Smith, C., *The Reason Why* (1953).

5 ART, CULTURE AND RELIGION

Best, G. F. A., *Temporal Pillars* (1964).

Boase, T. R. S., *English Art, 1800–70* (1959).

Brose, O. J., *Church and Parliament* (1959).

Briggs, A. (ed.), *William Morris: Selected Writings and Designs* (1962).

Clark, K., *The Gothic Revival* (new ed., 1962).

Burrow, J. W., *Evolution and Society* (1966).

Chadwick, W. O., (ed.) *The Mind of the Oxford Movement* (1960).

Chadwick, W. O., *The Victorian Church* (vol. I, 1966).

Chapman, R., *The Victorian Debate* (1968).

Furneaux Jordan, R., *Victorian Architecture* (1966).

Hitchcock, H.-R., *Architecture: Nineteenth and Twentieth Centuries* (1958).

Houghton, W. E., *The Victorian Frame of Mind, 1830–70* (1957).

House, H., *The Dickens World* (2nd ed., 1942).

Inglis, K. S., *Churches and the Working Classes in Victorian England* (1963).

Newsome, D., *Godliness and Good Learning* (1961).

Pevsner, N., *The Buildings of England* (many vols.) (1951–).

Pevsner, N., *High Victorian Design* (1951).

Pevsner, N., *Pioneers of Modern Design* (1960).

Rothblatt, S., *The Revolution of the Dons* (1968).

Thompson, P. R., *The Work of William Morris* (London, 1967).

Willey, B., *Nineteenth-Century Studies* (1949).

Willey, B., *More Nineteenth Century Studies* (1956).

Williams, R., *Culture and Society, 1780–1950* (1958).

Index

Black figures refer to main entries